Praise for
Walking the Path of the Jewish Mystic

"A luminous guide on the spiritual journey of self-discovery and expansion of consciousness.... Will greatly enrich readers across religious traditions."

—**Dr. Maria Reis Habito**, Zen teacher,
Maria Kannon Zen Center; international program
director, Taipei Museum of World Religions

"Filled with rich images and solid scholarship.... Leads us through the complexities of the historical Kabbalah with extraordinary adeptness.... Brings new light to an ancient wisdom."

—**Rabbi Ted Falcon, PhD**, coauthor,
Finding Peace Through Spiritual Practice:
The Interfaith Amigos' Guide to Personal, Social and
Environmental Healing

"In a generation threatened by so much spiritual exploitation, it is rare to see such responsibility and integrity in a teacher.... Translate[s] the highest and most complex esoteric wisdom into soul-bites that can be comprehended by all.... Will draw you to be your highest self and connect to your ultimate truth."

—**Reb Mimi Feigelson**, lecturer of Rabbinics and
Chassidic Thought, American Jewish University

"Powerful.... A profound discussion of the truths that underlie the human condition. A wonderful book that you will return to again and again."

—**Nan Fink Gefen, PhD**, author,
Discovering Jewish Meditation: Instruction and
Guidance for Learning an Ancient Spiritual Practice

"A combination of laser-like clarity and gentle authority.... A provocative vision, grounded in serious scholarship and supported by a thousand years of esoteric understanding."

—**Mirabai Starr**, author, *God of Love: A Guide to the*
Heart of Judaism, Christianity and Islam

"A uniquely valuable spiritual resource that masterfully interweaves Kabbalistic teachings with esoteric wisdom from other traditions.... A profoundly rich and evocative guide for the expansion of individual consciousness, as well as for the spiritual evolution of humanity as a whole."

—**Dr. Yehezkel Landau**, director, Building Abrahamic Partnerships; associate professor of interfaith relations, Hartford Seminary

"This book is to be treasured, placed on one's nightstand to be read frequently for spiritual elevation. Not only does this book transmit deep Kabbalistic teachings, the reading of the book itself places the reader in a wonderful meditative state."

—**Melinda Ribner**, author, *The Secret Legacy of Biblical Women* and *New Age Judaism*

"Opens the door to a world that is inaccessible for most people.... Makes personal transformation attainable to the one who is ready to do the work.... A gift to the soul and the mind."

—**Rabbi Marcelo Bronstein**, Congregation B'nai Jeshurun, New York City

"An excellent guide.... Shares a profound understanding of the paths of ancient wisdom while leading us onward toward the higher awareness that can become a catalyst for spiritual evolution and growth."

—**Rabbi Shefa Gold**, author, *The Magic of Hebrew Chant: Healing the Spirit, Transforming the Mind, Deepening Love*

"An exceedingly rare, inspiring integration.... Clarity and conviction with ecumenical universalism."

—**Dr. J. H. (Yossi) Chajes**, University of Haifa; author, *Between Worlds: Dybbuks, Exorcists and Early Modern Judaism*

"Informed by a depth of meditation practice and spiritual learning, Rabbi Glick's mystical and yet accessible teaching offer[s] an illuminating portrait of the planes of inner human topography, the multifaceted nature of Divine energy, and the unfolding of creation."

—**Rabbi Elie Kaplan Spitz**, author, *Increasing Wholeness: Jewish Wisdom and Guided Meditations to Strengthen and Calm Body, Heart, Mind and Spirit*

Walking the Path *of the* JEWISH MYSTIC

How to Expand Your Awareness
and Transform Your Life

Rabbi Yoel Glick

For People of All Faiths, All Backgrounds

JEWISH LIGHTS Publishing

Woodstock, Vermont

Walking the Path of the Jewish Mystic:
How to Expand Your Awareness and Transform Your Life

2015 Quality Paperback Edition, First Printing
© 2015 by Yoel Glick

Figures 5–11 created by Navonel Glick, modified by Michael J. Myers.

Library of Congress Cataloging-in-Publication Data
Glick, Yoel, 1954– author.
  Walking the path of the Jewish mystic : how to expand your awareness and transform your life / Rabbi Yoel Glick.
       pages cm
  Includes bibliographical references.
  ISBN 978-1-58023-843-4 (pbk.)—ISBN 978-1-58023-846-5 (ebook)
  1. Spiritual life—Judaism. I. Title.
  BM723.G564 2015
  296.7'12—dc23
                                    2015014307

10 9 8 7 6 5 4 3 2 1

Manufactured in the United States of America
Cover design: Tim Holtz
Interior design: Michael Myers
Cover art: © Hakki Arslan / Shutterstock, modified by Tim Holtz

For People of All Faiths, All Backgrounds
Jewish Lights Publishing
A Division of LongHill Partners, Inc.
Sunset Farm Offices, Route 4, P.O. Box 237
Woodstock, VT 05091
Tel: (802) 457-4000 Fax: (802) 457-4004
www.jewishlights.com

For my sons, Adir and Navonel,
passionate seekers of wisdom and truth

Illustrations

Contents

Introduction

Awakening the Higher Knowledge (*Daat Elyon*)

The purpose of this book is to create a foundation of understanding about the nature and workings of the inner life and the higher realm for spiritual seekers. It is not an exhaustive study, nor is it an authoritative treatise on the subject. It is a window into another reality; a door that leads to a different way of looking at life.

The Kabbalah, Jewish mystical teaching, speaks of two types of knowledge: *daat elyon*, the higher knowledge, and *daat tachton*, the lower knowledge. The lower *daat* relates to intellectual ideas, facts, and figures. The higher *daat* is something else entirely. It is an intuitive impression of the essence of a person or an object. *Daat elyon* is a direct experience where we merge with the object of our investigation and comprehend its true nature as it exists in the mind of God.

A common analogy that is used by the mystics to explain this type of knowledge is Genesis 4:1, "And the man knew his wife Eve." It is this kind of intimate knowledge that is at the heart of the inner life. This higher knowledge leads to a transformation in awareness that becomes the catalyst for spiritual evolution and growth.[1]

One of the keys to opening the door to *daat elyon* is the study of spiritual wisdom. As we enter into the wisdom teachings, the celestial worlds become alive for us. Our consciousness expands and our understanding deepens.

This type of study is not accomplished by intellectual learning, though the intellect has a part to play, but through contemplation and meditation on the higher truths. The exploration of the nature of consciousness, the anatomy of the soul, the geography of the higher worlds, and the structure of the supernal planes are all an integral part of such religious investigation.

The approach of this book is focused on awakening *daat elyon*. Four principles are employed to actualize its intuitive power. These four principles form the conceptual foundation for the teaching.

The First Principle: A Universal Approach

The essence of the spiritual life is the expansion of our consciousness. God's consciousness is all-inclusive and the divine love is all-embracing. If we want to join with the Eternal One, then we need to become all-inclusive and all-embracing as well.

The mystical teachings of the various religions are each like one of the proverbial blind men trying to describe an elephant.[2] Each religion gives us one perspective of the greater picture. No one religion has all the answers. We can discover the contours of the overall outline, however, by incorporating the insights from these different paths. The synthetic vision that arises from this interreligious investigation will begin to provide us with a comprehensive view of God's universe.

Judaism has its own unique insights to contribute to this larger picture. Certain ideas in the Kabbalah have a universal appeal. These concepts resonate with the teachings found in other world faiths. They attest to the common basis of understanding among the traditions, while imparting their own perspective on the nature of the world. These Jewish beliefs offer a vision that emerges out of our particular experience as a people and the distinctive qualities embodied in our religion.

Rebbe Nachman of Breslov, the late-eighteenth-century Hasidic master who was known for his innovative and insightful interpretations of scripture, teaches that diversity in religious approaches is the outward expression of a profound spiritual ideal. When we accept that different opinions are part of one single, indivisible Truth, we are revealing the unity behind the multiplicity of physical manifestation. The more that we can hold different opinions, and at the same time work together with a sense of unity and love, the more God's Oneness will be revealed in the world. This unity in diversity, Rebbe Nachman believes, represents a divine manifestation that is superior to having everyone follow the same religious path.[3]

Reb Gedaliah Kenig, one of the modern-day leaders of the Breslov Hasidim in Israel, had a wonderful way of expressing this vision: The people of Israel are like a great tree. The tree has one main trunk from which sprouts a multitude of branches, with an abundance of leaves and flowers on every branch. Each branch is different from the other; each leaf and flower has its own individual shape, color, and fragrance. They all contribute their unique character and personal qualities to the tree. This is what gives the tree its beauty and its grace.[4]

Reb Gedaliah used his metaphor to talk about different paths in Judaism. We can apply his metaphor universally. Then the wisdom teachings of the world religions will truly become a Tree of Life.

The Second Principle: An Approach Attuned to Our Present-Day Awareness

Today no nation lives alone. International communications and diplomacy have transformed the world into an intimate place. We may not yet have realized the concept of a global village, but we are well on the way in that direction. What happens in one part of the world affects peoples thousands of miles away. The influence of ideas and technology crosses all borders. There is access to the thought and lifestyles of hundreds of cultures and many different religions. The contribution to humanity's spiritual wealth of great teachers from all over the globe is an acknowledged fact. We are aware of religions that were unknown to the people of ancient Israel, religions whose teachings have hundreds of millions of followers across the globe.

Our self-identity has drastically changed. We incorporate into our self-conception identities as members of the human race and as one creation in a universe of billions of worlds. We are citizens of earth and citizens of the universe.

In the past, human consciousness was confined to the limits of one's own village; today we look to the stars for our future. We travel from one end of the globe to the other with amazing ease. We have even begun to explore other worlds. We think of life in much broader and grander terms.

We have also touched the world of the invisible. We can picture the universe of the microscopic. The unseen lives of bacteria, viruses, and one-celled creatures are part of our everyday existence. The realm of atoms and subatomic particles has become a natural component of the way we understand the intrinsic structure of the world.

The forces of gravity, electricity, and atomic energy have changed the way we view power. We have learned that we live in a world of many unseen forces that permeate and influence our lives.

The insights of psychology, philosophy, and other social disciplines have deepened our understanding of the nature of human beings and their inner world. We are far more conscious actors in our lives than were our forefathers and foremothers thirty-five hundred years ago when the Jewish people was born. Our inner world has evolved with almost as great an intensity as our outer reality. Our ideas about life have expanded exponentially. Our concept of God and the spiritual realm needs to mirror this growth in consciousness.

The Third Principle: The Two Paths to the Supreme

Sri Ramakrishna, the nineteenth-century Indian saint who was known for his profound knowledge of the inner reality, recounts a parable related to the experience of God, about a man who saw a chameleon:

> Once a man went into a wood and saw a beautiful creature on a tree. Later he told a friend about it and said, "Brother, on a certain tree in the wood I saw a red-coloured creature." The friend answered: "I have seen it too. Why do you call it red? It is green." A third man said: "Oh, no, no! Why do you call it green? It is yellow." Then other persons began to describe the animal variously as violet, blue, or black. Soon they were quarrelling about the colour. At last they went to the tree and found a man sitting under it. In answer to their questions he said: "I live under this tree and know the creature very well. What each of you has said about it is true. Sometimes it is red, sometimes green, sometimes yellow, sometimes blue, and so forth and so on. Again, sometimes I see that it has no colour whatsoever."[5]

There are two paths toward the Supreme: the personal path and the impersonal path. The personal approach is like the various colors of the chameleon. The impersonal route is when the chameleon has no color at all.

On the personal path, we strive toward the Sovereign of the universe using personal imagery and devotion. We speak of the individual soul, the group soul, and God. On the impersonal path, there is no soul; there is no other. We commune with the Infinite and become one with the Absolute.

On the personal path, we draw near to the Omnipotent and Omniscient by building an intimate relationship. We talk with God as naturally as we would with a family member or a dear friend. We see our relationship as that of a child and parent, or as a servant and master, or as two lovers. We feel the Divine Presence beside us, walking with us through life. We share our hopes and dreams with God, as well as our fears and disappointments. Through our devotion, we forge a spiritual link with our holy Beloved. The One who is pure love then turns toward us to bestow blessings and inspiration.

On the impersonal path, we are not looking for a personal Deity to call our own; we yearn to unite with the Infinite. We want to touch and then abide in a Reality that is beyond all thought or image. We seek the Timeless Consciousness that fills and transcends the whole of the universe but that cannot be named or described.

On this austere path, we do not go toward any personal aspect of the Godhead, but reach instead toward God in the abstract. We concentrate on the *Ein Sof*—that which is without beginning or end—and strive to ascend into the realm of unity and oneness as far as we are able. Rather than forming a relationship with our Creator, we desire to become one with the Boundless Ocean of Being.

For most people, the impersonal path is very difficult to follow. The majority prefer a personal approach to God. In Hinduism, the need for a personal relationship with the Overarching Presence is understood implicitly. The masses are therefore encouraged to worship the One worthy of adoration in many names and forms. The worship of the deities is seen as a step toward a more elevated form of devotion that will arise naturally later on.

For the spiritually evolved, however, Hinduism preaches the path of non-dual Vedanta. In non-dual Vedanta, seekers attempt to move beyond all aspects and appearances to unite with the consciousness of the Absolute. This sublime consciousness of Oneness is considered to be beyond the reach of the average human being.

Judaism follows the inverse process. On the one hand, normative Judaism teaches the worship of a formless God. The Supreme Being does possess attributes, but the creation of images is strictly forbidden. All devotion is addressed to the Higher Power who is Master over all.

In the teachings of the Kabbalah, on the other hand, this strict adherence to formlessness breaks down. A rich array of different aspects to the Godhead suddenly appear: there are the ten *sefirot*, or supernal emanations; the *partzufim*, or divine countenances; the *Shekhinah*, the feminine aspect of the Deity; and *Adam Kadmon*, the Primordial Human Being. It seems that Judaism believes that only the spiritually mature seeker is ready to cope with the paradox of the many forms of a formless God.

These two approaches are not conflicting truths; rather, they represent two aspects of one reality. In the personal mode, we ascend toward the Infinite through a progression of divine aspects. On the impersonal route, we look past all changing temporal manifestations and identities and strive to merge with the substratum of Pure Consciousness that underlies all that is. There are two separate paths, but both paths ultimately lead to the same Eternal Source, where all distinction between personal and impersonal becomes obliterated.[6]

The Fourth Principle:
The Ultimate Truth Is Beyond Description

Truth is beyond all words and understanding. Whatever system we may master, it is just a system, an artificial construct that tries to describe something that is unbounded and timeless. We give different names that suit our background and culture to this reality, and that is who and what we encounter when we "meet" God. Each paradigm is the expression of a certain conception of reality. Each model reflects another stage in the development of human awareness.

When God first reveals the Ineffable Name *Yud Heh Vav Heh* to Moses at the burning bush, the Almighty says, "*Zeh shemi l'olam*— This shall be my Name forever" (Exodus 3:15). The Baal Shem Tov, the eighteenth-century Jewish mystic who is esteemed as the founder of Hasidism, teaches that this verse has another hidden meaning. To understand its hidden meaning, we have to read the Hebrew word *l'olam* (forever) according to its literal sense—"for the world." The interpretation of this verse then becomes: The Name of *Yud Heh Vav Heh* has been given to the people in this world so that they can call on the Holy Blessed One and draw down the divine blessing. But, in truth, the Illimitable Spirit is above all names, even the Sacred Name of *Yud Heh Vav Heh,* which is called in the holy books "God's Essential Name."[7]

Yud Heh Vav Heh is the highest name or aspect of the Godhead that we on the physical plane can link to and draw on. But it is not the final name—there are aspects or names that reach much farther out into the infinite. As the Baal Shem states, *Yud Heh Vav Heh* is the Name for this world, but there may be other names for other higher worlds. And the Ageless Unchanging Reality is beyond all names and forms.

According to Rebbe Levi Yitzchak of Berditchev, another great teacher of the early Hasidic movement, who was known for his vibrant inner life, this is the true meaning of the name God reveals to Moses at the burning bush, *Eheyeh Asher Eheyeh* (Exodus 3:14). Rather than the traditional translation of the name as "I am that I am," Rebbe Levi Yitzchak reads the name in the future tense as "I will be what I will be." The Most High, he explains, is in essence saying to Moses, "Don't try to fit me into a name or form or idea or attribute; I am ever more than anything that you are able to grasp."[8]

Spiritual knowledge is ever changing. The truths that we hold dear today are a reflection of our present level of development. They are but a momentary glimpse of a reality that is infinite and eternal. The more we advance along the path, the more our understanding will deepen. The more we progress as souls, the more we will be able to tap the inexhaustible wisdom in the universal mind of God.

There is no ultimate model for reality. We can acquire only a foundation of understanding that can be applied to the various systems and mystical traditions. The study of spiritual wisdom is a never-ending process. Our understanding needs to constantly grow and evolve.

Though we will discuss many different kinds of heavenly beings and a multitude of supernal worlds, underlying all is the awareness that there is only one Reality. As you study the various physical details and descriptions, it is important to always keep in mind that the one Reality is inexpressible in words and concrete ideas; it is unknowable with our lower minds.

Which brings us back full circle to *daat elyon. Daat elyon* is about direct experience. It is about an inner encounter with the wisdom—a meeting with the One Truth seated in the hearts of all. To fully benefit from this book, you should not approach it as information to be assimilated, but as wisdom to be contemplated and meditated upon. Real understanding dawns through communion with exalted ideas. Then the intimate knowingness of *daat elyon* is awakened, and God and the inner realm become intensely alive.

The Structure of the Book

This book is divided into four parts. The first part, "Made in the Image of God," looks at the *Etz haChayim*, the Kabbalistic Tree of Life, and the *sefirot*, or energy centers, that make up the tree. This part opens the door to the understanding that we live in a world of energies and consciousness where a vast exchange of energies is going on at every level of existence.

"The Science of the Soul" delves into the nature of the soul and its subtle bodies. It reveals the truth that we are multidimensional beings on a journey of self-discovery and this world is our school. It explores the forces that propel us on our spiritual voyage and determine our path and trajectory.

"The Divine Structure of Reality" explores the nature of the *partzufim*, the divine countenances, and the four realms of our wider reality. Through our encounter with these archetypal beings, we realize that all of life is joined together in an interdependent, interlocking community that spans countless worlds and planes of existence. We also enter into the domain of the angelic kingdom and discover the crucial role angels play in the maintenance of all the structures and forms in the universe.

"Revealing the Kingdom of Heaven on Earth" investigates the unfolding relationship between the lower and the higher realms. It explores how this relationship is fostered and developed through the concepts of the *Shekhinah* (the feminine Divine Presence), the Temple, and the Messiah. It teaches us how to harness the power of the Infinite inside us and infuse that power into our life and our world.

Notes

The notes at the end of the book serve a variety of functions. They act as proof texts, guidelines for study, personal reflections, insight into various processes, or simply suggestions of a different way of looking at a subject that expands the mind. Some will have a strong basis in rigorous textual analysis, while others will be based on inner experience and intuition. I encourage you to delve into the notes, to see them as an integral part of the book.

The Scope and Approach of the Teaching

Walking the Path of the Jewish Mystic presents the spiritual principles that I received from my teachers as I have come to understand them through my own personal study and experience. The teachings encompass many types of knowledge. Though I focus primarily on Jewish sources, the book also includes material from Hinduism, Buddhism, Christianity, and other world religions, as well as ideas from a wide spectrum of modern esoteric traditions.

Many of the classical texts delineate complex and elaborate models. In some cases, I have distilled these complicated concepts down to their essential elements to make them more accessible and understandable. I believe this approach to their wisdom provides a more direct and potent tool for study and contemplation. I also believe that this is the approach that is needed in our time, not because people have less ability to comprehend concepts—on the contrary, they have a more expansive outlook and a wider range of knowledge—but because people today want clear, relevant, and unembellished answers to life's great questions—answers that go right to the heart of the matter and provide insight and inspiration. This is the type of teaching I have tried to offer.

Writing *Walking the Path of the Jewish Mystic* has been an amazing experience for me. I have been transported to new worlds and a multitude of different states of consciousness. Working on the book has enriched my life and deepened my understanding. It has opened up my heart and stretched my mind.

This voyage of the spirit is intended to take you back to the beginning of creation and forward to the transformation of our world. We will delve into the workings of the Kabbalistic Tree of Life—the body of the *sefirot*; follow the soul on its passage from incarnation to incarnation; explore the hidden worlds of the *partzufim*—the great archetypes who make up the cosmic Godhead; and enter into the living presence of the holy *Shekhinah*—the Universal Mother whose creative power upholds the universe. Walk the path of the Jewish mystic with me: expand your awareness and transform your life.

A Note on Language

All the translations of the Hasidic, Kabbalistic, and Rabbinic texts are my own, unless otherwise indicated. All biblical quotations, unless otherwise indicated, are adapted from the 1917 version of the JPS Hebrew Bible. Although I love the poetry and nobility of the 1917 translation, I have adapted certain parts of the archaic language to make the passages more accessible to the modern reader.

In order to present each thinker with integrity, I have retained the original male gender bias in all of my translations and quotations, including the biblical passages. My own writing follows a gender-free style, except when specifically indicated by the subject matter.

In terms of the transliteration of the Hebrew and Aramaic, I have followed the *Encyclopaedia Judaica* general transliteration guidelines. However, for technical reasons, I have used *ch* for the letter *chet* instead of *h* with a subdot, and *tz* for the letter *tzadi*, instead of *z* with a subdot. Also, I have diverged from the *Encyclopaedia Judaica* guidelines in cases where a different form is in common usage, such as "Hasid," *neshama*, and *Knesset Yisrael*. In these cases, I have used the common spelling instead. I believe this approach provides a greater ease of reading.

For Sanskrit terms, I have used the spelling or transliteration as it appeared in the Hindu sources that I used. I apologize to my more knowledgeable readers for any inaccuracies that might have occurred in this regard.

Gender and the Kabbalah

The traditional Kabbalistic texts present a major dilemma regarding the issue of inclusivity. Central elements of the Kabbalistic description of the higher reality utilize gender-specific terms such as the "beard of God." I decided that the best approach was to keep the sections about the *partzufim*, or divine countenances, in their male- and female-specific forms, as they constitute essential aspects of the Kabbalistic vision of the dynamics of the universe. This choice does not reflect any opinion on my part about the gender of God or human beings. The changeless and ever-present Reality at the heart of the universe is beyond all names and forms.

The Garden and the Cosmic Vessels

Two Ancient Paradigms That Define Our Existence

What is the essence of a human being? Why are we here in this world? These are the key questions that any serious seeker asks him- or herself. The Jewish tradition explores these questions using the events described in the biblical story of the Garden of Eden and the story of the creation of the universe as described in the teachings of Rabbi Isaac Luria, the figure at the center of the Kabbalistic circle in Safed during the sixteenth century.

The Garden of Eden

"In the beginning," the Hebrew Bible tells us, "God created the heavens and the earth" (Genesis 1:1). The Divine Architect formed both the physical planes of this world and a higher plane in the heavens, to which scripture gives the name the Garden of Eden.[1]

The earth was meant to be the dwelling place of the mineral, plant, and animal kingdoms. The Garden of Eden was established as the home for the human race, a new form of life that was to be the next step in the evolution of consciousness.[2]

Humanity was a unique creation. Human beings were given a spark of the universal mind, which enabled them to develop individual awareness and to think, analyze, and perceive.[3] This divine spark also brought humanity in direct contact with the Kingdom of Souls and made it possible for humans to communicate with these more evolved beings.

The plane of Eden had similarities to our physical world, but there were also key differences: In Eden we were at peace with ourselves and with the animal kingdom. All our needs were taken care of. We did not have physical bodies, but rather bodies made of light. And most important of all, in Eden we could walk and talk with God.

The Fall

When humanity was created, the desires of the animal body lay buried in its nature. Its evolutionary goal was to overcome these physical remnants and turn its heart and mind wholly toward the spiritual. The "humans" who were born into the realm of Eden, however, were led astray by the power of these desires. They misused the *Shekhinah* energy, the creative energy of the universe, whose mystical symbol is the serpent, by turning its power downward to the sexual impulses, and not upward toward eternal spirit. This drew them into the animal way of life until the matter of their bodies became too gross for them to exist in the higher realm. As a result, humanity was banished from the Garden of Eden and made to live in this lower world.[4]

The temptation and fall of the first humans was not just a question of uncontrolled desire. A yearning for wisdom also played an important role in the events that took place in the Garden. The creative energy that is aroused in physical union can also be used to stimulate mental creativity. It can be utilized to acquire understanding, awaken new ideas, and create great works of beauty and art. When the first humans began delving into this energy in Eden, they had high aspirations. The problem was that as they strove for wisdom, their lower instincts also became aroused. These urges took over their behavior and altered their minds until they could no longer remain in their heavenly home.

Exchanging Forms of Light for Bodies of Skin

The fall from Eden, then, was the fall of humanity from a sublime spiritual existence into the harsh reality of this physical world. Humankind was condemned to a life of struggle, to earn its bread by the sweat of its brow. Humans lost their intimate relationship with Divinity and the peace that sublime bond brought to them. They were forced to give up their bodies of rarified spiritual matter and take on bodies made of a dense physical substance. As the Midrash (Rabbinic allegorical tradition) explains in its interpretation of Genesis 3:21, "*Vayaas Adonai Elohim le'adam ulishto katenot or vayalbishem*—For the man, and also for his wife, did the Lord

God make coats of skins and clothe them." If the Hebrew word *or* is spelled with the letter *ayin*, it means "skin," but if it is spelled with the letter *aleph*, though it sounds the same, it means "light." As a result of the banishment from Eden, humanity exchanged bodies composed of light for bodies made of skin.[5]

Three Realizations about Life on Earth

The story of the Garden of Eden gives us the key to understanding the human race. It leads us to certain realizations about ourselves and about the nature of our world. It provides us with a perspective on life that forms the foundation for the spiritual path.

The first realization is that every human being is divided in two. One part of us is attuned to animal life, with all of its pulls and desires, and a second part is a spark of the Divine that knows a higher reality and a more refined type of existence. We are constantly struggling with this dual nature within us. These two halves of our being battle for control of our life: one part is trying to anchor us on earth, and the other is aspiring to reach the heavens.

The second realization is that we were not meant to be here. We are not meant to inhabit these bodies composed of flesh and blood that need to be fed with the dead bodies of plants and animals in order to survive. We were not meant to have bodies that are subject to all kinds of infection and disease and that decay and fall apart over time. All of these difficulties are a result of "the Fall." They are part of an unnatural situation that we continually struggle to overcome.

The third realization is that this plane is one of suffering that is unfit for humans to inhabit. Animals do not undergo the same mental anguish; they do not have the conscious awareness of pain that humans do. They are not concerned when they do not know from where their next meal will come. They quickly forget the existence of the children to which they have given birth and then lost. They are not haunted by memory and conscience. They remain detached from the pain they cause to other animals. The law of survival rules their lives.

Human beings, by contrast, have a highly evolved mental awareness. And the more our divine aspect is developed, the more sensitive we become to the suffering in this world. Spiritually evolved individuals are increasingly aware of the many levels on which people are in pain. They are increasingly sensitive to the rough nature of our existence. They feel acutely the daily aggressions on their person. They cannot cause others pain without deeply suffering themselves.

The Lurianic Creation Narrative

There is another dimension to humanity's peculiar condition as well. The cosmology of Rabbi Isaac Luria, also known as the Ari (the Lion), describes the first few moments of the creation of the universe. In an act reminiscent of the big bang of the physicists, God sent an *or yashar*—a burst of light and energy directly from the realm of the Infinite and the Absolute—into the fragile vessel of the newly formed universe. This fragile vessel could not withstand the tremendous force of the divine light, and a great shattering took place. As a result, our universe was left in a broken condition, where sparks of divine light, *netzutzot*, were fused with shards of concrete matter, *klipot*, and everything that existed became a mixture of light and darkness, good and evil, joy and sorrow, success and failure.[6] As a result of this cosmic shattering, nothing in this universe can be perfect; nothing can be whole. Everything in this universe is in a state of essential brokenness.[7]

Our incarnation into physical existence is a reflection of this cosmic shattering, this fall into the *klipot*. The literal meaning of the Hebrew word *klipah* is "shell." This physical world is just a shell, a hollow exterior that covers over the true reality within. It is the liberation of the *netzutz*, the divine spark trapped within our animal existence, that is the goal of life. We need to break through the hard exterior of the shell and reveal the shining light that is within us—to return to who we really are and where we truly belong.

Repairing a Broken World

This labor of *aliyat hanetzutzot*, "raising the sparks," is the Ari's great message of hope. Though we live in a broken world, our brokenness is not irreparable; amid the fragmentation there is the possibility of *tikun*—of fixing and wholeness. We can lift ourselves out of our fallen state by awakening the divine attributes that lie buried within us. Using the power of heart, mind, and soul, we can overcome the limitations of our animal nature and transcend this material existence.

Our tremendous sensitivity to the suffering of this world can be transformed into a spiritual force that arouses our innate divinity, an inner prod that stimulates the virtues of love and compassion inside us, inspiring us to try to relieve the suffering of others—to support and comfort them in their sorrow and their pain.

Life Is a School

Genesis 28:12 describes the patriarch Jacob's vision of a ladder reaching from the earth to the heavens, with angels ascending and descending upon its rungs, and God looking down from above. The medieval text *Olelot Efrayim* teaches that Jacob's vision is a metaphor for life on our physical plane of existence. This whole world is a ladder of ascension. Each life is an opportunity to take another step. We move from one incarnation to another, climbing from one rung to the next, until we reach the top of the ladder and enter into the glory of the divine embrace.[8]

Ethics of the Fathers (*Pirkei Avot*) 4:16 describes this world as a *prozdor*—an entranceway or vestibule that leads into the world to come. We cannot look at this life in isolation; it needs to be seen in the context of a greater reality that includes all of the higher worlds. This life is not a separate, self-contained existence; it is part of a process that began before we entered into this world and that will continue on after we depart. This world is a school where we come to learn and gain experience. We keep on returning to this school in incarnation after incarnation, in order to gather new wisdom, evolve, and grow.

Two hundred years ago the Hasidic rebbe Asher Zvi of Ostroha taught that the difficulties we face in our life are the key to our spiritual evolution. They are the specific challenge that we must confront; they embody the work of *tikun* or transformation that we have come into this world to fulfill.[9]

The spiritual paths outlined in the great world traditions have been created to guide us in that process, to show us how to accomplish this work of *tikun*. The religious life teaches us how to purify the animal side of our nature and develop the divine attributes within us. It teaches us how to convert ourselves into beings worthy of living in the higher realms once more.

This work of personal *tikun* is a source of great strength and hope not only for us, but also for the repair of the rest of creation—the work of *tikun olam*. Through the spark of the Universal Mind within us, we can act as a bridge between the supernal kingdoms and the kingdoms of this physical plane. We can strive to care for the planet and all of the lifeforms upon it. We can labor to uplift our world. In this way, we will fulfill the original task that God gave us in Eden: to "tend and watch over [the Garden]" (Genesis 2:15).

Made in
the Image
of God

Of all the Kabbalistic concepts, the idea of the ten *sefirot* is probably the most well known and widely studied. For a thousand years people have been intrigued and mystified by the *sefirot*, striving to understand their structure and workings. The first part of this book takes an in-depth look at the nature of the *sefirot*—their composition, development, and purpose. It explores their place in the life of the individual and the cosmos and answers the age-old enigma of how we are made in the image of God.

1

The Body of Spiritual Centers

How Are We Created in the Image of God?

In the account of the Creation story contained in the book of Genesis, the Hebrew Bible makes an astonishing statement:

> *And God created man in His own image;*
> *in the image of God [He created him].*
> *(Genesis 1:26)*

The Creator, Sustainer, and Destroyer of All does not have a physical image. How are we to understand this enigmatic statement?

The Boundless One does not have a corporeal appearance but does possess a body of manifestation. The Divine has a vehicle through which it manifests in the physical. If we understand the nature of this body of manifestation, we will understand how we are made in the image of God.[1]

The *Etz haChayim*—the Kabbalistic Tree of Life

According to the science of Yoga, beneath a human being's physical frame is a subtle field of energy centers (see figure 1). These centers infuse the physical form with life and consciousness. In Sanskrit these centers are called *chakras*.[2]

3

In the Kabbalah, the mystical teachings of Judaism, we find a similar description of a network of energy centers. Sometimes they are depicted as the limbs of a heavenly body, and sometimes they are portrayed as the trunk and branches of a celestial tree, *Etz haChayim*—the Tree of Life. In Hebrew, these energy centers are called *sefirot*.[3]

Underlying all of creation is a web of power and light that is structured around a series of spiritual vortexes. These vortexes or centers form a body of manifestation for both God and a human being. Our body of *sefirot* is created in the divine image.[4]

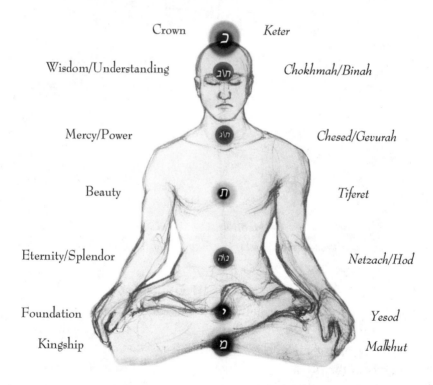

Crown — כ — *Keter*

Wisdom/Understanding — חו\בי — *Chokhmah/Binah*

Mercy/Power — ח\ז — *Chesed/Gevurah*

Beauty — ת — *Tiferet*

Eternity/Splendor — נה — *Netzach/Hod*

Foundation — י — *Yesod*

Kingship — מ — *Malkhut*

Figure 1. The Yogic/Kabbalistic *sefirot.* Illustration by Moriah Halevi.

The centers, or *sefirot*, have two major functions. First and foremost they are conduits for the passage of energy. Every living thing is composed of energy. There is a dynamic exchange of spiritual power flowing back and forth all the time. Everything is emanating and absorbing the life force at every single moment. Each *sefirah* is composed of a particular energy, and this energy is of a grosser or more refined nature depending on our state of evolution. Our goal in life is to develop our centers until they are composed of pure spiritual force. We then become effective instruments for the distribution of this refined energy into the greater world around us.

The second function of the centers, or *sefirot*, is to establish the nature of our consciousness. Each *sefirah* has its own characteristic state of mind. Each center is given a name that reflects the particular state it embodies. There are many different gradients to the awareness that is evoked in each center. We determine the quality of the consciousness in our centers through the actions of our daily life and the intensity of our inner strivings. The balance of spiritual forces in our *sefirot* and the stage of their development will define the natural resonance of our mind. This, in turn, will determine the manner in which we experience reality and our capacity to reach up into the spiritual realm.[5]

The Centers: A Foundation

The spiritual centers in our subtle body run along the spinal column, from the base of the spine to the crown of the head. They are interconnected with each other through a network of energy pathways that flow between them. The whole body of centers and pathways is called the *Etz haChayim*—the Tree of Life.

According to the Yogic model, the major centers are seven in number. There is the crown center at the top of the head; the *ajna* center, or what is called the third eye; the throat, heart, and solar plexus centers; the sacral or genital center; and the center at the base of the spine.[6]

The Kabbalah speaks of not seven but ten *sefirot*. The reason for this discrepancy is that each of the centers has a left- and a right-hand component to its makeup (see the next section, "The Three Energy Pathways"). In three of the centers, the difference between the left- and the right-hand components is so marked that the Kabbalah considers each side of the center as a separate *sefirah* in itself. Yogic teaching, on the other hand, continues to think of the left- and right-hand components of these three *chakras* as two halves of a single whole. This accounts for the addition of three extra centers in the Kabbalah.[7]

Traditional Kabbalah identifies the ten *sefirot* with the different limbs of the body. *Keter* is the top of the head. The right brain or eye is *chokhmah*, and the left brain or eye is *binah*. *Binah* is also sometimes identified with the heart. *Chesed* is the right arm, and *gevurah* is the left arm. *Tiferet* is the heart or sometimes the whole torso. The right leg is *netzach*, and the left leg is *hod*. *Yesod* is the sexual organ, while *malkhut* is the feet.[8]

In the seven-center Yogic/Kabbalistic framework, the *sefirot* are associated with the different *chakras*. These are the names for the *sefirot* as expressed within this seven-center system: *keter*, crown—the crown center; *chokhmah/binah*, wisdom/understanding—the third eye; *chesed/gevurah*, mercy/power—the throat center; *tiferet*, beauty—the heart center; *netzach/hod*, eternity/splendor—the solar plexus center; *yesod*, foundation—the sacral center; *malkhut*, kingship—the center at the base of the spine.[9]

How Does a Spiritual Center Form and Develop?

The centers are living vortexes of spiritual energy. Each begins as a small nucleus of gathered forces, which is composed of three elements. These three elements reflect the three lines of energy flowing on the left, right, and up the center of the body (see the following section, "The Three Energy Pathways"). A spark of each of the three combines to create the basis of a center. The quality of these sparks is determined by the nature of the energies that will form the center.

We can think of the composition of an atom as a useful model. In the atom we have an electron, a proton, and a neutron. There is a positive and negative force, as well as a neutral third element. The centers are based on a similar structure—a left-hand or negative component, a right-hand or positive component, and a powerful middle component. Like the atom, the different elements of a center are in constant motion, interacting around a central focus of energy. This movement gives them an ever-changing form.

Where do these elements come from? They are formed in embryo at the moment of the creation of the soul. They are part of our *Etz haChayim* that stays with us until the moment of union with our spiritual source. They are built up and developed into fully functioning *sefirot* over many incarnations.

Each center contains within it all of the other centers. There is, for example, a *malkhut* aspect of the *sefirah* of *chesed*, and a *keter* component as well. At different times in a center's evolution, different components are dominant.

The *sefirot* in our body of centers will be at different stages of development. One of us may have a well-functioning solar plexus center but a poorly functioning third eye, while another has an open and flowing third eye, but a heart center that is completely closed down. A higher center can be emanating at a low vibration at the same time that a lower center is radiating very refined energy. Everything depends on our specific stage of individual and sefirotic evolution.

The centers will also assume a different appearance depending on the quantity and the quality of the energy that is flowing through them. The centers enlarge and take on new forms as they develop over time.

The expansion of a *sefirah* has been described in various fashions by different spiritual writers. Some speak of a *sefirah* as a wheel of light turning in upon itself, moving from being two-dimensional to four-dimensional, recalling the wheels in Ezekiel's vision of the Heavenly Chariot. Others compare the development of a *chakra* to the unfolding of the petals of a lotus, with each layer of petals embodying a different quality of consciousness. Still others have described a center as a cluster of whirling light that continuously shifts its shape and pattern. What all these descriptions have in common is that they seek to express the fundamental changes that take place as a center develops. These modifications reflect the center's ever-greater capacity to absorb and emanate energy of a higher quality and quantity.

An Interlocking Network of Spiritual Forces

At the same time, each *sefirah* is not an independent system; it is part of an interlocking network of forces.[10] Each individual center is affected by the functioning of the other centers. They interact like molecules in a complex chemical reaction, where each component contributes to the creation of an overall effect.

Every interaction with the environment around us, both human and otherwise, has an effect on the field of light and energy that surrounds each of us. Our body of centers is one small component of the vast field of energy and light that encompasses all life on this planet. A constant stream of spiritual force enters into the body of the Tree of Life and circulates through our *sefirot*. A continual emanation of power flows out from our centers into the surrounding environment.[11]

Some of the incoming energies are used for the maintenance and well-being of the individual; others pass directly from the individual out into the wider world. Both the composition and the vibration of each *sefirah* are constantly changing. At every moment, the centers are being modified and transformed. The picture is one not of a static skeleton, but of a circulatory system where the blood is always flowing, with oxygen, food components, chemical enzymes, and their by-products entering and exiting the body at all times.

A *sefirah* is like a whirling centrifuge. At any given moment, many different types of energy will come flowing into a center. Incoming energies are either absorbed into the *sefirah* or cast aside, depending on their rate of vibration. A more developed *sefirah* will turn at tremendous acceleration, throwing off all but the most refined forms of energy. A less evolved *sefirah* will turn at a slower rate, enabling all kinds of energies to be absorbed into its structure, even energies that may be harmful to us.

There is another level at which the centers evolve. In the early stages of human evolution, the consciousness of a human being is focused in the lower centers below the diaphragm. As we reach toward soul contact, a shift in our consciousness begins to occur. Gradually our awareness is drawn toward the vibration of the higher centers. The *sefirot* above the diaphragm—*tiferet*, *chesed/gevurah*, *chokhmah/binah*, and *keter*—become the focus of our life. As these centers become vital and radiant, a radical transformation takes place in the body of *sefirot*. All of the energies that formerly were directed toward the lower centers are now channeled into the development of the higher ones.

This transformation in the body of the *sefirot* is comparable to the changes that take place in a company that has switched from manual manufacturing to high-tech production. All of the old jobs become automated and no longer need human attention. The human input now goes fully into the creative, management, and distributing aspects of the work.

The Energy Signature of Our *Etz haChayim*

In our efforts to define and identify the nature of the *sefirot*, we tend to forget the actual complex reality that they represent. Not only are the centers constantly changing and shifting, but also the exact composition of each center will vary from person to person. Just as no two people are alike, no two spiritual bodies are the same. The spiritual body of every living thing has its own unique signature of energy patterns. A realized teacher will see these patterns with etheric vision; others may develop an inner sensitivity to the spiritual vibrations that they radiate. These impressions will provide the observer with an indication of the individual's spiritual development, a "snapshot" of the soul as seen by the inner eye.

The Three Energy Pathways

There are three energy pathways that run through our spiritual body. The Kabbalah speaks of them as three columns. The left-hand pathway is called the column of *din*, or judgment. The right-hand is the column of *chesed*, or mercy. The middle path designates the column of *rachamim*, or compassion. It is also called the path of the *Shekhinah*, the Divine Presence.[12]

Yogic teaching identifies three subtle nerves, or *nadis*. Along the left-hand side runs the *nadi* of *ida*, the subtle nerve associated with cooling and the moon. On the right side is the *nadi* of *pingala*, the subtle nerve associated with heating and the sun. Up the middle passage ascends the *sushumna nadi*, the subtle nerve associated with the *kundalini* or serpent power.[13]

Esoteric wisdom defines three vehicles for the spiritual energies. The left side is the vehicle for the psychic energy. The divine energy passes on the right side. The creative energy flows up through the central channel.[14]

All three descriptions are expressing the same reality.

Judgment and Mercy: A Balance of Forces

The left-hand path is one of raw, neutral energy. On the one hand, the power of *din* (judgment) can flow through all of the different centers, but its basic quality will remain neither good nor bad. On the other hand, *din* needs to be tempered by mercy (*chesed*). The right-hand path brings in the positive power of spirit. If the energy of *din* combines with the energy of *chesed*, then it is converted into a force for good. However, if the power of *din* is used on its own, it can be turned into a force for evil. The following analogy illustrates this point.

Two cases come before a court of law. The first case is a mother who stole a loaf of bread because her child was starving. The second case is a

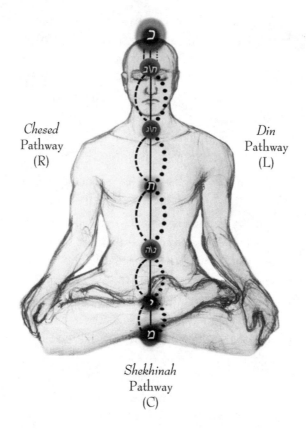

Chesed
Pathway
(R)

Din
Pathway
(L)

Shekhinah
Pathway
(C)

Figure 2. The three energy pathways. Illustration by Moriah Halevi.

wealthy man who stole from his business partner out of envy and greed. How should the court deal with these two cases?

Judgment is neutral; it does not discriminate between individuals. If we steal, then we are punished. Judgment will condemn both equally, resulting in a travesty of justice. Mercy, on the other hand, demands that we act with discrimination. It draws on the wisdom of experience and the compassion of a loving heart. It will soften the judgment of the woman in view of the circumstances and will punish the wealthy man with severity.

Compassion and mercy are an essential part of our existence. Without these divine qualities, the world would destroy itself through the sheer power of judgment. As the midrash *Bereshit Rabbah* states:

"These are the generations of the heavens and of the earth when they were created, in the day that *Adonai Elohim* made the earth and the heavens" (Genesis 2:4).

[It is comparable to] a king who had empty goblets. The king said [to himself]: If I put hot [liquid] into them they will crack; cold [liquid], they will collapse. What did the king do? He mixed together hot and cold and put them [into the goblets] and they endured.

In a similar manner, the Holy One, blessed be He, said [to Himself]: If I create the world with the attribute of compassion, there will be too many sinners; [if I create it] with the attribute of judgment, how will the world endure? Therefore, I will create it with the attribute of judgment and the attribute of compassion, and hopefully it will endure.[15]

The Psychic: Energy of Supernatural Experience

The left-hand energy is also referred to as the psychic. This is because it provides the medium for supernatural experience. The left-hand energy gives form to vision and inspiration. It opens the door to other planes of existence and enables us to contact those planes.

On its own, the psychic energy merely provides an open door. Therefore it can be dangerous. We need the overshadowing protection of the divine kingdom to make sure that the proper door is opened and that we contact the correct plane. Without this protection we can end up anywhere, contacting a disembodied being on any plane, including planes beneath our own.

The right-hand path provides us with this crucial spiritual protection. It guides us to our spiritual home. Providing such protection is one of the major roles of the traditional religions. When Jews pray to God as *Yud Heh Vav Heh*, or Christians pray to Jesus, or Buddhists meditate on the Buddha, they are linked to their spiritual source by a pathway that is formed of all the souls who have come on their particular line. Jews connect with all the prophets, rabbis, and great souls that have come to help and guide the Jewish people. Christians link with all of the Christian saints. Buddhists join with all the incarnations of the Buddha and bodhisattvas.

In this way, our prayers have a specific address to which they go. They are not just a message in a bottle haphazardly blown across the waves of an ocean, arriving, if we are lucky, on a distant and random shore. Our prayers are like a letter taken from our hand by the mail carrier and passed on directly to the post office. We can be sure that it will go to the right place and the right person, because it has a name, an address, and a zip code.

Great Ones who have founded or revitalized a religion act as a "safe pair of hands" to oversee our petitions. They make sure that our prayers arrive at the right destination. This is also the role of spiritual teachers. They protect us during our inner journey. The firm spiritual link that they have established provides a clear pathway into the supernal realm. Like telephone switchboard operators, these meditation guides connect us to the divine communication network.[16]

The Influence of the Psychic on Behavior and Religion

Whereas the spiritual force of the right-hand side plays a central role in human development, the left-hand energy has a powerful influence on the animal kingdom. The animal kingdom is identified with the solar plexus center, *netzach/hod*. This is the *sefirah* where the psychic energy is most potent. Animals have a strong psychic side that gives them a sort of sixth sense. This sixth sense helps them to be aware of their surroundings and provides a form of communication between the animals and their overshadowing angelic presence.

The psychic energy is also highly developed in primitive peoples. This is why their religions tend toward voodoo, trances, and the use of loud drumbeats. Though these practices can seem exotic and enticing, they bring with them certain potential risks. They work almost exclusively through lower psychic energy that exposes the practitioner to influences from the less-evolved planes that resonate with such vibrations.

The psychic energy itself is greatly influenced by the moon. The night-time brings an increase in the power of the psychic. Our auras expand in the dark, making us more aware of psychic phenomena. The full moon further intensifies this effect, bringing this energy to a potent pitch. As a result, the full moon is a time of strange and wild behavior in animals and even human beings. In fact, the old term used to describe people who have lost their sanity recalls the effect of the psychic on human beings. Such people were called lunatics. *Lune* is the French word for the moon.

The full moon is also the designated time for many religious festivals and celebrations. This fact once again underlines the two sides to the psychic energy, as well as the Divine's attempts to take care of us. The psychic energy facilitates our contact with the higher planes of living during the festival. The religious prayers and rituals protect us from any possible negative influences.

The *Shekhinah* Energy: The Creative Force of the Universe

As mentioned at the beginning of the chapter, there is a third path that flows up the central column in the body of centers. In Kabbalah, this middle path is called the path of *rachamim*, or compassion, and also the path of the *Shekhinah*. The *Shekhinah* energy ascends through this central passageway. In the Yogic system, the term used is the *sushumna nadi*. The *kundalini* energy flows along this subtle nerve. The *Shekhinah* or *kundalini* energy is seldom used beyond the lowest two centers of *malkhut* (kingship) and *yesod* (foundation). As *malkhut*, the *Shekhinah* serves as the basic energy that holds together material existence. In *yesod*, it stimulates the physical creation of life.[17]

The *Shekhinah* energy is the energy that binds the atoms of the universe together. It is the power that is released when an atom is split. Its glory is like the blazing light of a thousand suns. When the *kundalini* energy flows into a center, the *sefirah* is dramatically stimulated. If this spiritual force is raised to unite with the crown center *keter*, then the individual human consciousness merges into the universal consciousness of the Divine.

This is the great promise of this energy, and also the great danger. If the *Shekhinah* energy is used correctly, an ordinary individual becomes transformed into an enlightened soul. But if the energy is used wrongly, the person can be destroyed. This is why the knowledge regarding how to raise this energy has been so carefully guarded over the millennia. Today, the power of the *Shekhinah* is so seldom aroused that the knowledge of its use has been forgotten in most spiritual circles, or else its existence is simply denied.

The relationship of the *sefirot* to the centers in the body has also been forgotten by contemporary Kabbalists. The *sefirot* have become heavenly forces, a subject for intellectual and mystical speculation, devoid of any relation to experience. The schools of the prophets in biblical times trained individuals how to stimulate the centers in their spiritual bodies and raise the energy of the *Shekhinah* up the spine.[18] Since that time, however, reason and study have taken over from meditation and other related spiritual practices, and this vital knowledge has become totally obscured.[19] (The nature and workings of the *Shekhinah* energy will be explored in greater detail in chapter 13.)

According to the Jewish tradition, prophecy ended with Malachi, the last of the biblical prophets, and despite the wonders of the Rabbis of the Talmudic period, the mystical experiences of the medieval Kabbalists, and the ascensions of the Hasidic masters, true prophecy has yet to return to Israel.[20]

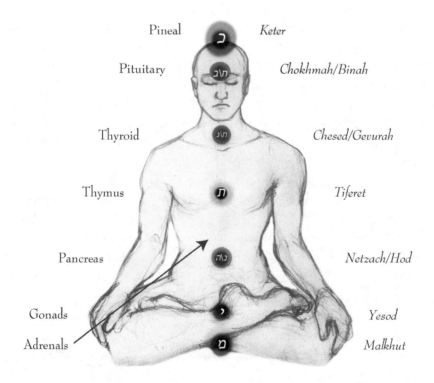

Pineal   Keter

Pituitary   Chokhmah/Binah

Thyroid   Chesed/Gevurah

Thymus   Tiferet

Pancreas   Netzach/Hod

Gonads   Yesod

Adrenals   Malkhut

Figure 3. The *sefirot* and the endocrine glands. Illustration by Moriah Halevi.

The Influence of the Centers on the Physical Body

The spiritual centers exert an important influence on the physical body. A properly functioning network of *sefirot* provides a beneficial flow of vitality and health to the whole metabolism of the body. An excessive activity of one *sefirah*, on the other hand, creates an imbalance and disturbance in the entire system.

A spiritual seeker will feel the effects of the spiritual life reflected in the physical body. Energy received by the centers first affects the glandular system, which then excretes hormones into the bloodstream. The blood, in turn, circulates the glandular influence throughout the rest of the body. Deuteronomy 12:23 tells us, "*Hadam hu hanefesh*—The blood is the life force." The blood carries the energy through the whole of our physical system. This is why, as part of the laws of kashrut (dietary laws), the holy scriptures forbid us to eat blood; we do not want to absorb the lower energy vibration of the animal that is concentrated in the blood.[21]

Energy stimulation affects the organs that are in physical proximity to the major centers. This is the reason why speech, activity, and diet all need to be carefully regulated during periods of intense spiritual practice. The flow of spiritual force through the *sefirot* also has an effect on the nervous system. According to the science of Yoga, there is a network of subtle nerves, or *nadis*, that underlie the entire nervous system. The Kabbalah also speaks about thirty-two energy pathways that connect all of the *sefirot*.[22] When the *chakras* or *sefirot* are stimulated, they send energy coursing through these subtle pathways, or *nadis*. This current of spiritual power then penetrates into all of the nerves.

As the spiritual seeker evolves and is able to assimilate and emanate more refined energies through the centers, the physical body also changes and evolves. Over time, every cell in the body is transformed, reflecting an increased level of purity and efficiency in fulfilling the energy requirements of the seeker's spiritual evolution and work.

2

The Centers

A Detailed Exploration of the Sefirot

Each of the centers in our body of *sefirot* is a world unto itself, with its own qualities and purpose. In this chapter, we investigate the nature of each center in detail—the energies the *chakra* emanates and the state of consciousness it arouses.

The Center at the Base of the Spine: *Malkhut*—Kingship

The first of the major centers is the center at the base of the spine, *malkhut*, kingship. *Malkhut* is the earth pole of the *sefirot*. It is the embodiment of the earth and all that is in it.[1] *Malkhut* is the seat of the *kundalini* or *Shekhinah* energy.[2] In the sacral center, the center above *malkhut*, this energy is utilized for the creation of life.[3] *Yesod*, or the sacral center, is the only center where the energy of the *Shekhinah* is normally active in our bodies.

The raising of the *Shekhinah* energy was taught in ancient Israel and India. It was an unusual occurrence for someone to raise this potent spiritual force even in ancient times. Today, it is very rare indeed. To rightly develop the power of the *Shekhinah* requires a great deal of spiritual training. Its development needs to be overseen by someone who carries this energy and has been instructed in the technique of its arousal and progression.

Malkhut embodies the female or mother aspect of Deity.[4] Like a mother, the energy of this center feeds and nourishes the material form. The energy of *malkhut* underlies the whole of God's physical kingdom.

This center is aligned with the crown center, *keter*. If *malkhut* is the earth pole, then *keter* is the pole of heaven. Like the ladder of Jacob's vision—set on the ground with its head reaching to the heavens—the goal of the spiritual life is to raise the energy along the axis of *malkhut* to *keter*.

Malkhut draws the energy of the "will to be,"[5] the fundamental desire to live, from *keter* and infuses the whole of the body with it. In the beginning of the incarnation process, which can last multiple lifetimes, we dwell in a semiconscious state, with only the will to live animating our being. This most basic form of existence is maintained by the *sefirah* of *malkhut*, drawing on the most rudimentary aspect of the energy of *keter*. Later, as the incarnations progress, the energy of consciousness flows into the centers and becomes the focal point for human life and evolution.

The Sacral or Genital Center: *Yesod*—Foundation

Yesod (foundation), the sacral or genital center, is the focus of the physical creative process and the foundation of all life. The power of *yesod* joins two opposites together. We all know the strength of its pull. It is the source of the great profusion of lifeforms on this planet. Without its "magnetism," there would be no life.[6]

When the sexual energy is sanctified by love, it is a gift of great joy. When there is love between two people, the sexual act can raise the *Shekhinah* energy to the heart center, *tiferet*, and stimulate a great expansion of the heart.[7] If, on the other hand, the sexual act is drawn down into the lower emotions of lust, jealousy, and envy, if our sexuality becomes entangled with negative psychological processes, then it becomes an act that is debasing—it is then a debilitating and destructive force.

This center also holds the energy of order. The Baal Shem Tov calls *yesod* "*koach hahitkashrut*—the power to connect."[8] *Yesod* is the cohesive force that binds spirit and matter together to create a living entity. The power of *yesod* gathers the diverse components of our reality and organizes them into a world of vitality and activity. *Yesod* transforms thoughtforms in mental matter into ideas and binds these ideas to form—be it the form of a body, an organizational structure, or a written page.[9]

Yesod is a very potent center at this time in human history. As many of the old ideas and structures of traditional society are disintegrating, this energy plays a central role in helping to organize and build new structures and ideals to replace them.

During the evolutionary process, the energy of the sacral center is shifted to the throat center—the *sefirah* of higher creativity. In this manner, the creative energy of *yesod* is redirected into intellectual and intuitive activity. New music, art, and science take the place of the act of physical procreation. The focus of our creative work is raised up from the plane of the dense physical into the realm of ideas and thoughtforms. In this manner, we move one step further along the path of our spiritual development, one step closer to the higher plane of living where we truly belong (see the section "The Throat Center").[10]

When the *sefirah* of *yesod* is brought to its highest fulfillment, the full creative power of the human mind will be awakened. At that time, the thoughts of the Kingdom of Heaven will penetrate into the minds of the thinkers of humanity, and the plan of God will come to fruition.

The Solar Plexus Center: *Netzach/Hod—* Eternity/Splendor

The solar plexus, *netzach/hod* (eternity/splendor), is designated as the third center in the seven-center framework. It is the center of emotions, the seat of the consciousness that allows us to become immersed in feeling.[11] When the power of the mind joins together with the emotions, we get a very potent force.

The consciousness of the majority of people is focused on the emotional level. Most of our life is spent thinking about our desires and how to fulfill them. Both in our fantasy life and in the real world, we are preoccupied with ourselves, with what we want and how we feel. Other people usually enter into our consciousness when they intersect with our needs.

The solar plexus is the gathering point for the energies of the centers below the diaphragm. Through the activity of this center the whole of our animal nature is unified and organized. The Hebrew word *netzach* has two meanings. It means "eternity," but it also means "victory." The solar plexus controls the lower instincts in a human being. In this center we vanquish our lower instincts and emotions.[12]

The *sefirah* of *netzach/hod* is the clearinghouse for our negative feelings and glamorous illusions. As *netzach/hod* evolves, it absorbs these lower emotions into itself, purifying and then transmuting them. When these energies have been fully purified, they are transferred up into the next center, *tiferet*, the heart. There they are used to evoke the higher emotions of love and compassion.[13]

As our solar plexus center develops, the quality of our emotions and desires starts to change. Our feelings become more subtle and mature. We become more aware of others, more sensitive to their needs. We seek a more refined way of living. We look for intellectual and artistic stimulation. We want to succeed, but equally we yearn to contribute.

The higher aspects of physical life now attract us. We search out more advanced material goals. Fame and fortune take the place of greed and lust. We think about becoming a great artist or a famous politician. We want to build a financial empire; we desire to leave our mark on society. These powerful emotions motivate us to live by more elevated ideals. Though we still have material desires, they epitomize the highest aspirations of the personality.

At this point, the focus of our consciousness shifts from the solar plexus to the heart center. As this occurs, we experience a sudden change in our perspective. Our ambition to succeed becomes a desire to serve. A businessman will turn into a generous philanthropist. A politician will take up the defense of the disenfranchised. Selfish desire is redirected into selfless service. These changes in our behavior are the outward signs of the profound inner transformation that is starting to take place.

The solar plexus center also serves another significant function. This center enacts an important role in the inner life of all spiritual seekers. *Netzach/hod* is the *sefirah* where the psychic energy is most powerfully stimulated.[14] It provides the pathway for the psychic energy into the body of centers. As we start out on the path, the psychic energy provides us with much needed encouragement in the way of spiritual experiences. Then, at a later stage, the psychic becomes our gateway into the Kingdom of Heaven and the conscious experience of the divine realms. This is why this *sefirah* is called *hod* or splendor, because through its medium we experience the celestial splendor.[15]

In its role as a spiritual doorway, however, the psychic also introduces certain dangers. Since the psychic energy merely provides an open passage into other worlds, we can end up anywhere, including planes beneath our own.

Contact with lower planes occurs more often than most people realize. When people interact with the lower psychic, they become hypnotized by the energy. Immersed in a world of illusion and half-reality, they are lost in a state of semi-trance.

This is not the only hazard. In their eagerness to get close to God, some seekers are drawn into a relationship with disembodied beings from these planes. These spirits play on their egos, convincing them that they are great spiritual beings. They are misled into believing that they have contacted the higher worlds of the Kingdom of Heaven. As a result, their inner development becomes misdirected, and their spiritual growth is derailed.[16]

In the worst cases, such individuals can be persuaded by their so-called inner guides to commit terrible crimes and engage in immoral acts. The Hebrew Bible speaks about the corrupt cults of ancient Canaan where adherents threw their children into the fire for the god Molech and took part in wild orgies in the name of the goddess Ashtoret. All of these base forms of idol worship were a product of such lower psychic alliances.[17]

When the lower psychic overshadows a large group of people, the consequences can be catastrophic. Whole populations can be led into spiritual darkness. The scriptures struggle at length with how to deal with such a city, finally deciding that it must be destroyed.[18]

Nor are such stories restricted to ancient myth and scripture. The great political rallies of Nazi Germany are an example of the modern use of the hypnotic power of the psychic to overpower the will of people's minds. These methods influenced the soul of a whole nation, inducing unthinkable, immoral behavior in otherwise ordinary human beings.

Anyone engaged in meditation and the development of the inner life needs to be overseen by a teacher. A teacher will provide guidance and spiritual protection for the seekers as they progress along the path. A competent spiritual director will know when individuals need careful overseeing and when they are capable of pursuing inner contacts on their own.

Many of the great spiritual masters have left us with clear instructions about how to distinguish between higher spiritual contacts and lower psychic phenomena. The teachings of the Baal Shem Tov provide us with valuable information in this regard. The best defense against spiritual problems, the Baal Shem tells us, is a dedicated life of purity and holiness. To be worthy of higher contacts, he explains, we need to fully attune our minds with God. Once we naturally turn to God for everything and at every moment, then we can trust the inner guidance that we receive.[19]

The books of the Christian mystic Saint Teresa of Avila are a helpful source of practical advice for dealing with a seeker who has become unhinged by the psychic. Among other advice, Saint Teresa makes clear that the nun in question needs to be prevented from spending too much time in meditation and prayer. She should also be given lots of practical work to occupy her. Saint Teresa also warns us not to argue with the troubled individual about her visions and heavenly voices; it will only make matters worse. The soundest counsel, she says, is to pay no attention to her psychic experiences; only in this manner will they quiet down. Saint Teresa admits that in some instances, she had to apply very harsh treatment to these disturbed souls. It caused her great pain to do so, she says, but the danger to them and to all those around them was too great to chance any other course. In most cases, Saint Teresa was able to gradually restore these wayward sisters to a healthy inner life. Her writings present us with an excellent example of the power of evolved spiritual teachers to guide those in their care.[20]

The solar plexus is one of the most vital centers in our spiritual body. It serves a crucial function in both our emotional and our inner life. *Netzach/hod* is an extremely active center in the spiritual body of the individual, as well as in the body of all of humankind. Raising our consciousness from the solar plexus up to the heart center, *tiferet*, is the spiritual goal before us all, as individuals and as a race.[21]

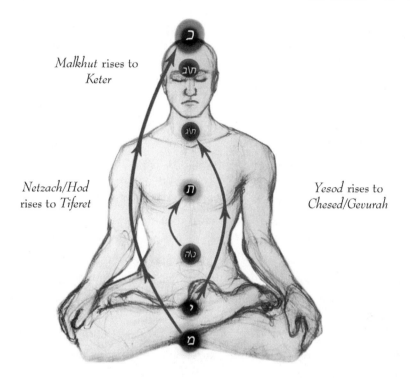

Malkhut rises to *Keter*

Netzach/Hod rises to *Tiferet*

Yesod rises to *Chesed/Gevurah*

Figure 4. The evolution of the *sefirot*. Illustration by Moriah Halevi.

The Heart Center: *Tiferet*—Beauty

Like its physical counterpart, the heart center circulates divine livingness throughout the whole of our subtle body. *Tiferet* is the central organ of the body of centers. It is a potent force in our spiritual advancement.[22]

The energy of the heart center is the energy of love. This magnetic power draws everything into its orbit. Love draws disciples to the teacher. Love pulls humanity toward God.

The heart center plays a pivotal role in the religious life. The development of a loving and compassionate heart is critical to our spiritual evolution. The first instruction given to any seeker is to learn how to love. Learn to act with selflessness, learn to give without thought of return; learn how to open your heart.

The heart center brings in the power of the right-hand side. Once *tiferet* is open and flowing, then we can be easily overshadowed by our soul. This higher presence provides us with inner protection from the negative influences of the psychic side.

We tend to think of love as a feeling. In fact, love is a state of consciousness. The development of the heart center is primarily an expansion of the mind. True love arises out of the inner experience of the Oneness of all being. We love others because we have discovered our common divine essence—because we realize that they are really ourselves.

Attaining this consciousness of love is a multistage process. We begin with a narrow, self-centered mind where we are unaware of anyone but ourselves. As our mind begins to expand, we start to notice other people. We become aware of their feelings, sensitive to their needs. We also start to care about their well-being and the quality of their lives.

At first, this broadened awareness touches only our close friends and family. Gradually, however, it reaches out to include larger and larger circles of people. The more our mind expands, the more our heart widens with it, and our feelings of love begin to deepen and grow. We start to feel love for our communities, love for our nation, and finally love for all beings everywhere.

It is through this expanding circle of love and inclusiveness that we join with the One who is the source of love. The Divine Consciousness is all-inclusive and all-embracing. If we want to join with God, then we need to become all-inclusive and all-embracing as well. The more we broaden our sense of inclusiveness, the more we will feel love for others. As our love approaches the all-encompassing love of the Creator, we will merge into the Boundless Ocean of Grace.

This process of the expansion of our consciousness and the circle of our love is also taking place within the larger human community. As technology has brought events around the globe into our living rooms, we have begun to identify with the struggles and hardships of people everywhere. We feel the pain of total strangers who live on the other side of the world. These feelings arouse in us a desire to alleviate all human suffering. We want to eradicate hunger, poverty, and ignorance. We have come to realize that we all belong to one human family. We have come to understand the precious value of a human life.

This growth in compassion and the broadening of our sense of inclusiveness mark an important step in human spiritual evolution. These developments are the external signs of the gradual opening of the heart center in the body of humankind.

The opening of the heart center reflects a shift of the whole of our perception out of the lower centers into the higher ones. It represents a definite move away from the lower self and its physical desires. The energy and mind-set in the lower centers attune us to this physical reality. The heart puts us in resonance with the Kingdom of Heaven.

When the heart center is open and flowing, we awaken to the higher aspirations. The development of religious virtues becomes our objective. Prayer and meditation become our form of relaxation. The service of God's plan becomes the focus of our work.

The consciousness of the heart center links us to who we truly are. *Tiferet* reveals the beauty of our soul. Indeed, the heart center is the first truly human center or *sefirah*. It is the heart that raises us above the animals and binds us to our Eternal Source.[23]

The Throat Center: *Chesed/Gevurah*—Mercy/Power

The throat center, *chesed/gevurah* (mercy/power), is the center of the teacher. It is the *sefirah* where the power of speech is mastered.[24] This means more than simply the capacity to be an excellent orator. The mastery of the throat center is the power to give authority and life to one's words. When the throat center is fully flowing, the words have purpose and relevance, captivating everyone who listens to them.

Chesed/gevurah is the center of human creativity. The energy of this *sefirah* attunes our creative imagination to the influence of divine inspiration.[25] *Chesed/gevurah* is the spiritual force behind the great artists, musicians, and thinkers. As noted earlier, the energies of the lower sacral center are shifted into the throat center as our spiritual evolution progresses. It is therefore understandable that there has always been such a close link between the artistic lifestyle and sexuality. There is a constant tension in the life of the artist between these two poles of creativity.

The throat center is the place where love and wisdom combine to guide and nurture seekers. Wisdom is the quality of the center above—the third eye, or *chokhmah/binah* (wisdom/understanding). Love is the quality of the center below—the heart center, or *tiferet* (beauty). Love and wisdom join together in the throat to create *chesed*, or mercy, the unique quality of this *sefirah*.[26] Individuals who work from this center have loving compassion for our suffering and merciful wisdom for our earthly struggles. They pour out their love on us. They teach us how to sanctify our existence. They strive with compassion to alleviate our sorrows. They work with mercy to ease our burdens, to lighten the load we carry in our lives.

Chesed/gevurah is the center of healing. Through this center all great acts of healing are done. When the energy of the throat center combines with the creative power of the *Shekhinah*, it generates an extremely potent spiritual force. This powerful energy wipes away all personality impurities and heals illness and disease.[27]

The actual work of healing is accomplished in conjunction with the angelic kingdom. Through the medium of the throat center, the creative energy of the angelic lives is directed toward the healing and repair of the sick individual's physical and subtle bodies.[28] This intricate spiritual work entails strong coordination between the two kingdoms. It requires a highly evolved instrument who is both carefully trained and very pure. Otherwise, what began as healing can quickly deteriorate into greater illness and suffering (see chapter 10, "The Angelic Kingdom").

The full vivification of the *sefirah* of *chesed/gevurah* is the source of a well-known spiritual discipline. This is the discipline of self-imposed silence. This practice is far more than a method to control our words. During extended periods of silence, the throat center can be stimulated in ways that are impossible when it is being utilized for speech. Individuals who take a vow of silence have given over their throat centers to higher service. They have renounced their voice for the sake of divine purpose.

The throat center is a multifaceted center of immense spiritual power. This is why it is called *gevurah*, or power, in the Kabbalah. The throat center radiates the vital force of healing and the living spirit of the higher creativity. It awakens the transformative energy of *chesed*, of love combined with wisdom, and the strength of the spoken word to uplift and inspire. From this *sefirah* emanate forth great words of power—the might of the divine utterances that created the world.[29]

The Third Eye: *Chokhmah/Binah—* Wisdom/Understanding

The *sefirah* of *chokhmah/binah*, wisdom/understanding, is the main center of meditation. Through this center we enter into the world of the mind, and through the mind we penetrate into the higher planes. Many forms of meditation instruct us to concentrate on the area between the eyebrows, where *chokhmah/binah* is located. Some believe this center to be the site of the soul, or more accurately, the gateway to the soul.

Through the *sefirah* of *chokhmah/binah*, we tap into the power of the creative imagination and the gift of inner sight. The third eye opens the door to new horizons and fresh possibilities. By focusing the energies of our mind on this center, we forge a pathway in mental substance between the physical and spiritual realms. The science of meditation is the science of the formation and utilization of this connecting "bridge." All visualization and concentration exercises are meant to help push this process forward.[30] (For an in-depth look at the process and role of meditation, see my book *Living the Life of Jewish Meditation: A Comprehensive Guide to Practice and Experience*, published by Jewish Lights.)

There are three stages to the development of this center. In the initial stage, *chokhmah/binah* serves as the door into our interior world. During this phase, all of our efforts are concentrated on building the mind bridge. Many hours are spent in this endeavor; it is a long and slow process, but there are "sweets" along the way. These are gifts of spiritual experience that give us consolation and encouragement. These experiences are the preliminary indication that the first strands of the bridge have been laid in place.

The second stage of the development of this center begins when clear spiritual contact has been made. This occurs as the bridge nears completion and a solid link has been established between the higher and lower minds. A stream of pure inspiration then begins to flow between these two aspects of the mind, putting the spiritual seeker into contact with the light of the soul. This is the reason why the third eye is called *chokhmah/binah*, because through this center we tap into the infinite wisdom and understanding that is in the universal mind of God.[31]

Now that the bridge in mental matter has been firmly formed, the higher self can pass the more rarified energies of the supernal planes to the lower self in incarnation. These energies are gathered into the sixth center and then projected out into the wider world. This is the final stage of this center's development, where the *sefirah* of *chokhmah/binah* is transformed into a spiritual transmitter and not just a receiver. It has become a great emanating station for the creative energy of God.

At an advanced stage in this process, the third eye is consciously used to direct energy toward a specific individual. It can even be used as a vehicle for the emanation of the *Shekhinah* energy. A direct influx of *Shekhinah* energy in this manner will create an incredible stimulation in the recipient's centers. It will propel the person forward into a state of higher consciousness. It is rare indeed for someone to reach the stage where his or her third eye is used in this manner. But it is a reality that is attested to by the scriptures and by the great teachers throughout history.[32]

When the development of this center reaches its highest fulfillment, the left-hand and right-hand components of the third eye come together, and the *Shekhinah* ascends to *chokhmah/binah*. When this occurs, we become conscious in the Kingdom of Heaven and can see God.[33] This is the meaning of the prophetic state of being "face-to-face" described in the Hebrew Bible. As the Holy Blessed One declares in reference to the prophet Moses, "My servant Moses, who is like a trusted servant throughout My house. With him I speak face-to-face, in a vision not containing allegory, so that he sees a true picture of God" (Numbers 12:7–8).[34]

The third eye plays yet one other vital role in the spiritual life of humanity. This center is the focal point for the energy of peace.[35] Shalom or peace is not just an energy; it is a state of being—a world where calm, stillness, and tranquility reign. Through *chokhmah/binah* we link our minds with this plane of total harmony and draw its power into our consciousness, thereby blessing us with a peace *m'ein olam habah*—a serenity from the higher worlds. Learning how to access and radiate this transcendental peace is of supreme importance for the future well-being of the human race.

The many facets of the third eye make it one of the major centers of the body. Other centers, like the throat and heart centers, provide great spiritual benefit, but the *sefirah* of *chokhmah/binah* is the agent of spiritual initiation. It is the central divine vehicle for the enlightenment of humanity.

The Head Center: *Keter*—the Crown

The center at the top of the head is a complex and sensitive instrument. Yogic teaching describes this *chakra* as a lotus composed of a thousand petals that need to be unfolded one by one.[36] This spiritual blossoming is a long and slow process that rarely comes to fruition in one lifetime.

A fully functioning head center is the distinguishing characteristic of the great prophets and teachers of humanity. It is an expression of the merging of the individual with God and marks a complete transformation of the physical human being. This momentous event is the culmination of an extended period of intense spiritual practice. It is the ultimate goal of the religious life.

This process of at-one-ment is portrayed in a symbolic manner in the mystical literature. The Kabbalah speaks of the mystical union of the bride and groom, the celestial meeting of the queen and king. The Hindu scriptures describe the joining of the Deity with his female *Shakti*, or power. Christians speak about the mystical union of Christ with his bride. All of these images are in reality describing a scientific process that takes place in the body of spiritual centers whereby a human being is joined with God.[37]

As we evolve along the spiritual path, our consciousness rises from center to center, uniting the left and right components in each of the *sefirot*. When this process reaches the highest center, the *Shekhinah* energy ascends through the middle passage to the *sefirah* of *keter*, the crown center, and a corresponding infusion of divine energy pours down into the top of the head from the highest aspect of the soul. When these two streams of energy, from above and from below, merge together, all of the centers fuse into one great *sefirah* in the head, and the body becomes filled with light. The power of this fusion bridges the gap between the physical and spiritual planes, and we become conscious in the Kingdom of Heaven.[38]

As a result of this spiritual union, we are transformed from an ordinary human being into a God-realized soul. Our will is now totally bound to the divine will. Our separate identity is submerged in the Infinite Consciousness that underlies all of existence. Enough personality is retained to enable us to function in the world, but this is only a facade. In truth, the individual personality no longer exists. All that remains is a pure instrument.[39]

The opening of the crown center and the awakening of the energy of the will of God are closely linked with the experience of suffering.[40] This is because our inner strength is galvanized in times of adversity. When circumstances arise that push our capabilities to the limit, we are forced to dig deep into our inner self and find new strength that we never knew we possessed. This new strength comes from the activation of our crown center, and it is our dire need and the suffering we endure that bring it to the fore. The trials and tribulations of life build up within us a great reservoir of willpower.

Or perhaps it is more correct to say that it is not our will that dwells in *keter* at all, but only the will of God. As a result of great suffering, the ego is shattered and faith in our own will is drastically shaken. In that moment, when the hold of the lower self has been weakened, our higher self can break through and reach us. Then the eternal will of God can come through our soul and inspire us. This is the reason that the development of the crown center is intrinsically linked with the experience of suffering.

The Hidden *Sefirah*: *Daat*—Knowledge

The Kabbalah speaks of one other major *sefirah* that is not included among either the ten *sefirot* or the seven-center framework. This is the *sefirah* of *daat*, or knowledge. *Daat* is a hidden and mysterious *sefirah*. It manifests in ways that are hard to understand and expresses its nature in seemingly contradictory fashions.[41]

To begin to unravel this mystery, we turn to Genesis 4:1, where the Bible tells us, "*Veha'adam yada et Chavah ishto*—And the man knew his wife Eve." On the highest level, *daat* manifests as the knowledge that comes from direct experience. It is a sense of knowingness that arises out of intimate and profound interaction.

In its purest manifestation, the *sefirah* of *daat* is formed when the *sefirah* of *chokhmah* unites with the *sefirah* of *binah* and then fuses with *keter*. *Keter* then becomes the apex of a triangle of energy in the head. It is no longer called *keter*—it is now designated as the third of the three aspects of the mind: *chokhmah*, or wisdom; *binah*, or understanding; and *daat*, or knowledge.[42] This is *daat elyon*, the higher knowledge.

The center of *daat* also manifests in another quite different manner as *daat tachton*, the lower knowledge. *Daat tachton* is the vessel through which the spiritual power of the head center is channeled into the rest of the body. *Daat tachton* arises when the subtle concepts of wisdom and understanding become concretized in tangible knowledge that we can apply to our lives. When it plays this role, *daat* is identified as a hidden *sefirah* that develops between the shoulder blades. This newly unveiled *sefirah* becomes a gathering point or way station for energies to move between the higher and the lower aspects of a human being.[43]

The *sefirah* of *daat* functions in this manner during the process of the emanation of the divine attributes from the *Ein Sof* (the Absolute) down into *keter*, and from there into the body of *sefirot*. This occurs when the *Etz haChayim* (Tree of Life) is first stimulated and aligned.

Later, during the process of personal spiritual evolution, the center of *daat* works in the opposite direction, raising the energies of the body up into the head. Here *daat* acts as the bridge between the intangible and the concrete. It is the knowledge that lifts the physical up into the spiritual realm.

When *daat* reaches its highest level of development, *daat elyon* and *daat tachton* merge together to lift us into the spiritual realm, while simultaneously drawing the reality of the supernal worlds down into our physical awareness.

This fusion of *daat elyon* and *daat tachton* is destined to occur on both the individual and the collective level. When this unification takes place on a global scale, the whole of humanity will be raised up toward the heavens, and the Kingdom of Heaven will descend upon earth. As Isaiah 11:6–9 prophesies:

> The wolf also shall dwell with the lamb, and the leopard lie down with the kid; and the calf and the young lion and the fatling together; and a little child shall lead them. And the cow and the bear shall graze; their young ones shall lie down together; and the lion shall eat straw like the ox. And a babe shall play on the hole of the cobra, and an infant shall put his hand on the viper's nest. They shall not hurt nor destroy in all My holy mountain; for the earth shall be full of the knowledge (*daat*) of God, as the waters cover the sea.

The Importance of the *Sefirot*

The study of the *sefirot* is the key to understanding consciousness and to comprehending the method by which all life evolves. The centers define our state of awareness. They determine our likes and dislikes, attractions and repulsions. Ultimately, the state of our spiritual centers decides the course that we will follow in our life.

The body of *sefirot* is an essential element in our comprehension of the structure of the cosmos. Understanding the workings of the Tree of Life clarifies the organization of the supernal realm and systematizes the varied lifeforms in the universe. Without its guiding hand, everything would remain a mystery.

The *sefirot* are a crucial part of our approach to God. Through meditation we awaken the energies in the centers and raise our awareness onto higher planes. In this manner, we join with our soul, and through our soul we merge with God. As we evolve, we reach ever further into the divine unity and encompass ever greater breadths of life within our consciousness.

———— ⬡ ————

The Science of the Soul

The spiritual literature of the world's mystical traditions describes the character of the human soul in many different ways. The number of components that make up the soul changes from system to system. For Buddhism, there is no individual soul at all, only a universal essence. For Hinduism, there is the concept of both the *jiva*, or individual soul, and the Atman, or universal Soul—the Self of all that is.

Within Judaism there exist numerous approaches to this issue. The number of levels to the soul depends on the system, with each level having its own function and coloring. Yet there are certain conceptions that are crucial to any understanding of the soul. I have chosen to use the terms *nefesh, ruach, neshama, chayah,* and *yechidah* to express these essential elements of the soul's structure. This terminology follows the teachings of the Ari and therefore employs the terms used by much of the subsequent Kabbalistic schools that follow him.

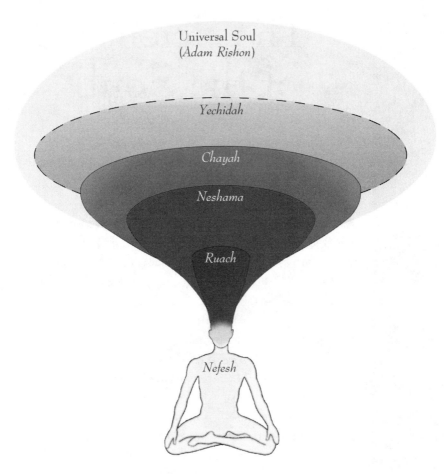

Figure 5. The five levels of the soul

3

The Nature of the Soul

We Are a Multilayered Being

In Judaism the higher nature of a human being is divided into five major components: the *nefesh*, the *ruach*, the *neshama*, the *chayah*, and the *yechidah*.[1] Each of these expresses a different aspect of the soul.

The *Nefesh*, or Personality

The *nefesh* can be considered as synonymous with the personality or intellect. It is the thinking, feeling human being in the world, the component that makes us the creative, active creatures we are.[2] The personality is the expression of the soul as it is reflected in one incarnation. It is a garment that the soul puts on in order to clothe the higher self in a body. It provides a vehicle for our true self. Without the vessel of the personality, we could not function on this physical plane. Our personality is composed of those characteristics that will aid us in our life's work. It is the repository of the necessary tools for the job that we need to accomplish in this incarnation. When this life is over, it is the *nefesh*, or personality, that dies.[3]

The *Ruach*, or Individual Soul

The second level of the soul is the *ruach*. This is the name for the spark of God within us all. It is our individual soul, the personal expression of the greater Life in which we live, breathe, and have our being. The *ruach* is the real human. It is the part of us that undergoes reward and punishment when we pass away.[4]

The *Neshama*, or Group Soul

The *ruach* cannot be understood without reference to the *neshama*—our true soul. The *neshama* is the larger soul to which we belong and from which we come. Like a pomegranate that contains many individual seeds, a *neshama* is composed of a number of separate souls who share a similar spiritual background and are bound together into a single unit or group.[5]

Initially, the souls that dwell within the *neshama* live in a consciousness of oneness and have no separate identity. A *ruach* is formed only when one spark of the group soul is broken off to fulfill a particular purpose. In order to accomplish this goal, this spark is given individual consciousness. The *ruach*, or spark, then descends into the physical world and evolves through its own series of incarnations and experiences.

The *ruach* goes from life to life, gaining knowledge and wisdom and developing purity and other virtues, which gradually are incorporated into its nature. When the *ruach* reaches the desired point of development, the barrier that separates the individual soul from the group soul is shattered. The *ruach* then is reabsorbed into the greater soul from which it originally was created. And the spiritual qualities and wisdom it has gained become part of the storehouse of knowledge and energy in the Divine Consciousness.

The *Chayah*—the *Neshama* of the *Neshama*

There are a multitude of different *neshamot,* or group souls, in the higher worlds. Each single *neshama*, or group soul, is part of an even greater group soul, which in turn is part of an even greater group soul—a process that goes on ad infinitum. As we progress in our evolution to become one with the source of our *neshama*, we reach up into the higher source from which our *neshama* has come. The *neshama* of the *neshama*, the greater group soul from which our own *neshama* was created, is called the *chayah*. We see an expression of this process in the life of Abraham, or Avraham (in Hebrew the letter *b* becomes *v*).

Avraham's original name was Avram. This name is composed of two words: *av*, "father," and *ram*, "high or esteemed." Together they form "father of many" or "high father." This formidable name indicates that Avram was connected to the source of his *ruach*, or individual soul, his *neshama*. (The full significance of this title will be further explained in the next chapter.)

Later in life, Avram underwent a spiritual initiation in which he was linked with the source of his *neshama*, or group soul—his *chayah*. As a symbol of this spiritual ascension, God added the Hebrew letter *heh* to Avram's name, so that he became Avraham. The letter *heh* is part of the Sacred Name *Yud Heh Vav Heh*. Its addition powerfully expresses the depth of the bond that was now forged between the Holy One of Israel and Avraham.

Each *chayah* or *neshama* has a specific quality that makes up its essential nature. These qualities are composed from the essence of the different *sefirot*. One *chayah* or *neshama* will embody, for example, the quality of *chokhmah*/wisdom, while another *chayah* or *neshama* will have the characteristics of *chesed*/mercy. Each *chayah* or *neshama* has its own *sefirah* from which it is formed.

Of course, given the complexity of the spiritual worlds, each of these group souls is composed of qualities from more than one center. For example, there may be one group soul that embodies the *chesed/* mercy aspect of the *chokhmah*/wisdom energy, while another soul expresses the *netzach*/eternity component of *chokhmah*. Though each group soul has components from a number of aspects of different centers, there always remains one center that dominates the soul. This central quality is then subtly colored by other complementing or contrasting elements.

A *neshama* is like a symphony with a central recurring theme that blends with a variety of melodic lines or "voices." The theme is sometimes buried amid the other notes, but it is always present and will resurface again. The harmony and contrast between the elements of the symphony give it its beauty and its distinctive sound. From this spiritual foundation, we get the wide range of individuals who manifest on this plane of existence. They are reflections of the many aspects of the Divine, each created with its own task and purpose.

The Soul and Religion

The *chayot* and *neshamot* have to do with the organization of the King-dom of Heaven and the purpose of religion. Each of us belongs to a particular group soul that is an expression of our essential nature. We are perfectly attuned to the quality of this soul; for us its vibration is home. It is the path of harmony and purpose that pulls us toward God in the most effective way.

Each religion is aligned with a particular vibration and energy. The different sects in each religion represent different approaches within the overall path that are suited to the various aspects of human nature. At the same time, as in life, not all of us gain the most by staying at home. Sometimes we will achieve greater progress by taking on a different religious tradition than our own. Often the knowledge and energy we acquire are then useful for our original natal faith.

Conversely, converts often bring with them a spiritual quality that is missing from their adopted religion. This has been a frequent occurrence in Judaism, where converts have played an important role in bringing new ideas and energies into the tradition. The biblical Ruth and the Tal-mudic Rabbi Akiva are two good examples: King David is descended from Ruth, and Rabbi Akiva, the son of converts, was arguably the great-est and most innovative of the Talmudic figures.

Whatever path we may take in a particular life, our group soul plays a central role in our evolution and is the ultimate home to which we return.

Not only do individuals come from different soul groups; different souls are at diverse points in their evolution. Some of us have progressed a long way in our journey through many incarnations; others are just starting out. This will be reflected in the nature of our lives and the work we have to do in the plan of God.

Some individuals come from group souls on a very high plane. Their birth and incarnation has been carefully planned, and a great deal of effort will be exerted to bring their life to fruition. Others come from group souls that were recently formed and are just at the beginning of their pilgrimage. Every individual, however, is precious and important. Every life has a purpose. Every soul plays a part in the divine scheme.

The *Yechidah*—the Root Soul

The last aspect of the soul is called the *yechidah*. The *yechidah* relates to the Universal Soul from which all of humankind has emerged. In the Kabbalistic tradition this soul is called *Adam Kadmon*, the Primordial Man, or alternatively, *Adam Rishon*, the First Man. Each human being is a spark of this vast soul. The *yechidah* is the *shoresh neshama*, the supernal root from which our soul has originated—the specific part in the body of *Adam Rishon* to which it can be traced. Our *yechidah* expresses our ultimate identity as part of the great Oneness of all life.

The Ari divides the different soul groups—the *neshama* and *chayah*—of each soul according to their location in the body of *Adam Kadmon/Rishon*. One person will be part of the shoulder; another, part of the heel; and so on. Each part is then a whole *partzuf*, or body, in itself, divided into a head, torso, legs, and so on. There are 248 limbs and 365 sinews in the body, which together form 613 major *shoreshim*, or soul roots. And these major *shoreshim* are then divided into smaller *shoreshim*, or roots, numbering up to 600,000.[6]

The Evolution of Our Soul

These five aspects or levels to the soul exist simultaneously on different planes. The two higher aspects of the soul, the *chayah* and *yechidah*, rarely become active factors in our awareness. They are relevant to the lives of great souls like Abraham. For the majority of us, the main focus of our spiritual life is the three lower aspects of the soul: the *nefesh*, *ruach*, and *neshama*. These three dimensions of the soul will be at a phase of integration into a unified whole in accordance with the stage of our own spiritual evolution.

In the beginning, the two lowest aspects of our soul are disconnected and vaguely formed. Our soul is but a simple spark, not yet aglow with the power of experience and refinement, and our personality is still unformed, not yet tested in the crucible of this world. However, over many incarnations, we will be transformed from a disparate and fragmented individual into a perfected divine instrument whose soul and personality are fused into one single consciousness. Our separate existence will then drop away, and our individual soul will be reunited with its greater source. We will be consciously aware on the higher planes and be able to communicate with the life that inhabits them. We will be alive in both heaven and earth—a powerful tool of the Almighty Architect that brings the presence of the spiritual realm down into this physical reality.

4

Our Soul Family

We Have a Higher Home in the Heavens

Each of us has a place that we call home in the supernal realm. In that place dwell the souls that are part of our *neshama*, or group soul—our soul family.[1] All the members of our *neshama* carry different aspects of the same energy. For example, if the underlying quality of our soul is love, then one individual soul in the group will embody pure love; another soul, love and wisdom; still another, love and strength; and yet another, love and beauty—each soul will express the quality of love in its own unique manner.

Our Relationship with Our Soul Family

Though each member of the soul is an individual with a separate identity, they all work together in a spirit of harmony and unity of purpose. They all are perfectly attuned to one another. Each of them naturally knows which role and function to take in order for the greater soul to achieve its goal.

The members of our soul family know our heart, because it is their heart. They understand our mind, because it is their mind as well. Our soul family shares the same aspirations and values. They feel our joy and experience our sorrow. They love us with a profound and unconditional love, because they know that we are one.

41

On this physical plane of existence, we are constantly struggling to reach each other across the great divide of the personality. In order to build a group relationship, we need to first overcome our natural inclination to protect our fragile egos. Then we need to negotiate the emotional minefield of other people's desire for recognition and control. Finally, we need to slowly build mutual trust and develop understanding, while trying to avoid unnecessary conflicts and arguments.

On higher planes, our relationship with others is on a completely different level. In the heavenly worlds, we relate as souls, not as personalities. There is no need for us to defend our personalities or promote our egos. There is total trust and cooperation among all of the members of a soul.

In this material world, we are each enclosed in our separate individual awareness. We are sealed off within our own personal reality. This "mental bubble" in which we live creates a barrier between us and those around us. Interaction and communication with other human beings often become difficult and filled with misunderstandings.

In the spiritual realm, there is no such barrier between ourselves and others. We share a common vision and a collective reality. Communication takes place through direct contact between minds. There is no chance for misunderstanding or misinterpretation. Interaction moves freely without veils or filters. A united state of being is experienced by all.

The Process of Merging with Our Soul Family

This "unity in mind" plays an important role in our spiritual evolution. Our spiritual evolution is essentially a process of merging our limited consciousness into the broader awareness of the group soul. This absorption into the greater soul takes place over many lives or incarnations. Each step that we take in our inner journey takes us one step closer to the goal.

We begin our soul voyage as one small part of the greater soul that has been broken off in order to create a separate individual life. As we strive and grow along the path, we start to reach out and touch our heavenly source. At first, our contact is only with the outer rim of the soul family. Yet this contact represents an important spiritual milestone. It marks our penetration through the barrier that has been imposed by physical incarnation. This penetration enables us to consciously link with our soul. It allows a flow of more rarified energy and awareness to reach us from the supernal source.

As time goes on, we are able to reach further into the center of our family and make elevated contacts within our group soul. When we have forged a link with the more evolved parts of our soul, we commence a process of "soul fusion." The higher link that we have made becomes the source for an increasingly vibrant contact between our group soul and ourselves. As we develop further, the contact intensifies and the alignment with our heavenly source is perfected. Once we have completed this attunement of energy vibration and awareness, we then merge into the consciousness of the higher source.

The Ari's Three Stages of Union

The teachings of the Ari describe three stages to this process of union in consciousness. The first phase he calls *neshikin*, kisses. In this stage, there is a momentary connection with our soul, an exchange of breath or energy. A new link in consciousness has been forged.

The second stage the Ari names *chibbuk*, the embrace. In this phase, love and light flow out to us from our soul, and we are enveloped in its presence. This stage also lasts only a short while, but its effects are more widespread and tangible.

The Ari terms the third and final stage *zivug yesod beyesod*—the act of physical union. We are now joined together with our soul and united as one. From this union, a new life and consciousness are born. We have climbed another rung in our spiritual evolution.

This process of contact and gradual unification continues on all levels of our soul until we have forged a link with the central core of our soul family, the highest aspect of our group soul. Our individual mind then fully merges into the awareness of the greater whole, and our separate self falls away.

Once this union has occurred, we have returned home and no longer need to go out again. Though our minds and hearts are one with the greater whole, we retain our individual identity. We bring the wisdom and energy that we have built up over our many incarnations with us into the family circle. At the same time, we are now able to fully share in the spiritual activity and richness of experience in the higher realm.[2]

Our Heavenly Family and Our Earthly Life

Our relationship with each member of our soul family or group soul is different. Each of the individual souls has its own specific task to fulfill. Some individuals within the soul may become our intimate companions in this incarnation, while others may have no close tie with us at all. It all depends on our state of evolution and the qualities that both we and they possess.

Our Guardian

We each have one particular soul from our soul family who acts as our guardian and protector. These souls take incarnation in a less refined subtle body (but not in gross physical form) in order to remain close and watch over us. They push and prod us as we go through life. They inspire and comfort us as we face the many challenges along our path. They share our trials and tribulations as we struggle through this worldly existence.

Our guardians act as our link with the elevated parts of the group soul. They function as a go-between and switchboard operator. They overshadow us with their presence, enabling others within the group soul to reach us. They help us to draw the aid that we need toward us and hold us close at important moments in our lives.[3]

It is their hands that we hold when we turn toward God. They are the presence that we feel surround us. They encourage us in our aspirations and weep with us when we are in pain. They remain close to us even when it causes great grief and suffering to them as well.

Special Friends

Apart from the soul guardian who is always with us, there are other beings that come to us at special times. These souls overshadow us during periods of intense stress and fear. They uphold us when we suffer a tragedy and strengthen us when we need to confront great obstacles in our lives. The more we turn to them, the closer they will be. The purer we live our lives, the higher will be the source in the Kingdom of Heaven from which they will come.

At times of spiritual initiation, there are three souls that surround us. Two hold us steady on either side, while the third acts as the agent of initiation. Through their instrumentality, God is able to apply the necessary initiatory force to our firmly anchored soul.

This work is a very special task, and those that perform it have a profound love and affection for us. Often they come from our soul family. At other times, they come from a completely different source in the heavens. Whatever the actual source, at the moment of our initiation they are like our family, escorting us down the wedding aisle to meet our spiritual groom or bride.[4]

Our Soul Father

In the Hebrew Bible we are told that when Joseph was a slave in Egypt, he lived in the house of a high Egyptian official. The man was so impressed by Joseph's intelligence and integrity that he put him in charge of the whole of his household. One day the official's wife grabbed Joseph by his tunic and tried to seduce him. The Talmud tells us that at this moment of great danger, the face of his father appeared in Joseph's mind.[5] The sight of his father filled Joseph with inner strength and courage. He sharply rebuffed the wife's advances and fled from the house.

The one who is the overshadowing presence and source of our *ruach* is called our Soul Father. It is toward union with our Soul Father that we aspire in meditation. He is our personal address in the Kingdom of Heaven. He is the gateway through we reach God in the Absolute.

At the critical moments in our lives, it is our Soul Father who comes close to overshadow us. We will experience this overshadowing in a manner that is appropriate to our present stage of spiritual development. However we experience His presence, we will be keenly aware that God is there with us, supporting us. There will be no doubt that something extraordinary has taken place.

The experience of our Soul Father's presence will propel our spiritual life forward. It will bring our personal life to a climactic intensity. It will open new doors for us and create unexpected opportunities. It is a moment that will radically transform our life.

People who have never experienced the presence of their greater soul cannot imagine its power and beauty. We pray and meditate and have all manner of experiences that we believe is the "presence of God." But when God truly descends from on high, these other experiences pale by comparison; they seem like a spark next to a flame.

When the love of our Soul Father comes pouring in, it fills us with abundant hope and courage. His unmitigated love wipes away all feelings of worthlessness or despair. His boundless love floods us with so much joy and light that we are lifted out of our body awareness and propelled into the subtle consciousness of the spiritual realm.

Our Soul Mother

There is also the higher feminine aspect of our soul—our Soul Mother. Our Soul Mother is the one who nurtures, inspires, and protects. She is the presence to which we turn for comfort and security. She provides the energy that is necessary for us to spiritually progress.[6]

In the Kabbalah, the *sefirah* of *binah* is called *Imma ilah*, "the higher Mother," and the *sefirah* of *malkhut* is called *Imma tatah*, "the lower Mother."[7]

From our Soul Mother we receive true understanding—*binah*. It is our Soul Mother who enables us to understand symbols, ideas, and ideals. She empowers us to see into the hearts of people, places, and creatures.

From our Soul Mother we receive the energy that enables us to experience the Kingdom of Heaven—*Malkhut Shamayim*. She bestows upon us a real and living faith.

We Are All Blessed with a Soul Family

While not all are blessed with a unified and supportive physical family, all of us are endowed with a soul family that is ready to bestow upon us its abundant love and help. It is a great comfort to know that there is another world to which we can turn for strength and succor. It is a joy to realize that a supernal refuge exists, where we can feel whole and at peace with ourselves and with others—a spiritual home where we truly belong.

Spiritual Contacts

All life within the Kingdom of Heaven is bound together in a unity of consciousness called *Ruach Kodesh*, or the Holy Spirit. All souls and all manifestations of the Godhead are part of this great spiritual body. When some aspect of the Holy Spirit overshadows an individual personality, this presence is called a *ruach kodesh*, a spirit from the realm of holiness.[8]

Contact with a *Ruach Kodesh*—a Holy Spirit

Normally the *ruach kodesh* comes from our own *neshama* and is an expression of the level of spiritual evolution that we have reached. But sometimes a soul from some other root is brought in to overshadow us, to provide a particular energy or spiritual capacity. This overarching *ruach* can be a momentary presence, or it can become a more permanent part of our soul/personality link that remains with us throughout the whole of one lifetime.

This process of overshadowing is overseen by the souls who are closest to us within our group soul—our soul family. Our soul family wards off the effects of any negative influences by bringing us under the protection of its aura. It also makes the decisions about any outside influences that are brought in from the Kingdom of Heaven to help us as we advance along the path.

Contact with a *Ruach Ra'ah*—a Negative Spirit

Wrong thought and action can lead us in a completely different direction. Instead of reaching into the Kingdom of Heaven, we can contact beings on lower planes. These beings can be benign, or they can be evil. Overshadowing by beings from outside the Kingdom of Heaven can lead us to embrace ideas and act in ways that are negative or harmful, because we believe that they have been given by God. These may be simply bizarre behavior or outright immoral and unethical acts.

In Talmudic times, people were much more open to psychic influence, and instances of manipulation and even possession by "disembodied spirits" were quite common. There are a number of sections in Rabbinic literature that deal with how to avoid evil spirits and how to protect ourselves from them. There are many stories in the Gospels as well about driving out evil spirits from individuals who are possessed. The Rabbis defined the impingement by such a being as an assault by a *ruach ra'ah*, "a negative spirit." They suggest, among other possibilities, that we recite the *Shema*, the central prayer of Judaism, as an antidote to such a visitation.[9]

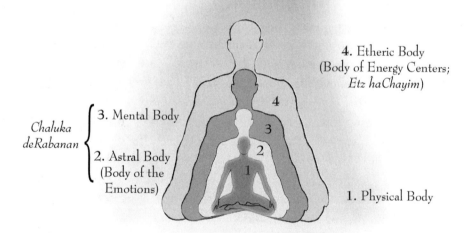

Soul Body
(*Tzelem*)

Divine Spark
Individual Soul
(*Ruach*)

4. Etheric Body
(Body of Energy Centers;
Etz haChayim)

*Chaluka
deRabanan*

3. Mental Body

2. Astral Body
(Body of the
Emotions)

1. Physical Body

4

3

2

1

Figure 6. The five bodies of manifestation

5

The Garments of the Soul

Five Bodies of Manifestation

Judaism, Hinduism, and Buddhism postulate different conceptions of our spiritual bodies. However, each of these religions addresses the need for a body that passes energy from the higher realms to the physical plane. They all agree that we create with our thoughts, feelings, and deeds. Each tradition speaks about a gross physical body that we inhabit in this world and a subtle body that we inhabit in the spiritual realm. Each teaches that we travel between worlds on flights of the spirit both in our sleep and when we leave the body after death.

We are accustomed to thinking of our physical body as the only form that we possess. In fact, we have a number of different bodies or sheaths that make up our vehicle for evolution. A human being has four bodies of manifestation in the physical world. We have a dense physical, an astral, a mental, and an etheric body.

The Kabbalah speaks of four realms or worlds: the realm of *Asiyah* (Making), the realm of *Yetzirah* (Formation), the realm of *Briah* (Creation), and the realm of *Atzilut* (Emanation). Each of our bodies is linked to one of these worlds. The physical body is linked to the realm of *Asiyah*, the astral to *Yetzirah*, the body of the mind to *Briah*, and the body of centers to *Atzilut*. (For more about the four realms, see the section "The Universe of *Tikun*" in chapter 9.)

The Physical Body

Each of our bodies of manifestation serves a different purpose, yet they all have a definite effect on our life and spiritual development. The physical body allows humans to function on the physical plane. It enables us to interact with the material reality that surrounds us. Our physical form puts us in touch with the space/time perception of four dimensions. It awakens us to the experiential world of the senses.

From a spiritual point of view, it is the glandular, circulatory, and nervous systems that are of importance. These systems serve as the conduits for the transmission of the higher energies into the body. Through their medium, the different energies maintain our physical well-being and health.

The Astral Body

The astral body is a corresponding vehicle composed of our emotions and desires.[1] It is linked to the astral plane, where emotion and desire form the substance of that realm. Astral matter is a fluid medium that takes whatever shape we give it. Our astral body too continually shifts and redefines. The astral body connects the etheric and physical bodies. Its constant fluctuations affect the quality of energy that we receive.

Each astral form has its own particular coloring, which reflects our emotional condition at any particular moment. Its color provides a clear indication of our spiritual development and is a direct expression of our thoughts, words, and deeds. When psychics see different colors surrounding people's physical bodies, it is their astral aura that they perceive.

The astral body has many different functions. It is the body of light that we inhabited in the Garden of Eden, our vehicle of ascension during meditation, and the form we use after our death to travel to other planes and worlds. In the same way that the bodies of water on the planet act as systems for the transportation of people and goods around the globe, the astral plane serves as the "transportation system" in the spiritual realm that allows souls to move between worlds. The astral plane is the higher correspondence to the nervous system in the physical body. It facilitates the passage of the energetic impulses from our thoughts and feelings from one level of reality to the next.

The Mental Body

The mind is what we refer to as our mental body, though in some ways it is not really a body at all. Our mind is the body of our intellect in the sense that it holds all of our thoughts. These thoughts build forms composed of mental matter—thoughtforms that we take with us from incarnation to incarnation. These thoughtforms are the lens through which we experience the world around us. They define the nature of our reality and govern our capacity to contact the higher mind of the soul.

The *Chaluka deRabanan*: Our Spiritual Garment

> And he showed me Joshua the High Priest standing before the angel of the Lord, and the adversary standing at his right hand to thwart him.... Now Joshua was dressed in filthy garments, and he stood before the angel. And he [the angel] answered and spoke to those who stood before him, saying, "Take off the filthy garments from him." And to him [Joshua] he said, "Behold, I have caused your iniquity to pass from you; and I clothe you in festive garments." (Zechariah 3:1–4)

In Judaism, the combined emotional and mental body is called the garment of the soul. The idea of a spiritual garment for the soul is based on the *Zohar*'s interpretation of the above vision from the prophet Zechariah.[2]

According to the tradition, when our souls are formed, they are naked and have no garments in which to stand before the Sovereign of sovereigns. The needed garments are "woven" during our life in this world through the performance of the mitzvot, or spiritually potent acts.

The *Zohar* teaches that our souls possess both higher and lower garments. Our lower garments are made from the fulfillment of the commandments—our actions; the higher garments are made from the spiritual yearning and *kavanah* (intention) in our heart.[3] The spiritual garment that we create with our positive actions is called the *chaluka derabanan*, the garment of the soul (literally, the robe of the sages). The spiritual garment that we create with our *aveyrot*, our transgressions or negative actions, is called the *chaluka tzoim*—the dirty garment.

According to the *Zohar*, when we do a sin (*aveyrah*), it links us to the negative energy pathways (*tzinor mar*) of the realm of evil (*klipot*). As a result, the spiritual emanations (*shefa*) from our acts of intended holiness do not ascend into the spiritual realm, but flow instead to the powers of the "other side." This negative energy gradually forms into a "dirty garment," which envelops us at the moment of death. In other words, the negative vibrations created by our sins cause our consciousness to resonate with the sullied vibrations of the lower realms. As a result, we are magnetically drawn to this realm after death.[4]

The Etheric Body

The etheric body is perhaps the most important of all our bodies or spiritual garments. It is a form composed of spiritual centers, or *sefirot*, and is called in the Kabbalah the *Etz haChayim*, "the Tree of Life." The *Etz haChayim* is our eternal vehicle. The state of this body is a fundamental determinant in our spiritual evolution. The centers determine the quality of the energy that we take in and give out. They determine our state of consciousness. Our body of *sefirot* is the medium through which the souls on the higher realms can reach us while we dwell in physical incarnation.

Unlike the astral aura, the etheric aura is colorless. Only someone with highly evolved inner vision will be able to see this body and its aura. The nature of the *Etz haChayim* and its workings is discussed in great detail in the first part of the book, "Made in the Image of God."

The *Tzelem*: The Body of the Soul

Beyond the four bodies that are used in physical incarnation there is one other body that is part of the soul's manifestation. In each physical incarnation, the *ruach*, or individual soul, works through the personality and its bodies. In addition, the *ruach* itself has its own separate sheath or body on the mental plane. It is this body that enables the individual soul to progress from incarnation to incarnation, moving from one personality in physical form to another as it continues on its evolutionary journey.

This "soul-body" has been created to facilitate the work of the individual soul (*ruach*) as an intermediary between the group soul (*neshama*) and the personality (*nefesh*). Through its medium, the greater awareness of the *neshama* can influence the consciousness of the person in incarnation. The individual soul and body act as a step-down transmitter for the powerful emanations from the group soul. Without their existence, the personality would be cut off from conscious contact with its heavenly source.

In Judaism, the body of the individual soul is called the *tzelem* (image). The *tzelem* is described as an image from God that is engraved on our head. This image is the mold that the *neshama*, *ruach*, and *nefesh* are fixed upon. In the same manner that a silversmith first constructs a mold before creating a silver image, similarly the Creator first constructed the *tzelem*, or soul-body, before forming our other bodies and souls.

This *tzelem* exists before our birth. Until we are linked to our *tzelem*, our *neshama*, *ruach*, and *nefesh* cannot be attached to our body and we cannot be born. It is said that the *tzelem* leaves us thirty days before our death, as does the *neshama* and other higher aspects of our soul. It is this loosening of the connection with our higher aspects that leads to our physical weakening and subsequent death.[5]

The Disintegration of the *Tzelem*

As our individual soul progresses through its different incarnations, our consciousness evolves and expands. When the incarnation process reaches its final climax, our now purified *nefesh*, or personality, fuses with our *ruach*, or individual soul, and they become one integrated whole. Once this occurs, our *tzelem*, or soul-body, begins to disintegrate, as its purpose has been fulfilled, and our individual soul merges with our *neshama*, or group soul. A sense of individuality still remains, but our ordinary personality characteristics fall below the conscious level of recognition and become a subconscious, automatic part of our soul life. These traits now have a role akin to those of the automatic systems in the human body, such as breathing, digesting, and pumping blood—activities that go on without the soul having to consciously think about them. However, our personality characteristics can be returned to conscious awareness and control at any time, if such a need arises.

With the shattering of our *tzelem*, or soul-body, we are left without spiritual protection. At the same time, both our astral and etheric auras now encompass an enormous radius. This inner condition makes us highly vulnerable to all the varied energetic inputs coming from our surroundings. Therefore, we need a clear, unfettered space around us so our auras can expand in all directions and our consciousness can freely ascend to higher planes.

To facilitate this unusual life, we have to live in a contained and protected environment. All elements of our life need to be carefully regulated and monitored, with all input into our personal space thoroughly screened by those watching over us. In addition to the physical steps that are taken to protect us, there also needs to be a constant overshadowing by those who are overseeing our soul from on high.

When we reach this stage in our evolution, we have no life but our spiritual life. Our whole being is totally given over to God. It is the culmination of our pilgrimage of the soul, the prize attained after eons of effort. We think only of sacrifice and selfless service. We have been given the gift of the chosen few.

These are humanity's five bodies of manifestation. They are the vehicles that enable us to pass through the different stages of our evolution. All our bodies need to be properly cared for and developed if we want to succeed in our mission. Each form contributes to our overall well-being and growth. Learning to balance the relationships between the five bodies is one of the keys to spiritual progress and the maintenance of a healthy and harmonious inner life.

6

Incarnation and Evolution in the Human Kingdom

How Do We Grow and Progress as Human Beings and Souls?

We do not know why God created the universe. The answer to that question is hidden in the mystery of the Eternal One's own being. We do know that evolution is the key process whereby that purpose is being fulfilled. Evolution takes place on all levels of creation. It reaches from the smallest existing entity to the movement of the great galactic clusters. It is the central driving force of life.

Evolution is more than a physical process. It embodies many other types of growth. One level of development that is of vital importance for the spiritual life is the expansion of consciousness. This is the central measure of the success of our spiritual work. It is something that can be measured only by the results of a lifetime. It is part of a process that spans billions of years.

This chapter describes the nature of this work. It is an investigation into the dynamics of this process and how it occurs on the different levels of existence. It begins with a look at the development of our own kingdom, the human.

The Concept of Reincarnation (*Gilgul*)

Reincarnation, or *gilgul* (from the Hebrew verb *lehitgalgel*, to revolve or turn, and the noun *galgal*, wheel), is the key idea that allows us to expand the concept of evolution into the spiritual realm. Its central principle is that this life is only one part of a larger series of lives. We return to this world again and again over the millennia. We take up a multitude of bodies over numerous lives or incarnations, and we learn from each life through our triumphs and failures.

The experience we gain and the qualities we develop become the raw material for our growth in the future. We continue on with this process until we reach a point where we have learned all we can from this earthly existence. We then move on to life on higher planes.

Reincarnation can be compared to the different types of clothing we put on depending on the work we do. If we are a doctor, we wear one set of clothing. As a firefighter, we wear another garment. And as a football player, we put on a whole other type of apparel. Similarly, in different incarnations, our *ruach*, or individual soul, takes up numerous bodies with varied personalities and characteristics.

Another good analogy for reincarnation is the life of actors on the stage. During their career, actors will play all kinds of roles and wear any number of costumes. However, no matter what character they play or which costume they wear, it is always the same people who are doing the acting. Similarly, no matter what part we play on the stage of life, the same soul remains the dynamic force behind all of the different personalities.

The concept of *gilgul* is described at length in the section of the *Zohar* called *Sabah deMishpatim*, "the grandfather of [the biblical portion] *Mishpatim*" (Zohar 2:94b–114a). In this section, the concept of reincarnation is developed as an explanation for several biblical injunctions, including the commandment of *yibbum*, levirate marriage, and the admonition for a man not to send away the wife of his youth. In *yibbum*, or levirate marriage, the widow marries the brother of her deceased husband. According to the *Zohar*, the soul of the dead husband reincarnates as the child that is born from the union of the man's brother and his wife.

Therefore, it is crucial for the marriage to take place so that an appropriate body can be provided for him.[1]

The concept of *gilgul* is elaborated on in all the major mystical texts of the Jewish tradition that come after the *Zohar*. The Ari's ideas on the matter are explained through examples and teachings in the *Shaar haGilgulim (Gate of Reincarnations)*, by Chayim Vital. Certain central principles arise out of these writings.

The physical, emotional, and mental equipment that we possess when we enter into incarnation is of immense importance. We will be given the particular body, personality, and life circumstances that will enable us to further the evolution of our soul. Our body will possess the right physical characteristics to carry the energies that we will use in our spiritual lives. The glandular and nervous systems will be correctly aligned with our etheric centers. Our body will have the appropriate level of purity and sensitivity to be our instrument for the spiritual work that God has given us in this incarnation.

We will be provided with an emotional disposition that will help us tackle the various experiences we face in our life. Our mental makeup will have all the necessary characteristics we need to overcome the challenges confronting us. Each life will be planned in a manner that is perfectly suited to our present stage of spiritual development.

The nature of the environment in which we will be raised is another crucial factor to be considered. What kind of family will we have? What kind of education will we be given? What experiences will our family's circumstances enable us to have? What people will we meet, and what influences will be brought to bear on us? With what values will we be raised? What lessons will we learn?

These elements determine the incarnation that we will take. For each person and life, the balance of the various factors will be different. A great deal of effort goes into organizing an incarnation. The precise components of each specific life are largely defined by another important spiritual principle: the principle of karma.

The Law of Karma: You Reap What You Sow

There are certain fundamental cosmic laws that govern the working of our universe. The law of karma, or cause and effect, is one of the major principles that define the nature of spiritual evolution. It embraces all forms of relationship, on all levels of living. It is one of the prime factors determining our incarnations. It is a complex system of relationship that encompasses millions of lives in the task of overseeing its working mechanisms.

Karma is, in essence, a very simple idea. Every action has a cause. That action then becomes the cause of further actions, ad infinitum. For example, we feel hungry. This hunger then acts as the cause to motivate us to locate something to eat. If our cupboard is bare, then we need to go and buy food. To do so, we need to have money. If we have no money, then we need to devise a way to get some. To earn money, we decide to find work. We then use the money that we have earned to go out and buy food. The original feeling of hunger, then, has become the cause for a whole line of cause and effect that has led us to search for a job, engage in work, earn money, and buy food.

The same cause could have led to different results. We might have gone to our parents for food instead. Or we could have grown our own. Or we could have decided to steal some from the corner market. Each of these acts would then become the cause of further acts and their subsequent consequences. Through these expanding chains of action and reaction, we gradually build up our store of karma over the course of a whole lifetime. As it states in *Pirkei Avot* (Ethics of the Fathers) 3:20:

> Everything is given on collateral and a net is spread over all the living; the shop is open, the Shopkeeper extends credit, the ledger is open, the hand writes, and whoever wishes to borrow, let him come and borrow; the collectors make their rounds regularly, each day, and exact payment from man with or without his knowledge, and they have [a record] on which they can rely; the judgment is a judgment of truth; and everything is prepared for the feast.

The workings of karma can also be understood from the perspective of the science of energies. In our personal universe, there is a process of cause and effect that takes place through the constant exchange of energies between the surrounding environment and ourselves. Everything that we do, say, or think has an effect on us and on those around us. When we speak to another person, both of us are influenced by the energies that pass between us. When we smell a flower, both we and the flower are affected by the exchange. At any given moment, an enormous number of energy interactions are taking place in our life.

The nature of the energy we absorb from our environment directly affects the character of our centers. Over time, these energy intakes imprint a specific quality on our spiritual body. The quality of the energy in our spiritual body will determine our state of consciousness. Our state of consciousness, in turn, will draw us toward people, places, and experiences that are attuned to our own particular energy and awareness.

For example, it is a known phenomenon that once people have lived on the street they find it difficult to return to normal living. All the habits of an ordinary lifestyle feel foreign and unnatural to them. Even if they are offered a place in which to live, they still prefer to return to the street. The homeless pattern of living has become so ingrained in them that they cannot break free from its hold.

Soldiers returning from battle face a similar challenge. As a result of their war experiences, ordinary life often seems too sedate and dull to them. Daily existence takes on an unreal quality. Some soldiers even find themselves craving the adrenaline rush and excitement of battle. After everything they have been through, the value and meaning of life have changed. They question their former relationships, their families, jobs, and homes. Only after much counseling and struggle are the returning soldiers able to find their way back into the "normal" world again.

From these examples, we see how karmic consequences build up through everything that we do in our life. When the time comes for us to leave this world, we will have reached a specific point in our evolution. Our centers will have developed to a certain degree. Our awareness will have arrived at a particular plateau. These different factors, taken together, will determine the starting point for our next incarnation.

During our individual soul adventures, we will undergo many different incarnations. Each will have its own set of circumstances, its own possibilities and choices. What we do in one life will influence the elements that will compose the incarnation that follows. If there is a task we have not fulfilled in this life, we will return to fulfill it in the next. More accurately, we will return to face the same challenge until we have learned the lessons of that particular experience and developed the qualities, strengths, and purity that it offers to us.

We do not have to look to other incarnations to observe this principle at work. Often we can watch this phenomenon play out over the span of a single lifetime. If we do not succeed in facing a difficult situation the first time, then we will find ourselves confronting the same circumstances again at a later point in life. This pattern will continue to repeat itself until we have overcome the chosen challenge and fulfilled our designated task.

For example, suppose we have trouble confronting authority figures. At different stages in our life, we will be placed in situations where we are dominated and abused by people in authority. And we will continue to be put in this situation until we learn to stand up for ourselves. In fact, our circumstances will become increasingly precarious until finally we are forced to take action in order to survive.

In a similar manner, if we have not learned what we need to in this life, then the struggle will continue on in the next life as well. Each time we leave this world, we take with us the knowledge and experience that we have acquired. We also retain our increased capacity to absorb and radiate out energies. These gains become part of the essence of our *ruach* or individual soul. They will aid us in fulfilling the work of our next incarnation.

In the traditional perspective of karma, the principle of *tikun*, or fixing a past wrong, plays an important role. Vital's *Shaar haGilgulim* and the writings of the Hasidic masters are filled with stories that revolve around the fulfillment of such *tikunim*.[2]

For example, the belongings of one person are taken away in this life as payment of a karmic debt for a past life of miserliness. Another individual is offered a chance to show a great act of loyalty and patriotism to undo an act of cowardice and betrayal in a past life.

This is a very personal approach to the subject of karma and reincarnation. The law of cause and effect can also be viewed in a more impersonal fashion, as a precise science with its own specific laws and parameters. In the scientific approach, there is no necessity for karmic repair of specific actions. It is the effects of these actions on our centers and our consciousness that matter, not the particular details of our past mistakes and relationships. If we have been miserly in our past life, that shows a heart center that is closed down and blocked. Since the opening of the heart center is central to spiritual growth, in our next incarnation we will be given a life that will provide us with the opportunity to develop a loving and compassionate heart. What that will mean will be different for each of us. It will depend on the rest of our spiritual makeup, the point that we have reached in our evolution, and the work that we have to fulfill in the plan of God.

The workings of karma are not bound to personality relationships and individual acts of repentance. The law of karma follows a process of cause and effect that is overseen by a "department" in the organization of the heavens. This supernal department works with the balance of energies and the development of divine qualities in close cooperation with the eternal plan. Each action is recorded in the Book of Life—the "celestial computer." Each life is brought into alignment with the plan. Every individual is given a place within the divine structure. Every karmic event is integrated in a manner that will maintain the overall equilibrium of the universe.

The Kabbalah has a vast literature that portrays the organization that oversees the workings of karma in the higher realms. The *Idra* section of the *Zohar* describes the twenty-four supernal courts of judgment that reside in the Lesser Countenance.[3] The *Hekhalot* section spends much of its time enumerating the vast network of lives who mete out reward and punishment on the various planes. It also describes the power of prayer and repentance to overturn or mitigate that judgment—to bring in the redeeming power of mercy, compassion, and grace.[4]

A graphic description of the effects of negative karma on our soul is outlined by the sixteenth-century mystic Rabbi Moses Cordovero in his book *Pardes Rimonim* (Orchard of Pomegranates). When we do a wrong act, Rabbi Moses explains, our soul becomes wrapped in a *klipah*, or shell, formed of negative energy. This energy shell creates a partial barrier between the soul and its supernal source, which prevents the soul's spiritual emanation from flowing freely. In this spiritually weakened state, the forces of the "other side" are able to draw on the energy of our mitzvot, or positive spiritual acts, and use that energy for their own evil purposes. All is not lost, however, Rabbi Moses tells us. Despite the negative effects of our wrongdoings, sincere repentance can retrieve the soul's spiritual power and raise it back up into the realm of holiness again.[5]

Different Levels of Karma

Each incarnation that we undergo is governed by a number of levels of cause and effect, moving from the personal to the cosmic.

First of all, there are certain events that will occur to us in this life that are the result of what has happened to us in past lives. These events are a natural outgrowth of how we have lived in our other incarnations. They are karmic debts that we have to pay in order to move ahead.

There is also a positive side to karma. Each of us comes into this world with certain gifts that are the fruit of good actions taken during our former lives. We may, for example, have particular inborn talents or specific spiritual qualities that allow us to progress swiftly along the path. The twentieth-century Indian sage Sri Ramana Maharshi was known for his complete identification with the Self of all that is, and the profound inner peace that people experienced in his presence. The Maharshi spoke of two different kinds of spiritual aspirants. Some seekers are like gunpowder, he said; all that is needed is to light a match and they will "detonate." These individuals have done intense spiritual work in their previous lifetimes. This earlier work has prepared them for the breakthrough moment in this life. Other seekers are completely different; they are more like wet wood. These aspirants are only setting out on the path and will need a long period of drying out before they become ablaze.[6]

Sometimes a soul comes into this world with longtime companions—spiritual sisters and brothers with whom he or she has worked in other lives. Great teachers incarnate into the world with their eternal companions. Together they form a carefully honed nucleus of spiritual force.

Sri Ramakrishna had a vision of a higher realm, from which he called down one of his intimate disciples to come and incarnate with him in this physical world.[7] Sri Ramana Maharshi told a Western devotee that he had been one of his students in a previous lifetime and shared with him a vision of the two of them together in a large gathering of enlightened souls.[8] Rabbi Isaac Luria claimed that he and his followers were the *gilgul*, or incarnation, of Rabbi Shimon bar Yochai and his circle in the *Zohar*.[9] And the Baal Shem Tov disclosed to his Hasidim that his soul had refused to come down to this world until God gave him sixty advanced souls to incarnate with him, who would watch over the Baal Shem and help with his work.[10]

There are broader levels of karma beyond our own personal karma that also have a powerful effect on our lives. For example, if we are

Jewish, by birth or by choice, our own karma will be tied up with the karma of the whole Jewish people. Karmic forces at work in the history and spiritual evolution of the Jewish people will directly impact our lives, independent of anything that we ourselves might do or have done in the past. These forces were set in motion by the original divine impulse that formed the Jewish people thirty-five hundred years ago. They have created gigantic waves of cause and effect that have reverberated through the lives of the Jewish people ever since that time.

Then there are the karmic influences of the great civilizations throughout human history. The Egyptian, Greek, and Roman empires have all left their mark on human consciousness, as have the Indo-Chinese cultures of the East. The different "isms," such as communism, socialism, totalitarianism, and capitalism, have had an enormous impact on our perception of reality over the last couple of centuries. The humanistic ideas of the Renaissance and the societal changes of the industrial and technological revolutions have changed the way in which we interact with our world. All of this "global karma" has had a profound influence on our personal lives.

Being a human being also has its own particular karma. Humanity was originally meant to be the next step in the evolution of the kingdoms of earth. We were supposed to live on a higher plane of consciousness, but we were unable to maintain the necessary state of mind to remain in this higher world. As a result, we were forced back into the life of physical-plane existence and became the peculiar creatures that we are today. This karma in itself has had a deep effect on our being. It has shaped the manner in which we think, perceive, and interact with reality. We cannot even imagine what life would be like without the burden of this karmic debt.

Above and beyond our human karma, there is the karma of the great Divine Being who oversees our planet. The Guiding Force of the planet is also on a journey, with personal karma to work out. All the events that are occurring in our world are the expression of this karma. They represent the consequences of past incarnations and their imprint upon this present planetary life. Like us, the Holy Blessed One has spiritual lessons to learn and challenges to overcome, but on a much loftier level of consciousness. Like us, the Bestower of every blessing has brought unique gifts into this incarnation and is accompanied by spiritual "friends" who have come to help accomplish the cosmic work. (For more on this subject, see chapters 9, 11, and 12.)

Each of us will engage these different layers of karma in varying degrees. Some will concentrate their energies on bettering their present personal circumstances; others will immerse themselves in the destiny of their nation or people. And still others will commit their lives to the struggles facing all of humanity, to ensure the future well-being of the planet.

And then there are those who will turn away from all outward activity and focus on the inner life; those who will look beyond the body and the personality to explore the realm of the spirit and the soul. And finally there are those individuals who will strive to rise above the whole process of incarnation and karma, to become free forever from the endless cycles of birth and death.

The Choice to Incarnate

Each incarnation that we take is carefully chosen by us, together with those who are our guides in the higher realms.[11] All of our incarnations on this earthly plane are a means of achieving the necessary experience we need to evolve. The difficulties and tribulations of this world provide an excellent basis for growth and development. The intensity of the emotional and mental effects of earthly life on us stimulate quicker, more substantial progress than other planes of living.

Our physical world is only a minute part of a much greater reality. There are thousands upon thousands of other planes, both higher and lower than our own. In the overall scheme, this plane is one of the coarsest. We can characterize the choice to incarnate in this world as a leap into muddy waters to retrieve a precious jewel that is buried there. It is comparable to taking a steep shortcut up the mountain that is covered with brambles. We know that it will be difficult and that we will suffer, but precious time will also be saved.

In the early stages of incarnation, the cycle of lives progresses in rapid and frequent succession. We remain unconscious after we leave this world, held in a state of mental hibernation until we are ready to begin our next incarnation. The choice of life is made for us by our guides and soul family. We are not yet aware enough to be involved.

As we progress, we begin to awaken to life on higher planes. We become part of the activities happening all around us and participate in the spiritual work that is going on. The period between our incarnations is stretched out now. Each incarnation has clear objectives and specific goals. They are conscious choices that we make with the aid of our family. Every life is chosen with our active participation, in conjunction with advice from those we love and trust.

As our capacity to contact our soul increases, we begin to receive help and guidance from on high while in incarnation. We are guided in making our decisions, and everything we say and do takes on a greater significance. Gradually, we become useful instruments of divine service, potent vehicles through which the energy of the spiritual realm can pour forth into this physical world.

The more that we advance, the further we can reach into the Kingdom of Heaven. The higher we can reach, the more effective instruments we will be and the greater the work that we will be able to accomplish. Our life is now increasingly focused in the supernal regions. Our incarnations are a matter of personal choice rather than karmic necessity.

Finally, we arrive at the point where we are no longer bound to the physical world by desire or imperfection. We dwell and work wholly in the spiritual realms. If we incarnate at all, it is in response to an invocation from humanity and the strong urging of our greater soul to undertake a difficult task.

The Astral Body: Our Vehicle Between Worlds

When we depart this life and move on to the next plane of existence, we transit between worlds using our astral body or *chaluka derabanan* (astral and mental body combined).[12] The desires and emotions we have built up over our lifetime determine the plane of consciousness we will go to after we pass over. Our desires attune us to a certain way of living and spiritual vibration. The plane that corresponds to that vibration is the place to which we are magnetically drawn.[13]

There are many different heavens that resonate with the aspirations and mental constructs of various peoples. Religious Jews will go to a plane where they learn sacred texts, dwell peacefully under the shade of their grape vine, and meet the great teachers of their tradition. The same is true with respect to other faiths and religions. They each will experience the paradise that they expect to find.

We will be granted the specific heaven for which we are ready. If we have lived a life of refined values and aspirations, then we will ascend to a supernal plane that reflects those ideals. If we have lived a life that was filled with sordid morals and base desires, then we will descend to a lower plane where such qualities predominate, and where we apparently belong.

The different planes have diverse material compositions. Some worlds are very much like our own, with many of the same characteristics. There are landscapes, structures, and activities that resemble life on earth. Other planes are so unlike our own that it is nearly impossible to describe how they appear.

The astral body changes its appearance as the soul inhabits these various realms. On the planes closest to ours, it has a form that is similar to the physical bodies we now possess. As we move on to the higher planes, the astral body becomes increasingly differentiated from the figure with which we are familiar. On the highest levels, the astral body appears as a beautiful form composed of color and light.

If we descend instead into the lower worlds, the astral body takes on increasingly dense and grotesque forms. The astral body is always a true reflection of the thoughts and feelings that are in our hearts. Whatever qualities lie hidden behind our exterior facade will be plainly revealed when we leave this world.[14]

Our *chaluka derabanan* remains with us while we are in the higher realms. Once we are ready to take another incarnation, our old *chaluka derabanan* dissolves and a new one is created for us. This fresh spiritual garment will be shaped by all the desires, thoughts, and emotions that we experience in our next life. The state of our subtle body at the end of that life will determine our destination after we leave the world once again.

Our *Etz haChayim*, our body of spiritual centers, in contrast, remains with us from life to life. It is imprinted with the energies and qualities that we have developed over our many incarnations. And our *tzelem*, the body of our *ruach* (individual soul), remains intact until the individual soul has brought its mission to final fulfillment. When that climactic moment arrives, the *tzelem* totally disintegrates, and we are absorbed back into the body of our *neshama*, or group soul, even as we continue our earth-plane life.

Misconceptions

Today, the nature of our past lives has become a wildly popular area of speculation. Everyone seems to think they were last incarnated as some great spiritually evolved or historically renowned person. In fact, most of us were insignificant individuals in our last life. We probably did nothing of great importance and had the common failings and imperfections of the rest of humanity. Otherwise, we would not have incarnated in our present form.

This life is a school. We are here because of our imperfections. An incarnation on this plane of existence is an opportunity to rid ourselves of our flaws. If we were great spiritual beings, we would not need to be on this earth.

Think about how terrible we feel when some awful mistake that we have made in the past is brought to the fore. If this is how we feel about our mistakes in this life, imagine how we would react if all of our failures from our previous incarnations were recounted to us. It is better not to know about our former sojourns on earth. They surely were less evolved than our present one.

God has intentionally prevented us from remembering what happened to us during our past lives. The Talmud, *Niddah* 30b, tells us that when we were in our mother's womb we were taught Torah, spiritual wisdom, every day. Before we were born, however, an angel tapped us on the upper lip and made us forget everything that we knew.

Though knowing about our former incarnations sounds enticing, having such knowledge would only be counterproductive. Life would become very confusing. We would be constantly interpreting our experiences in terms of our past, rather than being fully present in the moment.

This is our task in life, to live in the here and now. We should concentrate on the challenges that we face in our current circumstances. They represent opportunities that have been specifically tailored to match our needs and potential. They are the way forward in our spiritual evolution.

7

Key Factors in Spiritual Evolution

What Determines Our Spiritual Growth?

The process of our evolution is dominated by several factors that exert a powerful influence on our movement through each lifetime. These larger forces affect our progress and balance our karma. Understanding their workings provides us with crucial perspective on the work we need to accomplish in this world.

The Law of Spiritual Reciprocity

We receive in order to give and give in order to receive; this is the cosmic law. If you have received, then God will put you into a position where you must give to others. And if you give, then the True Judge will make sure that you receive, even against all odds and without any effort on your part.

The Baal Shem Tov teaches that you must give to others if you want to receive, because this builds a pathway along which the supernal emanations may flow. In fact, if you receive divine blessing (*shefa*) but do not pass this abundance on to others, the blessing will stop flowing, because there will no longer be a pathway for it to follow along.[1]

We can understand this teaching from another perspective as well. If we have a job to do in the world, then the Provider of All will give us the necessary means to fulfill it. This can be a matter of monetary funds, learned skills, spiritual attributes, or individuals who will help us—whatever specific elements are required for our work. However, these gifts are not unconditional or irrevocable. If we turn away from the task that God has given to us and use the bestowed gifts for our own selfish purposes, then the Controller of Destiny will take those gifts away and give them to someone else who is willing to do the work. The Almighty's work will be accomplished; the only question is, who is ready to be a dutiful tool?

There are many ways that we can give to others. Some individuals follow the overt path of public roles like teachers, counselors, medical practitioners, or aid workers. Others labor on the inner side, consciously directing spiritual energies to further the eternal plan. Still others go about the world as lighthouses, quietly giving of their spiritual vitality to whomever they meet. These "lighthouses" may have no conscious knowledge of what they are doing. They may not even consider themselves to be spiritual or religious, but the work of emanating out energies will be invisibly going on all the same.

A vast network of interactions is continually taking place across the universe. Energy, light, and power are flowing back and forth within all of creation in a never-ending exchange of being. This interchange is the basis of all life and is the means by which the world lives, breathes, and evolves. The higher is giving to the lower, and the lower is striving toward the higher in a constant fulfillment of the divine command to seek the path of evolution and growth.

The time sequence for these acts of mutual reciprocity is not always readily apparent. Time has its own distinct pace in the Kingdom of Heaven; the greater picture is the focus of its vantage point. Therefore, an act of giving in one direction may not receive the return gesture until many years later in another time and place.

The nature of the giving may also be quite different. One person may give of his physical talents, while another may return with an offering of the heart. No matter what the specific elements of the give-and-take may be, there will always be a karmic balance. This is the fundamental basis of the law and the nature of its spiritual beauty.

Central to the give-and-take in all of the kingdoms is the law of sacrifice. This law states that each kingdom sacrifices its life for the kingdom above it. The mineral kingdom sustains the vegetable kingdom, the vegetable kingdom nourishes the animal kingdom, the animal kingdom feeds and clothes the human kingdom, and the human kingdom gives its life for the service and glory of the divine kingdom.

Sacrifice opens the door to blessing and allows the Divine Livingness to stream from one kingdom to another. It is the spiritual force that empowers the process of cosmic reciprocity. The Kabbalists call the sacrifice of the kingdom below for those who are above it *hitoruta deletata*, an arousal or awakening from below. This lower sacrifice evokes a *hitoruta dele'eila*, an arousal or sacrifice from above.[2] The most sublime expression of this higher sacrifice is the manifestation of the absolute God in finite creation. As a result of this divine act of *hitoruta dele'eila*, infinite love and compassion radiate throughout all of the worlds.[3]

The Spiral of Purification and Holiness

The spiritual life is a never-ending process of purification and growth. We continually ascend to ever-higher levels of holiness. Each step lifts us into new states of awareness and understanding. Each stage reveals another aspect of the divine reality.

Constant effort is required to transform our physical nature into a worthy vessel for the divine spirit. We work to eliminate the behavior and thought patterns that drag us down into lower consciousness and to replace them with habits and modes of thinking that will lift us into a higher state of mind. We strive to turn inward instead of outward, to raise the mind above the senses, instead of continually immersing ourselves in sensual experiences.[4]

The midrash *Mekhilta* states, "All beginnings are difficult."[5] The first steps on the path are challenging. Though we have made a mental decision to go toward God, our consciousness has run along a different groove for many lifetimes and will not so easily change its course. In the initial stages of the spiritual life, we are fighting against the predominantly physical character of our mind-set. Our thoughts stray in all directions, and our practice is a constant struggle. As we become attuned to the inner life, this sense of tension gradually disappears until only the pleasures of the spirit bring us joy.

Each time that we climb another rung on the ladder, each time we link into another state of consciousness, we go through a process of sanctification and transformation. The degree of holiness that we have reached suddenly feels inadequate to us. The purification that we have internalized seems insufficient for the next stage of our spiritual development. Our purity looks tarnished in our eyes. Our "selflessness" appears quite selfish, and our "enlightened understanding" seems like foolish ignorance.

This shift in our perception is due to the fact that we are looking at ourselves from a more evolved perspective. We are seeing ourselves with the eyes of the soul. As we link into ever more elevated aspects of being, we see with an increasingly clearer and more expansive vision, until ultimately we see with eyes that are eternal and become eternal ourselves.

During these periods of changing self-perception, a feeling of spiritual emptiness is experienced, where the normal avenues of approaching God are shut down and our inner contacts cut off. As a result, we are forced to delve deeper within to find new sources of strength and inspiration. This enables us to establish a more profound connection with our soul. It motivates us to discover new pathways into the higher realm. Every time we go through such an episode, we erase another layer of physicality from our consciousness. Each new level that we reach engraves the patterns of spiritual living more firmly in our hearts.

This human progression parallels the movement of the heavenly creatures in Ezekiel's vision of the celestial chariot, which constantly strive forth toward the supernal light and then withdraw again (Ezekiel 1:14). We too strive forward toward our ideal until we reach the limits of our spiritual capacity. We then withdraw to a place of quiet and stability before we begin our ascent anew.[6] Each ascent is a step forward toward perfection; each withdrawal a concession to human frailty and limitation. Each time we rise up to receive the revelation and then come back down again to assimilate and recalibrate. Our lives are made up of this constant inner movement, this pendulum of spiritual swings.

Yet these swings are not simply a cycle of "to and fro" that finds us each time back in the same place. The spiritual life is an upward spiral, a path of overall advancement and growth. Each time we strive, we reach a little higher; each time we come back down, our descent is a little less steep. Slowly, with perseverance and patience, we make our way toward our supernal home.

Every person has his or her own pattern of change. There is no set schedule for this process. We will all have periods of breakthrough followed by periods of integration, and there is no way to determine when these periods will happen or how long each will last. We need to constantly look toward heaven to identify whether it is time to remain where we are or to move on to a new spiritual destination. We need to be alert and receptive to what God is sending our way.

Learning how to negotiate these personal crossroads is a key aspect of our evolution. We achieve a state of preparedness by constant spiritual work. Through regular daily practice, we gradually transform ourselves into sensitive instruments that are finely tuned to the "divine frequency."[7]

All the varied religious practices have been created to help us fulfill this work. The experiences of our life have been placed before us to further our process of purification and ascent. Forging this inner alignment is the hidden purpose behind the many travels of our soul.

The spiritual path unfolds over many lifetimes. As we slowly make our way up the spiral of holiness, the divine spark at our core becomes increasingly potent. As the rate of our spiritual vibration quickens, its light shines forth, radiating with ever-greater beauty and brilliance.

Free Will

Deeply interwoven with the workings of spiritual evolution and karma is the operation of free will. How do we, as individuals, interact with the lives that God has given to us?

To properly discuss the question of free will, we need to understand the complexity of this issue and the various levels from which it can be approached. It is like the changing viewpoints that we get from different locations on a mountain.

If we are at the bottom of the mountain, we view the world from our accustomed angle, what we call normal life. We see an abundance of dwellings and other buildings, with large numbers of people moving about. Everything is accessible to us, and we can choose freely whatever we wish to do.

Once we move partway up the mountain, however, our perspective starts to change. There are far fewer dwellings and inhabitants. Life is more rigorous and our choices more limited. Our life is restricted to a smaller area of action. We now feel somewhat disconnected from the world below, with all of its activity. It takes a great effort for us to leave our dwelling and go down into the villages below. At the same time, we also feel closer to the peak of the mountain. The air has become purer. The view is now more open and expansive.

When we ascend onto the mountaintop, the perspective becomes even more extreme. Everything below us seems tiny and unimportant. All the dwellings and activity at the foot of the mountain seem insignificant compared to the grandeur and the power of the view from the mountaintop. We can see for miles in every direction. The air is so rarified that it may be hard for us to breathe. The landscape is much less hospitable to any type of lifeform. It is a rugged and austere landscape, where only a very few can endure.

These different viewpoints represent the various ways in which we can understand the nature of free will. Each viewpoint represents another stage in the human attempt to comprehend the paradox of human will versus divine will. Each perspective has its value, but they all are only temporary stepping-stones in the overall evolution of the soul.

From the angle of those of us who are living the ordinary life of this world, we can be said to have complete free will. We go about our daily activities and try to make ends meet. Our spiritual life consists of the choices we make. It is through our choices that we grow and evolve. The experience we gain as a result of our successes and failures enables us to acquire wisdom and to change our thinking and behavior. Our past karma will influence the way we see and experience the world. It will determine the spiritual equipment we begin our life with, but how we proceed with those tools is completely up to us.

Once we move partway up the mountain, once we begin to walk along the path of the spiritual life, our perspective starts to shift. We see that there are still many choices for us to make along the way, but it is God who sets the broad outlines of our life. Each choice we make will take us through its own distinct series of experiences, but all of the paths will lead us to our destination point.

There will be certain key experiences in our lives that are essential for our growth, specific obstacles that we need to surmount and people we have to meet, if we are to fulfill our purpose in this incarnation. Amid these crucial elements there will be many flexible circumstances and diverse relationships from which we must choose. Each choice will influence the way we move forward. Each direction that we turn will affect the qualities we absorb and the character of our day-to-day life. The manner in which we respond to our life experiences will alter the amount of time we take to progress. All paths may lead to the mountaintop, but each path follows a different route.

We can choose the path that gradually winds its way up the mountain. This is a sure and sound way forward, but it will take a very long time for us to arrive at the summit. Or we can choose an alternative route to the mountaintop. We can climb straight up the face of the mountain, scaling its heights using rope and grappling hooks. This way is much faster than the first, but the effort that it demands and the dangers that we will need to confront are far greater.

We have a similar range of choices on the spiritual path. Some people will choose to advance slowly through life. They will take incarnation after incarnation and make slow and steady progress toward liberation. Others will immerse themselves totally in the inner reality, forgetting everything else in their focused search. They will surge ahead in their ascent, leaping from level to level of experience.

Each of these paths will ultimately take us to our final destination. All of us will one day become enlightened. The question is one of time and suffering. How much suffering will we need to experience before we turn our minds toward God? How many more lives will we go through before we break the bonds of physical consciousness?

The essential question in any incarnation is not what we will do, but how we will do it. We can face the same conditions and do the same work on many different levels. For example, if we become a lawyer, we can pursue our career in a variety of ways. We can become a civil rights lawyer, a criminal lawyer, or a high-powered tax lawyer. Though we will be practicing law in all three cases, each of these choices will have different consequences for our life. Each choice will create its own lifestyle, values, and challenges. Each decision will present us with unique obstacles to overcome. Each option will transform us into a particular person and create its own distinct life.

Though elements of our life may be predetermined, the manner in which we respond to life's experiences is where we express our free will. Will we respond in the highest or in the lowest? Will we use our experiences as opportunities for new spiritual growth and divine service, or will we simply continue on living as we have always lived? This is the choice that is ours to make. This is the battleground of our free will.

From the highest perspective, from the dizzying heights of the mountain peak, we see that everything is in the hands of God. The Baal Shem Tov teaches:

> At every moment, a person should think that everything that is in the world is filled with God. As it says in the Torah, "Do I not fill the heavens and the earth?" (Jeremiah 23:24).
>
> And one must know that all things that are done through the thoughts and schemes of men all come from God—even the simplest of simple things that are done in the world all come from Divine Providence.[8]

The Hasidic master Dov Baer of Mezeritch, who was the successor to the Baal Shem Tov, teaches that if we all were in our natural and rightful state of consciousness, "each person would do the will of God in the same way that our limbs do the will of our mind—since God is our mind and we are His body, so to speak, and it is fitting that we should do His will."[9]

From the top of the mountain, we see that we cannot even raise our finger or think a single thought without the power of the Ineffable One infusing us. We understand that we are only instruments of the Supreme Being—the limbs of the divine body. It is the Higher Power that moves us, the Guiding Force that directs our lives. We have no free will of our own. Everything is part of the grand design. Our task is to rest in the All-Merciful's embrace, like a child resting in the arms of its mother, and accept everything that happens as the expression of Her will. Our mission is to find the divinity in every encounter, in every person that we meet. When we have completely surrendered ourselves to God's will in this manner, we will have fulfilled our lives.

The Talmud, *Brachot* 33b, states, "Everything is in the hands of the Heaven, except for the awe of Heaven." Some great teachers would argue that even the capacity to feel awe for God is not in our hands; it too is a divine gift of grace. All is determined, even the "simplest of simple things," as the Baal Shem has told us. But this perspective is not usually taught in religious texts or propagated by spiritual teachers, because it would undermine the very important principle of individual self-effort.

What the final word is in the reality of the Timeless Boundless One is beyond our ability to know. What we can purposely undertake is to strive to purify ourselves and progress along the spiritual path to the best of our ability, to become ever-clearer and more effective instruments of God. Just as a snake sheds its old skin when it grows a new one, we discard our old conceptions of free will and karma each time we take another step along the path. Each stage bestows its own new revelation of understanding and wisdom. Each revelation brings with it ever-higher contacts in the spiritual realm. One day we will reach the mountaintop and the lofty heights of divine union. We will then attain an understanding that no words or concepts can express.

Whatever Way We Live—All Life Is Divine

Life is a transcendental picture show. When we look at the world, we are looking at the Universal Being. When we see people competing, pushing, and fighting all around us, we are seeing "divine life." We are watching human beings work to repair the brokenness of their existence. We are observing embodied souls as they try, on whatever level they are able, to overcome their fallen state.

Some of us are happily immersed in this physical world, some are just enduring, others are struggling to prevail over their environment and their karma, and still others are striving to move beyond this material reality and become pure spirit. But all of us, no matter which path we are following, are part of God's eternal plan.

———— ◉ ————

8

Larger Group Souls / The Soul of Israel

Identity Beyond the Individual

Beyond the smaller group souls to which our individual souls belong, what we have called our spiritual family, there are much larger soul groupings that have been formed in the heavens.

These larger soul groups have been bound together to fulfill a divine command. In some cases, their activity is totally independent of life on this plane of existence. In other cases, they work together with those in incarnation to fulfill a mission for God. Among the greatest of the soul groupings that work in this world are the souls that have formed around the world's major religions.

The Formation of a Larger Group Soul and the Birth of a New Religion

From a spiritual perspective, a new religion is created when the Directing Force of the universe wants to introduce new ideas and energies into the consciousness of humanity. A plan is constructed to facilitate the revelation and growth of this divine imperative on the earthly plane. Then, a *shoresh neshama* (root soul) is formed to take up this spiritual mission and bring it to fruition in time and space.

Great souls from the higher reaches of the celestial planes are sent down to anchor the divine thoughtform in our world. The lives of these souls are filled with suffering and struggle, but they are lives where the Eternal Presence is real and tangible.

When these souls pass over, they form the spiritual nucleus of the religion in the higher realm. This nucleus becomes an outpost of energy and consciousness in the Kingdom of Heaven. It acts as an intermediary link between those on the physical plane and their supernal source.[1]

After the birth pangs of its initial inception, the new religion goes on to grow and spread on the physical plane. While this is happening, a concurrent expansion takes place in the spiritual regions. More and more souls are drawn into the vortex of energy created by the original nucleus until a great center of light and power begins to form in the heavens. This center of energy becomes the source of inspiration and spiritual force for the souls who have taken incarnation upon the physical plane. As an ever-sturdier bridge is built between the higher and lower worlds, the new religion is infused with further vitality.

However, just as the life of an individual human being is not all a direct ascent upward, there are also many twists and turns in the life of a religion. There are stages where the religion prospers and grows, and there are stages where it falters and takes a backward step. When this happens, the theology and practices become so concretized and fixed in material consciousness that a darkness or veil is formed, creating a barrier between the souls in the higher worlds and those on the physical plane. The religion then can no longer receive the full light from its supernal source.

When this occurs, God once again sends down teachers and prophets to inspire, purify, and reinvigorate the religion. These great souls bring in a new energy and a fresh teaching to stimulate an expansion of consciousness and understanding in those on the earthly plane. This energy then enables the members of the religion to clear away the spiritual blockage between the higher and lower worlds and begin to move forward again in the plan of God.

Soul of Israel (*Knesset Yisrael*)

To see how this process works, let us take a look at the Soul of Israel. How was this soul formed? How did it come into being?

First, the thought arose in the universal mind to create a kingdom of priests, a holy nation that would build a dwelling place for the Divine Presence in the world. The Holy Blessed One then gathered together great souls from a high plane of consciousness and gave them the task of anchoring this mission in our physical world.

The first of these great souls to incarnate was Abraham or Avraham. Avraham is the father of the soul and people of Israel. As was explained in chapter 3, this truth is expressed in the Hebrew Bible (Genesis 17:4–5) when the Guardian of Israel blessed Avraham that he would become a father of many nations and changed Avram's name to Avraham, by adding the letter *heh* (one of the four letters of the Sacred Name *Yud Heh Vav Heh*). By adding this letter to Avram's name, the Most High infused him with divine power. In this way, the first step in Israel's mission was firmly established.

The next step in the development of the Soul of Israel was to expand its members and augment its spiritual potency. This was accomplished through the incarnation of the two other Patriarchs and three other Matriarchs. If we take an unsentimental look at the Hebrew Bible, we will see that the three Patriarchs—Abraham, Isaac, and Jacob—and the four Matriarchs—Sarah, Rebecca, Leah, and Rachel—all had very difficult lives. They faced a constant stream of crises that forced them to continually turn toward God. Through this life of intense prayer and supplication, they forged a solid link with their souls. This inner connection later formed the foundation for the larger soul and mission of Israel.

Next, a number of new souls were brought down to join the people. Reuben, Judah, and all the twelve sons of Jacob were born, together with their families, until finally there were seventy souls who went down to live in Egypt.

We can gain an insight into the spiritual process that was taking place by looking at these numbers. There are seventy souls that go down to Egypt. Seventy is seven times ten. Ten is the number of centers in the Kabbalistic body of *sefirot*. Seven is the number of days in Creation and also the number of years in the agricultural cycle. Perhaps the number seventy is used to tell us that at this stage in the story of Israel, the spiritual nucleus or "critical mass" needed to create a vibrant soul in the heavens had been established. Now a nascent spiritual form could take shape in the higher realms.

The following phase in the development of the Soul of Israel was the long period of exile in the land of Egypt. Through hundreds of years of struggle and suffering, the seventy souls that made up the Children of Israel were transformed into a "great, mighty, and numerous nation" (Deuteronomy 26:5) with the spiritual power and the inner strength to take up the work of the Soul on earth. By the time that the people reached Mount Sinai and received the Word of God, the Soul's mission was fully vitalized.[2]

In Egypt, the people were organized into twelve tribes. The number twelve is also spiritually significant. It represents a powerful combination of energies. The number twelve is prominent in many groupings: the twelve tribes, the twelve constellations, the twelve months in a year, the twelve hours in a day, and the twelve hours in a night. In the Kabbalah, the twelve tribes are called the Chariot of God and also the Divine Seal.[3] Together they form a sturdy vehicle for the spiritual body of Israel that contains the full range of energies needed for God's work.

Since that time, the Soul of Israel has continued to flourish and mature. All those who have incarnated as part of the Jewish people have steadily built up its power. Today it is a tremendous vortex of light and consciousness that stretches way up into the Kingdom of Heaven, embracing all those who have shared in the mission and destiny of Israel. In the Kabbalah, this vast soul is called *Knesset Yisrael*, "the Assembly of Israel."[4] This is the true Israel to which we belong—the higher Israel. The Israel that we perceive in this physical reality is just a minute expression of this immense spiritual edifice. It is the outermost manifestation of its divine essence, the lowest expression of its mighty spiritual force. When we link ourselves to *Knesset Yisrael*, we harness the spiritual power of these lofty souls who live on higher planes. We draw on the strength and inspiration of their overshadowing presence.

The people and the Soul of Israel are of one and the same essence. They are different parts of a single whole that was created to hold the light of the Divine Presence. This sacred task is what unites the higher with the lower Israel. The greatest spiritual work that we can undertake is to bind our heart and mind to the supernal Soul. All of those in the Soul are waiting to pour their energy through us to help the people dwelling on this physical plane. All we have to do is to turn our minds in their direction. The more we bind ourselves to the higher Israel, the purer a vessel we will become, and the more effective an instrument we will be in the great work of uniting the two Israels together.

As this work of inner connection progresses, the higher and lower Israel will be drawn ever closer together, as the souls on the heavenly planes increasingly overshadow those who have incarnated in this world. The more the energy of the higher Israel flows through into the lower, the more refined the energetic vibration of the people will become. Finally, a time will arrive when the energy of the people will be raised to the highest level, and the two Israels will fuse together and become one. Then, in the words of the prophet Isaiah, there will be "a new heaven and a new earth" (66:22), and our entire reality will be transformed.[5]

The Divine
Structure of
Reality

When we embark upon the path of the mystic, a new world opens up for us. This earthly plane is no longer the focus of our lives. Rather, it is the invisible realm of the soul that draws us toward it. We become aware that there are worlds upon worlds beyond the material existence in which we live. An understanding of the inner reality is an essential part of our journey. This understanding provides the insight we need to expand our awareness, illuminating our ascent into the Timeless Expanses of Infinity.

9

The Organization of the Heavens

What Is Our Relationship to the Cosmos?

The evolution of life is an extraordinary process. From a single-celled creature we have evolved into the complex organism that is a human being. What began as a collection of separate lives, each living its own reality, was transformed through the evolutionary process into a single unified individual whose consciousness encompasses trillions of cells. Our individual mind directs and orders the body, sustaining and maintaining it, bending it to our will throughout the years of our life. This gathering of little lives becomes the vehicle for our wishes and desires, the instrument that allows us to dream and to fulfill our dreams. It is the vessel to hold our knowledge, wisdom, and understanding, and the instrument through which we express the creative energy infusing our heart and mind.

The Body of God

Our relationship with God works in a similar fashion. We are all part of the "body of God." We are the vehicle of manifestation through which this Cosmic Consciousness realizes dreams and gives form to vision. We are the instrument for fulfilling the supernal purpose and plan.

The divine awareness is the unifying principle that binds all of existence together. The infinite mind of the Sovereign of the universe underlies the life of all of the worlds. Like the cells in our body, we each have our own individual identity and consciousness. Yet all is overshadowed by the Ageless One and directed and guided toward the cosmic desires and goals.

Like the physical body, the body of God has a circulatory system circulating the divine life force through the body in the form of energy and light. There is a nervous system that binds all the different parts together into a unity of being and links them all to the universal consciousness. The heart and mind are the central organs of this body, providing life and awareness to the physical form.

Like our bodies, the body of God requires constant attention to keep it in good working order, to purify and align all the different parts to the divine will. As in any physical organism, there is a fundamental tendency toward chaos and dissolution in God's body that needs to be constantly controlled and kept in check. It takes enormous effort to keep this "body" vital and healthy.

Two Models for Reality

In his teachings, Rabbi Isaac Luria (the Ari) presents two models for the structure of reality: *igulim* and *yosher*—interlocking circles and straight lines.[1] The model of *yosher*, or straight lines, expresses a perspective where the universe is composed of individual beings, each with its own function, with all the different parts working together and existing as one unity of consciousness. In the Ari's system, these exalted beings are called *partzufim*, "divine countenances." This is the model described above.

The second model proposed by the Ari, *igulim*, articulates the truth that the whole of reality is composed of ascending circles of ever more inclusive awareness. This spiral of consciousness reaches from the minute to the Infinite.

The Spiral of Consciousness

The atom is a sentient entity. Each atom has an overshadowing mind that unifies all the particles that compose the atom into a singular whole. Each individual human being is a world. The human consciousness is the overriding presence that gives unity and life to the inconceivably vast number of atoms that make up the body.

There is a Divine Being who embodies the awareness of this planet, whose life force flows into all that is on the many planes of earth. The earth is the body of this Divine Being, and the lives on it are the cells that make up the skeleton, organs, and tissues of this body.

The solar system is the concrete expression of the life of the Sovereign of the sun. Each planet is a different center in the solar body. This is the true purpose of astrology, to give expression to the qualities and emanations that come from the different planets and to explain how these emanations affect our world. Just as the parts of our body are interrelated and have a mutual effect on each other, so do all the planets radiate energy and light that affect one another. The solar system is a distinct unit of being. It is a living organism that has a reality and spiritual evolution of its own.

Beyond this, the sphere of divine perception stretches out into the galaxies and mega-galaxies. Who can even begin to imagine the nature of the Being whose mind-stream encompasses all of this stupendous creation?

Yet, though we will be discussing the Sovereign of the world and the Sovereign of the sun, it is essential to always keep in mind that ultimately all these differentiations are an illusion. There is only one God, and all life on all of the planes is part of the One life and consciousness.[2] This is the reality of *igulim*.

Everything Is Endowed with Life and Consciousness

At the same time, we also need the model of *yosher* to remind us that even though inanimate objects may seem to be lifeless, they are in fact expressing life and cognizance on their own level. The electric interaction between positive and negative elements in an atom or the movement of molecules across the barrier of a cell wall in the body is as much a conscious choice as any of the decisions we make.

Conversely, we too respond to positive and negative stimulation, but of a much higher order. We receive the "electric" impulse of the love of God that continually draws us toward the Source of all love. We react to the input of positive and negative energy in the form of sensations, emotions, and thoughts. All human behavior, from the magnetic pull of sexual attraction between two individuals, to the migration of peoples across borders for economic opportunity or political freedom, can be seen as electrical phenomena.

On cosmic levels, the great changes of history and civilization on our planet are perceived as the actions and choices of an individual mind working through a "personal life." The life spans of galaxies and the creation and destruction of billions of stars are the framework for the evolution in consciousness of these great lives. Everything in the universe, from the minimal cognizance of the smallest subatomic particle to the infinite awareness of the Sovereign of all the worlds and planes, is in a state of constant progression.[3]

The Focus of Divine Awareness

The mind of God in the Absolute overshadows the mind of everything that lives and breathes. However, not all of creation occupies the conscious attention of that mind at every moment. Just as many activities in our body take place in an automatic fashion without penetrating the level of conscious activity, so each level of existence functions subconsciously with respect to the life of those beings whose awareness envelops theirs.

Much of life on this planet continues on levels that are "instinctive" for the Sovereign of the world. These activities do not penetrate the Great One's "waking consciousness." However, nothing would function or remain in cohesive form without the Overshadowing Presence. When the divine gaze turns toward a particular area of the body, tremendous effects are felt in that region, as when we turn our minds to one part of our own self. Concentration leads to a direct effect on the region of choice, for a human being and for God.

For example, normally we are unaware of the presence of our toes. We walk without thinking or concentrating on our feet. However, if we bang our toe, then our attention is immediately drawn there, and the full force of our being is directed toward alleviating the pain.

In a similar manner, God reacts to the different parts of the divine body. If an area is in distress and cries out for help, the supernal mind is focused there. Otherwise, the Eternal One's awareness is concerned with the greater picture and the well-being of the overall creation.

The Unique Role of Humanity

In this greater reality, human beings hold a unique place. Unlike the cells in our physical body, we have self-awareness.[4] On the one hand, this unfortunately means that we are continually trying to fulfill our own desires instead of the will of God. On the other hand, our self-awareness also enables us to strive to know the will of the One who oversees our lives. We can expand our field of awareness and attune ourselves to the purpose of the Higher Power; a cell cannot. The cells in our body are bound by their "cell cognizance" that stretches no further than responding to positive or negative electrical and chemical stimulation.

Humankind functions on two levels at the same time. On one level, we are self-conscious individuals with a will of our own. We make independent decisions that either advance or retard our personal evolution. We each have our own thoughts and feelings, our plans and dreams.

On another level, we are living components of the Sovereign of the world. We are cells in God's body, and our consciousness is a miniscule aspect of the eternal mind. We are each a chip in the divine computer that carries one bit of information.

Yet what we do has significance in the larger picture. Our personal purification is a small contribution toward the refinement of the planetary centers. Our growth is part of the evolution of the Sovereign of the world. The wisdom and experience we gain in this life add to the knowledge of the planet. The will and passion we put into achieving our life's goals add another spark to the creative process unfolding in the mind of the All-Encompassing One.

The individual human being can sometimes affect the body of God on a scale that far outweighs our place in the divine structure. One person who has reached a stage of great spiritual development can uplift millions of lives. Or one person who has turned to evil can influence whole nations to commit acts of cruelty and barbarism.

Just as the breath and blood circulate oxygen and nutrients throughout the body of a human being, a great soul pours life and energy into the body of God. Just as one cancerous cell can create a malignant growth that will spread disease throughout the body, one soul that has turned to evil can spread violence and destruction throughout the body of humankind.

Humanity has a special place in the plan of God. We fit a specific niche in the divine structure of reality. A clearer understanding of our role in the overall pattern will help us to better fulfill that task. Therefore, the next section is a description of the body of the planet and the nature of the process that vitalizes our earth with spiritual life.

The Body of Earth

> As I looked, thrones were placed, and the Ancient of Days did sit, whose garment was white as snow, and the hair of whose head was like the pure wool; His throne was fiery flames, its wheels being burning fire. A fiery stream issued and came forth from before Him; a thousand thousands served Him, and ten thousand times ten thousand stood before Him. (Daniel 7:9–10)

Overshadowing the whole of the organization of the planes of earth is *Atik Yamin*, the Ancient of Days. *Atik Yamin* is responsible for overseeing

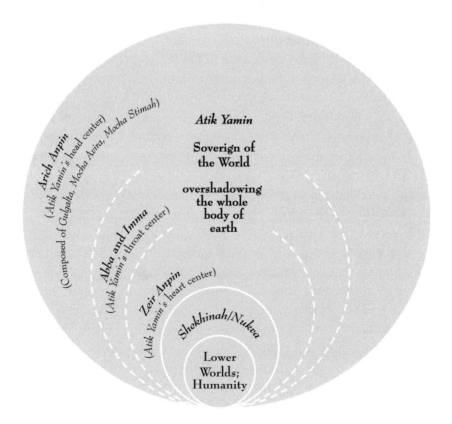

Figure 7. The body of earth

and caring for all life on our planet. He is the Sovereign of the world, the One in whom we live, breathe and have our being.[5]

The Organization of the Planes of Earth

In the *Idra* sections of the *Zohar*, *Atik Yamin* is described as seen in a series of visions by an evolved seer long ago.[6] According to tradition, this seer was the Talmudic sage Shimon bar Yochai, who spent seven years meditating in a cave.[7] These revelations, which were the fruit of his contemplation, describe the head of an exalted being who is the living abode of millions upon millions of lives. Some are emanating from the strands of His hairs, some compose His beard, others form the pupils and corneas of His eyes, yet others come bursting forth from His ears. They are formed into courts of judgment, messengers of mercy, witnesses of human actions, and emissaries of divine intervention.

The color of His eyes, hair, and beard change to reflect the particular energies that He is using. His hair either covers or reveals His ears and face to express the nature of the spiritual work that He is carrying out. And His forehead radiates forth light when the energy of the eternal will of God floods in to fill His being.

These descriptions are a symbolic representation of the organization of the planes of earth. They bring to life the structure of the celestial realms. They provide us with a dynamic and holistic vision of the supernal worlds.

Gan Eden Elyon—the Higher Garden of Eden; and *Gan Eden Tachton*—the Lower Garden of Eden

When we look at the spiritual body of earth, we can discern a number of major centers of life and activity. These centers form the equivalent of the body of centers in a human being. The centers are focused on the different planes of earthly existence. The "coloring" of each plane reflects the center in the body of God that it embodies. Each plane has its distinct form of life and level of consciousness. Certain of the planes are aligned with the human kingdom. They play a pivotal role in the life of this world.

As in any body, the central organs of life are the brain and the heart. In the body of *Atik Yamin*, the spiritual center that acts as the brain of the planet is called *Gan Eden Elyon*, "the Higher Garden of Eden," and the spiritual center that serves as the heart of the world is called *Gan Eden Tachton*, "the Lower Garden of Eden."[8]

These two great centers of light and consciousness maintain the life and health of the planet. *Gan Eden Elyon* infuses the planet with the will to live and the desire to fulfill the plan of God. *Gan Eden Tachton* provides the breath that circulates life and energy throughout the body of God.

The souls that dwell in the Lower Garden of Eden guide and inspire us, putting the breath of life into our physical existence. From the souls in the Higher Garden of Eden come the strength and courage to live that life and to strive toward ever-higher goals. *Gan Eden Elyon* is the mind that overshadows and gives cohesion and vitality to the body of God. *Gan Eden Tachton* is the loving heart that draws us to God and consoles us in its compassion and mercy.

Arich Anpin—the Greater Countenance

Each of these spiritual centers has its own particular structure and organization, which are described in the teachings of the Kabbalah. The whole of the center called *Gan Eden Elyon* is overshadowed by the presence of a divine being called *Arich Anpin*, "the Greater Countenance." He is the one who is responsible for the overall coordination and functioning of this spiritual plane.

There are three exalted beings who work together with *Arich Anpin* in overseeing the plane of *Gan Eden Elyon*—the head center. They embody the mind of God. Therefore, the *Zohar* depicts these three beings as corresponding to the three aspects of the head and brain of *Arich Anpin*: *mocha stimah*, the concealed brain; *mocha avira*, the subtle brain; and *gulgalta*, the skull that holds them. *Gulgalta* represents the *keter* or crown center of *Arich Anpin*. *Mocha stimah* is the *sefirah* of *chokhmah*, and *mocha avira* brings in the influence of *daat*, the direct knowledge of *Atik*, into the consciousness of the planet.

Together, these three might be called the "Royal Council," for they are the custodians of the will of God for the planet. They are responsible for keeping the purpose of the Guiding Life of the universe a vibrant and active spiritual force in the planetary consciousness.

Zeir Anpin—the Lesser Countenance

The second most important center of light and consciousness in the spiritual body of *Atik Yamin* is the heart center—*Gan Eden Tachton*, the Lower Garden of Eden. *Gan Eden Tachton* is at once an extension of *Gan Eden Elyon* and also an independent center in its own right. The task of those in *Gan Eden Tachton* is to organize the purpose of God into a concrete plan that can be fulfilled on the physical planes of earth.

Overarching the whole of the Lower Garden of Eden is the one called *Zeir Anpin*, the Lesser Countenance.[9] The sweep of His awareness embraces all of the life contained in this planetary center. *Zeir Anpin* receives the emanation of the will of God from *Arich Anpin* and emanates it out, in turn, to all those who live in His body, the plane of the heart.[10]

Two lofty souls aid *Zeir Anpin* in the direction of the Lower Garden of Eden. Together they wield the three energies of *daat* (knowledge), *chesed* (mercy), and *gevurah* (power). These three energies are then broken down into seven forces that form the focal points for seven groups of workers. The three directing souls can be thought of as forming the head of the *partzuf*, or countenance, while the seven lower groups make up its body. Together they provide the energy and guidance necessary to fulfill the spiritual mission of this plane.

Gan Eden Elyon and *Gan Eden Tachton* work in close cooperation. A constant flow of energizing life emanates out from *Gan Eden Elyon*, the Higher Garden of Eden, to produce an impression of the purpose of God upon *Gan Eden Tachton*, the Lower Garden of Eden. This emanation manifests at the heart of each of the seven groups as a reservoir of will or crown-center energy. This energy flows through to them from the *daat* (knowledge) of *Arich Anpin*.[11] It acts as the enlivening or energizing life of each group. This energetic transmission is distinct from the specific quality of energy with which the group works. It is the group's link to *Gan Eden Elyon* and the inspiration of divine purpose that unifies and empowers it.[12]

Abba and *Imma*—Father and Mother

The Kabbalah mentions one other major pair of *partzufim*, or "divine countenances," as part of the divine structure of reality. These divine beings are called *Abba* (Father) and *Imma* (Mother). They played a central role in the creation and development of *Zeir Anpin*. *Abba* and *Imma* dwell in *chesed/gevurah* (mercy/power)—the throat center—situated between the planes of the head and the heart. They were active at the time of the "birth" of *Zeir Anpin* and the formation of the heart center. Since that time, they have receded into the background. In the Kabbalah, *Abba* and *Imma* are placed underneath the beard of *Arich Anpin* as a symbolic expression of this spiritual fact and to indicate that they are under *Arich Anpin's* spiritual protection. At present, the primary function of these *partzufim* is to act as a relay station that directs the energies from *Arich Anpin* to *Zeir Anpin*.[13]

Nukva—the Female Counterpart to *Zeir Anpin*

The last of the divine beings called the *partzufim* is *Nukva*, literally "female." She is the female counterpart of *Zeir Anpin*, the Lesser Countenance.

In the higher *partzufim* of *Atik* and *Arich Anpin*, despite the use of the metaphor of an external male appearance, there is no actual separation of male and female—both aspects exist together within one being. The same is true of *Abba* and *Imma*. Even though they have been separated into male and female *partzufim*, they remain very much one united identity. This union of male and female aspects is the symbolic expression of the fact that all the souls that live in the bodies of these great beings are part of the unity of divine consciousness that is the Kingdom of Heaven.

When we reach the last two *partzufim* of *Zeir Anpin* and *Nukva*, however, there is a complete separation that occurs. *Zeir Anpin* and *Nukva* are each a totally separate *partzuf* with a life of its own.[14]

Zeir Anpin oversees the plan of God and emanates energy and consciousness into the lower worlds. The lives that dwell in His body, the heart center of the planet, all live fully within the consciousness of unity.

Nukva, or the *Shekhinah* as She is more commonly known, acts as a bridge between the spiritual and the physical worlds. She joins the divine kingdom together with the natural kingdom. She links the higher centers of the supernal planes—the head, throat, and heart—with the lower centers of the denser planes that make up our physical reality—the solar plexus, genitals, and base of the spine. The *Shekhinah* receives all of the emanations from the higher worlds and feeds them to the lower worlds. The beings who are part of the *Shekhinah* do not live fully in the consciousness of unity. They are both in the world and also in the higher realms. (We will explore the nature of the *Shekhinah* in greater depth in chapter 13.)

Humanity

Below the realm of the *partzufim*, humanity plays a key role in the organization and evolution of the planet. Our job is to bring the plan of God into physical manifestation, to concretize the divine vision in this material world. We are an extension of the immense centers of power and light called *Gan Eden Elyon* and *Gan Eden Tachton*. We are the go-between that relates the higher and the lower planes of living.

Humanity is uniquely suited for this mission, as we are both part of this world and part of the Kingdom of Heaven. We embrace within our being both a spark from the mind of God and also an animal body. Therefore, we can live with our minds in God and our feet on solid ground. We can convey the energy and ideas of the Kingdom of Heaven down to the earthly plane, and we can raise the activity and aspiration of the natural kingdom up toward the spiritual planes.

The Beard of God—the Great Compassion of *Arich Anpin* and *Zeir Anpin*

A Psalm of Ascension of David

Behold, how good and how pleasant it is
for brothers to dwell together in unity!
It is like the precious oil upon the head,
running down the beard of Aaron;
running down over the hem of his garment.
Like the dew of Hermon descending upon the
   mountains of Zion.
For there the Lord has commanded the
   blessing, even life forevermore. (Psalm 133)

The beard has a special significance in the Kabbalah.[15] In the *Zohar*, Psalm 133 is linked to the beard of the Greater Countenance. According to the Ari, the beard symbolizes the forces of divine compassion in the universe, the network of celestial workers who override all emissaries of judgment and destruction to come to the aid of humanity in times of dire need. Just like the anointing oil that runs down from the beard of Aaron in the Temple, these forces are described as thirteen wellsprings of anointing oil that flow down from the beards of the Greater and Lesser Countenances to illuminate the lower worlds.[16]

Kelim (Vessels) and Orot (Transmitters) of Light and Energy

How do we bring the power of the Kingdom of Heaven into this physical reality? How does energy and consciousness pass down through the worlds?

The *Idra* sections that describe the beards of *Arich Anpin* and *Zeir Anpin* are the *Zohar's* answer to these questions. All those who live in the higher worlds dwell in the unity of consciousness that is the universal mind of God. Yet each of these individual souls embodies its own transcendent state of mind. This state is the expression of the level that they have attained in the vast spectrum of being that stretches from the sentience of an atom to the infinite awareness of God. It is the result of the specific plane that they live upon and the parameters of cognizance that form the boundaries of that plane.

As these souls advance, their consciousness expands outward until they are able to transcend the boundaries of their own plane of living and contact souls who live in realms higher than their own. Once this breakthrough occurs, these souls become potential vessels, or *kelim*, to receive and distribute the energy and perception of the higher realm to their own world.

There is also another aspect to the spiritual evolution of the souls in the supernal realm. As their centers become more developed and their energy becomes more refined, some of the souls become *orot*—potential transmitters of the light and energy from their plane of consciousness to those who dwell in the planes below them. In this way, these souls become divine instruments that can both receive and transmit energy.

These spiritual contacts are used on a regular basis to transfer energy and guidance between souls on different planes. In a crisis, however, these soul contacts become a vital vehicle for sending help from on high to those who are in need. In a critical moment, these soul contacts form a chain of being that stretches from the higher reaches of the Kingdom of Heaven down into our physical world. This soul chain pierces through the barriers that separate the different planes to bring the power of love and compassion to transform the situation at hand.

This chain of soul contacts is what the *Zohar's* description of the beards of the Greater and Lesser Countenances attempts to portray. The hairs of the beard are symbolic of the *kelim*, the network of individual lives that act as vessels to carry God's light. The "holy oil" is symbolic of the *orot*, the actual light or energy that is transferred through this spiritual network.[17]

The *Idra* sections of the *Zohar*, as well as the *Etz haChayim* of the Ari, describe the beards of the Greater and Lesser Countenances in detail. The beard of *Arich Anpin*, for example, begins at the two *payot*, or side curls, on either side of the temples of His head. From the temples, the beard covers His face and then runs down across His chest. Each feature of the beard's form corresponds to a particular spiritual *tikun* (repair or redemption) that is accomplished through this network of souls. The beard of the Greater Countenance is composed of thirteen different elements, or *tikunim*. These thirteen *tikunim* are called the *shivcha deAtika*, "the praise of the Ancient One." Through the chain of energy and consciousness that is the supernal beard, the spiritual power of *Atik Yamin*, the Sovereign of the world, can reach anywhere in the body of earth.[18]

Two Prayers of Compassion

The Kabbalistic tradition provides us with a vehicle for evoking these spiritual forces in the form of two biblical prayers of compassion. The first prayer is taken from the story of Moses's second ascent up Mount Sinai.

After the sin of the Golden Calf, Moses once more climbed the mountain to meet with God. When he stood before the Ineffable One, Moses asked to see God's face. The Most High replied that Moses could not see the divine countenance, but God would show him the sacred beauty of the divine back. Moses then hid in the cleft of a rock as God passed the exalted glory over him. As God approached, Moses experienced a tremendous influx of spiritual energy and presence that totally overwhelmed him. Falling on his face in awe, Moses cried out:

> Lord, Lord, mighty, compassionate and gracious, long-suffering, abundant in love and truth, keeping truth to the thousands, forgiving iniquity, transgression and sin, and He cleanses....
> (Exodus 34:6–7)

This prayer is known in the tradition as the thirteen attributes of compassion. It is said to correspond to the thirteen aspects of divine compassion. It is the first of the two prayers that we use to arouse the heavenly powers embodied in the symbolism of the divine beard.

The second prayer that we use to awaken this spiritual force is taken from the prophet Micah. It represents another powerful evocation of God's compassion. Here is Micah's prayer:

> Who is a God like You, who pardons iniquity and forgives the transgression of the remnant of His heritage? He does not maintain His wrath forever, because He delights in mercy. He will again have compassion upon us; He will suppress our iniquities. And You will cast all their sins into the depths of the sea. (Micah 7:18–19)

The Ari explains that when we recite the thirteen attributes of compassion in the prayer of Moses, we bind ourselves to the chain of souls who form the *kelim*, or vessels, that connect all the worlds. When we recite the thirteen aspects of compassion in the prayer of the prophet Micah, we draw the *orot*, the divine light and energy that flows through this vast celestial network, down into our own being.

Just as there is an individual soul that envelops every human being, so there is the Kingdom of Heaven that overshadows all of humankind. When we turn our hearts and minds toward God in aspiration and hope, we join ourselves with the forces of love and compassion that live on higher planes. We become one link in the immense web of energy and consciousness that channels the spiritual power of the supernal realm down into our mundane physical reality.[19]

Divine Grace

May the Lord shine His face upon you
and be gracious unto you. (Numbers 6:25)

There are unexpected and inexplicable moments when God's grace comes pouring in, moments when light shines forth into the world for no apparent reason.

This section is about the dynamics that set divine grace in motion and the work that needs to be undertaken to create a vessel to hold it.

Darshan—Being in the Presence of Holiness

In India, there is a tradition that we receive a blessing merely by being in the presence of a holy person. They call this blessing *darshan*. *Darshan* is to "see and be seen" by a holy person and to receive his or her grace.[20]

This tradition is based on a basic understanding of the nature of holiness. What is it that draws us toward holy people? It is not their outer appearance that draws us, nor their human personalities; rather, it is the power of their souls shining through the outer appearance from within. People are holy because they have reached the stage in their spiritual evolution where they are overshadowed by God. Because of that overarching presence, the light of God shines through them. And we, in turn, desire to be in their presence, because then some of that light will enter into us. This is what it means to be blessed by *darshan*— to receive grace.

The *Zohar* provides us with a cosmic version of the process of *darshan*. In one of its more beautiful passages, the *Idra*s describe how in an *et ratzon*, a moment of grace, the face of the Lesser Countenance becomes illuminated as He is enveloped by the Greater Countenance. This light, in turn, radiates out from the face of the Lesser Countenance down through the worlds, filling the whole of creation with divine blessing and grace.[21] The Lesser Countenance is, in effect, receiving the *darshan* of the Greater Countenance. He then passes that *darshan* on to us.

Two Holy Apples

In the *Zohar's* description of the beard of *Arich Anpin*, the broad cheeks on either side of the face are called *trei tapuchin kadishin*, "two holy apples." This is because the energy of divine grace that sustains all the worlds is sent through the cheeks.

Even though we speak of seven major centers in our *Etz haChayim*, there are several minor centers located in other parts of the body. Two of the more prominent of these centers are located behind the cheeks. They are a focus for the emanation of the energy of the face and become fully activated during the advanced stages of spiritual development. One can see their influence radiating forth in a face that is filled with light. This is the underlying reason why many cultures have different forms of ornamentation for the cheek area. They have recognized the reality of this spiritual truth.

The seventh *tikun* of the beard is that the cheek area is completely free of hair. This *tikun* symbolizes the fact there is no obstruction to the passage of the divine light through the cheeks. The Ari expands on this idea: part of the light and energy of *Arich Anpin*, he explains, is emanated out through the beard, and part is directed through the cheeks. These two emanations originate in different parts of the mind of *Arich Anpin*, the Greater Countenance. The emanation that is imparted through the cheeks originates in *gulgalta* (the skull), the first of the three divine beings that embody the mind of *Arich Anpin*. The current that flows through the hairs of the beard carries the energy of *mocha stimah* (the concealed brain), the third of the beings that embody the greater mind.[22] The energy that streams through the cheeks is an outpouring of divine livingness that is of God's very essence. The energy that runs through the beard is the active response within the mind of God to a desperate cry for help.

Preparing to Receive Divine Grace

Moments of grace are a blessing. They are an unmerited gift from God. No one knows when such a moment will arrive. However, we can prepare ourselves for that time by forming a vessel to hold the grace. The amount of grace that we can receive and retain will be determined by the size and quality of our receptacle.

We build our spiritual vessel through three principal activities: by working to transform and purify our character, by engaging in spiritual disciplines, like meditation and prayer, and by studying and contemplating the wisdom in mystical traditions. Each of these practices will add to the strength and size of our container.

On a collective level, humanity needs to go through a similar process. We need to work on transforming human relationships so that they are founded upon a basis of moral and ethical behavior. We need to engage in practices that will bring us close to God—closer to our true self—such as meditation, prayer, and self-reflection. And we need to encourage the study and development of all forms of wisdom that expand human consciousness, such as spiritual teachings, philosophy, and science. In this way, we will forge humanity into a fitting repository for the light of the Kingdom of Heaven—a receptacle for the divine grace that flows down to our world through the Greater and the Lesser Countenances.

There are two cosmic mechanisms for bringing the power of the Kingdom of Heaven into the world: compassion and grace. The forces of compassion are activated by our prayers and our yearning for God. The energy of grace is bestowed upon us, when and how God chooses to do so. We can only make ourselves a worthy vessel to receive that grace whenever it enters into our lives.

The Mind of God

In the *Ein Sof*, the Absolute Reality, God is pure, infinite consciousness. The Ari asks: How did this infinite consciousness become embodied in a finite world? How did this finite creation arise out of an infinite Creator?

The Supernal Torah

The limitless becomes limited, the Ari explains, when the infinite undivided awareness becomes self-aware. This is accomplished through the formation of the divine mind—that is, by the containment of pure consciousness in a form of differentiated consciousness. The Kabbalah calls this original form the supernal Torah (holy scriptures).[23] It contains all the thoughts, wisdom, knowledge, and desires of the Creator.

The source of the scriptures is a higher reality that cannot be fully expressed in our space/time world. The Bible is the Word of God that created the universe and that infuses all of creation with purpose. Therefore, the laws that we were given on Mount Sinai can only be a reflection or partial expression of the "Divine Word." When we read the Hebrew Bible, we are reading only a small fragment of what is an infinite reality.

The *Etz haChayim*, the central text of the teachings of the Ari, states that the source of the Torah is the *daat* of *Atik Yamin*. The author brings as a proof text to support his claim the Talmudic saying in tractate *Sotah* 49a: "There is no knowledge (*daat*) but Torah." This subtle divine thoughtform is stored in the consciousness of *avira* (the subtle brain), the most hidden and unfathomable of the three beings who dwell in the head center of *Arich Anpin*. This concealed life holds the thoughtform of the supernal

Torah in a state of vibrant livingness, so that the whole of creation can be nourished from its boundless vitality.

Every Person Embodies One Letter in the Supernal Torah

The supernal Torah is not just an abstract concept for the Ari; it is an integral part of the essence of every human being. Each person, the Ari explains, has a letter in the supernal Torah that is linked to his *shoresh neshama*, his soul root.[24] Each of us is a spark of the divine mind. Hidden at the center of our being is the wisdom and knowledge of that Source. Through deep aspiration in prayer, meditation, and mental investigation, we can touch our source in the supernal Torah and bring the wisdom that is held within our personal supernal letter down into our human consciousness. The more we advance in the spiritual life, the greater the inner wisdom that we can bring through. Initially, we may get only occasional glimpses of that inner knowledge, but when our spiritual life is firmly established, this inner wisdom will become a natural part of our daily life.

In the case of a great soul, like Moses, the *ruach* (individual soul) and *nefesh* (personality) become one with the *neshama* (group soul) and *shoresh neshama* (soul root or *yechidah*). This links the soul-infused personality with the supernal Torah, or divine mind, and all of the knowledge, wisdom, and understanding that is stored there. This capacity to access all knowledge and all wisdom explains why it was Moses who brought the holy scriptures down into this physical world. Moses was able to accomplish this phenomenal task because he was one in soul and mind with the Torah's supernal source.

Rebbe Dov Baer of Mezeritch believed that the purpose of all of our spiritual work is to connect us back to this supernal Torah. In *Likutei Amarim* he writes:

> When a person does a mitzvah (a spiritual commandment), he should concentrate his speech, action, and thought—because thereby he will lift up the mitzvah and break it out of its physicality and bring it closer to its source and foundation in the higher worlds.[25]

The Torah in its essence expresses eternal truths. More than a system of laws, the Bible conveys the fundamental nature of reality, God, and life. Only as it descends into our physical world does the scripture become engaged in the details of physical existence. Because our understanding is physical and limited, the Bible needs to be expressed in similar terms. Our goal is to use the physical laws and teachings to expand our mind upward toward the Infinite—to unite back to our source in the Universal Mind and receive the *daat* of *Atik*, the infinite and eternal knowledge of God embodied therein.

The Universe of *Tikun*

According to the tradition, God created and destroyed several universes before creating ours. In the teachings of the Ari, the last of these worlds is called the World of Vowels or Dots—*Olam haNekudot*. This is the world in which the breaking of the vessels occurred. This shattering led to the collapse of *Olam haNekudot* and the scattering of the divine sparks.[26]

The World of Dots did not survive, according to the Ari, because of the lack of interconnectedness between its different parts. Each vessel, *sefirah*, or world of this universe was self-contained and separate from all others. This created a universe of chaos, or *tohu*, a universe where there was no balance or harmony.[27]

The Supernal Scales

At the beginning of the *Sefer Detzinutah*, one of the central sections of the *Zohar*, there is a description of the supernal scales, the *matkala*, upon which the whole of our universe is balanced.[28] On these scales there is a left-hand column of *din* (judgment) and a right-hand column of *chesed* (mercy) and a middle column of *rachamim* (compassion). A vast network of divine energy and light connects all of these different parts.

Our universe, therefore, is a universe of *tikun*, or repair. In this universe everything is aligned with each other. Everything is organized upon a *matkala*, a supernal scale.

This transformed reality is expressed in the imagery of *partzufim*—divine countenances or divine beings. Each level of interconnected life is described as the countenance and body of a great divine being. Each being has its overshadowing consciousness that brings cohesiveness to its entire spiritual body. As a single unified identity, the *partzuf* strives toward perfection in balance and harmony. Just like any other body, all the parts of the *partzuf* are interdependent and interconnected. Like in any other body, all the parts of the *partzuf* work together for the good of the whole under the direction of the overseeing presence.

Ours, then, is a universe of balance and harmony. It is a universe of interdependence. It is a universe of relationships. Balance, harmony, and relationship form the basis for the process of universal redemption and repair.

Structure of the Universe of *Tikun*

This universe of *tikun* is divided into four major worlds, realms, or levels of existence: the realm of *Atzilut*, or Emanation; the realm of *Briah*, or Creation; the realm of *Yetzirah*, or Formation; and the realm of *Asiyah*, or Making. Each of these realms has its own particular quality or essential character. Each of these realms is composed of seven major planes. The planes of *Atzilut* are called palaces, *hekhalot*, as are the planes of *Briah*. The planes of *Yetzirah* are called dwellings, *madurim*. The planes of *Asiyah* are called heavens, *rakiyot*.[29]

In classical Kabbalah, the six lower planes of each realm contain the lower seven *sefirot*, and the seventh and highest plane holds the upper three *sefirot*. If we follow our Kabbalistic/Yogic system, then the seven planes reflect the energies of the seven centers, beginning with *malkhut* and ending with *keter*.

The *partzufim* are the basic structure of this new reality. They exist in all four of the realms. They each, in turn, are composed of ten *sefirot*. Each *sefirah* expresses a different function and a different aspect of being in the body of the *partzuf*.

Above all of the worlds stands *Adam Kadmon*, the Cosmic Human, the Supreme Being about whom nothing can be truly said or known.

This is the fundamental spiritual structure of the universe. There are levels within levels to each realm, *partzuf*, and world. All of the *partzufim* that we have discussed in this section are only the *partzufim* of the realm of *Asiyah*. This provides us with a sobering perspective on our own relative importance in the greater scheme of the cosmos. Yet when we speak of the Sovereign of the world, *Atik Yamin*, we are speaking about a being whose consciousness holds all of the life on this planet as well as all of the seven planes of *Asiyah*. We cannot even begin to imagine what the mind of the Being whose consciousness holds all of the life on all of the planes in our galaxy might be like.

The Nature of the Four Realms

Atzilut (Emanation) is composed of pure energies. In this realm, nothing exists except the interaction between the divine emanations. Here we have the archetypes of the five *partzufim*.

Briah (Creation) is the realm of thought, the plane of the mind. In *Briah* everything is composed of mental matter. This is the world of souls. The souls dwell in the most subtle form of bodies composed of light. They communicate directly from mind to mind. This world is the destination of the humans who have passed out of incarnation.

Yetzirah (Formation) is the dominion of the emotions; it is the astral plane. The psychic is the main form of communication here. Therefore, the angelic kingdom predominates in this domain. The psychic is the medium of angelic communication. Both in the highest and the lowest, they rely heavily on this sense. This is where humans in physical incarnation make contact with the plant, animal, and angelic kingdoms—in the sphere of feelings.

The world of *Asiyah* (Making) is the realm of the concrete. It is the most densely physical of the worlds. It functions through the experiences of the senses. It is the region that we know best.

From one perspective, we can think of the four realms as four great planes, one higher or more refined than the other, with each plane containing seven sub-planes. From another vantage point, we should not think of the planes in a hierarchical fashion at all. The realms do not move from *Asiyah* to *Yetzirah* to *Briah* to *Atzilut*. Rather, each is a different mode of interacting with reality. Each one can take us a certain "distance" toward the essential nature of existence, as far as we are capable of perceiving it.

Asiyah is the physical dimension, the realm of form. We judge everything by spatial perception and by the input of the senses. Physical perception allows us to interact with the world of the five senses. It puts us into contact with a myriad of different sensations through touch, sight, hearing, smell, and taste. When we reach the edges of physical discernment, the physical laws begin to break down and our understanding becomes confused.

Yetzirah is the home of emotions. Form is no longer central to our awareness. Feelings guide our life and create the reality around us. Feelings can take us further than purely physical sensations. Emotion leads us into unseen areas of experience. But emotion can take us only so far, and no further. The grossness of feelings blocks our movement. At a certain point, we no longer receive clear and true information through feelings, and what we do receive becomes jumbled and distorted.

Briah is the birthplace of thought. Everything is composed of mind substance. Our thoughts mold our reality. The mind is dynamically creative and powerful; it has a more refined perception than feelings or physical sensation. We can travel a long way using our mind, but there still are limitations. A time comes when even the mind is stymied, where we reach a wall that we cannot scale.

Atzilut is the abode of pure energies. Here we use inner sight or etheric awareness to interact with the world around us. We observe a domain composed solely of light and consciousness. *Atzilut* takes us to the essence of reality as far as we can know it. It takes us to the edge of our manifest universe.

Beyond *Atzilut*, there are other realities that transcend light and darkness, form and formless. This is what we touch upon when we experience the Self—the awareness of the Absolute. We leave behind everything that we know and reach out to realms and levels of perception of which we cannot even begin to conceive.

———— ◎ ————

10

The Angelic Kingdom

The Spiritual Dimension of the Natural Realm

T he angelic kingdom is a vast and powerful dominion. It encompasses all the varied lifeforms in the universe that are not part of the human evolution. The entire natural world is part of this realm, and much more as well. In some ways, the life of the angelic kingdom overlaps with the life of the human kingdom, but in most respects, each lives within a completely separate reality.

The Keepers of Form

The key word in this domain is "form." The angelic kingdom is responsible for the form side of life. It nurtures, protects, and constructs out of its own nature the bodies that make up all life. Be it the body of a human being, the body of an animal, the body of a plant, or the body of an atom, it is the angelic kingdom that gives the body its existence.

The Kabbalah tells us that everything contains a spark of the Divine. What this means, in essence, is that every created thing is composed of angelic lives. There are angels that vitalize the wood and rocks that form our houses. There are angels that embody the air we breathe. Angelic lives form our currents of electricity and other forms of energy. There are even angels that fill the empty space between the stars.

The Collective Consciousness of the Natural Kingdom

The angelic kingdom oversees the evolution of all of nature. Midrash *Bereshit Rabbah* 10:6 states that every blade of grass has an angel that taps it on the head and commands it to grow. What the midrash is explaining to us is that unlike humans, the lower lifeforms in the angelic kingdom do not possess self-awareness. They experience life as part of a larger group consciousness.

The animal kingdom also experiences reality through group consciousness. This truth is expressed in the group behavioral patterns of different animals. The perfect flight formation of a flock of birds and the complex social organization of a hive of bees are both examples of the workings of such a "collective mind."

Each of these animal or plant groupings is overseen by a more advanced angelic being. Each angel works with a different part of the realm. There are separate classes of angels for water life, mineral life, plant life, animal life, human life, and many other forms of life that are unknown to us.

Humanity's folklore is ripe with depictions of the inhabitants of this magical empire. They are called angels, but also fairies, elves, dwarves, and many other names as well. The elves and fairies of folklore are the guardians and tenders of the natural world. They are portrayed as small, gentle beings with a playful and mischievous quality—an attempt to describe a consciousness that is entirely different from our own.

This idea is also expressed through tales like Shakespeare's *A Midsummer Night's Dream*, where the wrong person is given a love potion, and other tales of blunders being made by angels through a lack of capacity for humanlike thinking. We also read about the tricks that those in the angelic kingdom enjoy playing on humans and of their special love for riddles and jokes. In the Midrash and Talmud we find passages that depict the angels making careless mistakes as God's messengers. The Talmud, *Hagigah* 4b, tells the story of an emissary of the Angel of Death who brings the soul of Miriam the nanny instead of Miriam the hairdresser. All this is a way of indicating that the minds of those in the angelic kingdom work in a manner quite distinct from that of a human being.

The descriptions of these beings that we find in ancient tales and mythology give us an indication of their role. They also reveal a lot about the character of the angelic lives and the organization of their communities. The whole of ancient literature is a mine of information concerning this dominion.

Angels in the Jewish Tradition

There is also a great deal of knowledge regarding the angelic within the Jewish tradition. A look at some of the roles played by angels in the Hebrew Bible will give us a glimpse of the breadth of understanding there was about this realm.

When Adam and Eve are banished from the Garden of Eden, God places angels, the *keruvim* (cherubs), with the bright blade of a revolving sword to guard the entrance to Eden and the Tree of Life. Three angels come to Abraham to tell him of his wife's pregnancy and to carry out the destruction of Sodom and Gomorrah.

When Jacob flees his father's house, he sees a vision of a ladder with angels ascending to and descending from heaven. On his way to confront his brother Esau, Jacob meets an angel in a deserted wadi, who wrestles with him all through the night. In the morning, Jacob is alone and lame in one thigh. But before he departs, the angel gives Jacob his blessing and also a new name and identity: Israel, one who has wrestled with God.

An angel appears to Moses in the burning bush, the Angel of Death sweeps through Egypt to kill the firstborn of the Egyptians, and an angel leads Israel through the desert. As Joshua gazes upon Jericho, he meets the captain of the angelic hosts, with his sword drawn before him, and the angel informs Joshua that God has given Jericho into his hands.

In the Hebrew Bible, angels are wielders of power. They are guardians and protectors, beings with the strength to defend against any enemy. They control the energy of destruction and the energy of healing. They have the ability to bestow spiritual blessing and divine revelation. These are clearly not the playful elves of folklore, but beings who embody awesome spiritual force.

The Rabbinic sources expand upon the biblical stories about angels. The midrash *Bemidbar Rabbah* 2:10 explains that there are four hosts of angels under the direction of the four archangels who oversee the whole of this kingdom: Michael, Gabriel, Uriel, and Raphael. The midrash also ascribes specific roles to each of the archangels in many of the biblical narratives. *Bereshit Rabbah* 48:9–50:2 tells us that Michael, Gabriel, and Raphael were the three angels who came to visit Abraham after he was circumcised. Raphael came to heal Abraham, Michael came to announce that Sarah would give birth to Isaac, and Gabriel came to destroy the cities of Sodom and Gomorrah. In this way, the angels in the various biblical stories become personalized for us, and the character of their different roles is revealed.

The angelic kingdom also receives a large amount of attention in the medieval Jewish writings. The Kabbalah is filled with teaching about this invisible realm. The *Hekhalot* (Palaces) section of the *Zohar*, for example, describes the nature of the seven heavenly worlds. As part of its description, the *Zohar* goes into remarkable detail about the angels who inhabit and work in these worlds. The *Zohar* discusses a whole variety of different types of angelic beings, called *ruchot*, *chayot*, *serafim*, *ofanim*, *malachim*, and *galgalim*. On each of the planes, there are exalted angelic beings who are in charge of the work on that level, as well many other beings who work under them, performing a variety of tasks such as guardians of the gates, messengers carrying divine decrees, and simple laborers who maintain the activities in each *hekhal*.

Every angel has its individual name, its own specific color or colors, and its particular directional location and position within the palace. These details designate the type of work they do, the nature of the *sefirot* that they embody, and the level of spiritual energy they carry. An in-depth study of the *Hekhalot*, as well as the many other texts about angels within the *Zohar* and the rest of the tradition, will provide a rich harvest of both information and understanding regarding the structure and character of this remarkable class of beings.[1]

The Work of the Angelic Kingdom

The numbers of angels involved in the organization of this kingdom is immense. The diversity of life is extraordinary. The angels provide all of the workers and builders needed in the grand labor of creation. On each level of life, the angelic collective is organized to undertake and oversee the work of converting the images in the divine mind into a material form.[2]

In the mineral kingdom, angels supervise the various levels of metal formation. They give gold its glitter and silver its shine. They oversee the gradual transmutation of plant life into coal and oil over a period of millions of years. A great angel stands behind the range of the Himalayas, watching over and shepherding all of the life upon her slopes.

The angelic kingdom oversees the evolution of water through its various stages of moisture, evaporation, and condensation again as moisture. It controls the balance of life in rivers, lakes, and ponds. There is a high angelic being that cares for the Amazon River and all of its plant and marine life. And there is a glorious angelic lord who overshadows each of the oceans of the world.

In the plant kingdom, the angels labor tirelessly to provide the color and form that give this domain its beauty and appeal. There are myriads of angels that work to create the bouquet of flowers that adorn the fields and forests of the world. They are directed by higher angelic beings that mold the lower angelic lives into the harmonious landscapes and vistas that give humans such peace and joy.

In the animal kingdom, there are angels that are responsible for tending the herds of animals and flocks of birds. They guide and nurture them, making sure that they get the protection and the nourishment they need. There are angelic beings whose job it is to help the animal kingdom to diversify and evolve. Their task is to develop new kinds of evolutionary species and to weed out old ones that have completed their usefulness on this plane.

Angelic beings are responsible for the major weather patterns and climatic phenomena around the globe. These great angels of power work under the guidance of the archangel Gabriel ("God is my power"). This task draws on the energies of the *Shekhinah*. Under Gabriel's direction, millions of angelic lives carry out their mission.

When there is a natural catastrophe or man-made disaster, there are special angels whose job it is to repair the damage and devastation. They work under the guidance of the archangel Raphael ("God heals") to heal disease and suffering. Multitudes of angelic lives work to reestablish health where there is sickness, well-being where there is sorrow and pain. They are with every doctor and healer, with every individual who works to bring order and healing to the creation.

One has to wonder if there is not a new order of angels that has been formed to combat the damage that humankind has done to the planet—specialists in pollution and environmental repair, who have been trained to counteract the folly of humankind.

The Angelic Kingdom and Humanity

The nature of the angelic mind is little understood by humanity today. This was not always the case. In ancient times, when human life was more closely linked to nature, there was greater awareness of and understanding about this realm. There was also more contact between the two types of lives. This higher level of contact was partly due to a greater psychic openness among human beings, which provided a medium of communication between the two kingdoms.

During this period, the sighting of angelic beings was not that uncommon, and a certain sympathy developed between these different domains. There are many stories about the help and cooperation that took place between humans and angels. Such folktales as the cobbler and his elven helpers are a product of this collaboration. The great myths that inspired Tolkien in his writings, such as *The Lord of the Rings*, all arise out of this shared past. The insights of herbal medicine may have also come from this time of angelic contact, when humanity maintained a more intimate relationship with the angelic lords of the plant kingdom.

Reestablishing Contact Between Humanity and the Angels

In the past century, there have been numerous groups that have attempted to reopen this dialogue. The Findhorn community is one notable example. Having entered a region where the angelic kingdom was still exceptionally potent, the members of the community made contact with the angelic life that dwelled there and gained their aid in growing the community's food crops. The gigantic fruit and vegetables that resulted from this partnership astonished everyone.

Many other groups have also explored the relationship between humanity and this kingdom. There are scientific groups that have tried to determine if plants have awareness and feelings. A number of well-known anthropologists have forged a profound link with specific animal communities in the wild. Each of these attempts at human-angelic contact has reopened the door of relationship between the realms. They have led to many similar spiritual experiments in countries across the globe. Who knows what the eventual results of these new contacts will be, what unique spiritual opportunities these encounters will provide to the members of the two kingdoms?

There is fresh air and beauty in nature, but there is also the blessing of the angelic kingdom that we receive in their domain. A desire for contact with this realm motivates many people to seek the outdoors. Only in virgin nature can the angelic allow its full presence to be manifest. This fully manifest presence creates the feeling of peace and the expansion of consciousness that we experience in such an untouched natural environment.

This same angelic influence is the reason why many spiritual seekers prefer to meditate outdoors. By sitting in nature, they are drawing on the help and energy of this realm to reach toward the Divine. This contact leads them to richer experiences and deeper meditations than when they meditate in a closed room. There is less of an impediment to the flow of energy in a natural setting, and the energy is purer and more concentrated. It is no accident that most monastic centers are located in beautiful, isolated locations in nature. This is the right environment for intense contemplative work.

Approach the Angelic Kingdom with Respect and Love

Despite all of the positive benefits that we receive from contact with the angelic, this domain needs to be approached with considerable caution. There are many dangers involved in interaction with the angelic. The lesser angelic lives are completely instinctual in their behavior. If we turn to these angels with anger or if we come with the intent to harm them, there will be an immediate reaction. If the might of this dominion were accidently aroused against us, the consequences could be devastating.

The angelic kingdom functions according to a different logic and another law. In our ignorance, we can cause serious harm to this kingdom and create grave danger for ourselves. There are numerous folktales about humans who brought disaster on themselves through too strong a curiosity regarding this realm. We need to approach the angelic life with humility and caution.

Where there is the willful manipulation of the power of this domain, then it is no longer called ignorance, but black magic. A black magician utilizes his command of the angelic lives to manipulate the forces of nature. The story of the eleventh-century Tibetan saint Milarepa is a poignant example of the negative karma that arises when the power of this kingdom is abused.

Milarepa was born into a happy, prosperous family. He had a joyful childhood until the age of seven, when his father suddenly died. Before Milarepa's father's death, he entrusted all of his wealth and business affairs into the hands of his brother and sister-in-law. He instructed them to take care of his wife and two children until Milarepa reached the age of manhood and could assume responsibility for the family. However, Milarepa's uncle and aunt betrayed his trust. They stole the family's wealth and property, leaving Milarepa, his mother, and his sister in abject poverty and then forced the family to be their servants.

When Milarepa grew to manhood, his mother commanded him to go study black magic with a sorcerer so that they might take revenge on her husband's brother and his family. Being a loyal and obedient son, Milarepa followed his mother's advice and went to seek a teacher. After learning the black arts from his teacher, Milarepa returned to his native village and brought forth storms and earthquakes to destroy his uncle and aunt and their home and property. In the ensuing calamity, thirty-five people were killed, and the harvest of all the villagers was destroyed.

When Milarepa saw the tremendous loss of life and the great suffering that he had brought about by his magic, he felt profound remorse. Tormented by the horrendous consequences of his actions, he set out on a long quest for personal redemption. Milarepa spent many painful years going through much trial, tribulation, and penance to wipe away the karmic debt that he had created with his black work of destruction.[3]

The angelic dominion is not ours to command. Our relationship with the angels needs to be based on love and respect. Any help that they give us is a precious gift that we should accept with gratitude. For most of us, it is probably better to avoid too keen an interest in the workings of this realm. It is only necessary that we understand the great benefit and blessing that we receive from this kingdom in God's manifold creation.

11

Incarnation and Evolution in the Divine Kingdom

Can God Evolve?

The evolutionary cycle of the divine kingdom is a revolutionary idea. For many, the idea that God can evolve is blasphemous; God is perfect, and there can be no need to add to or change anything.

On one level, God in the *Ein Sof*, in the Absolute, is already perfect. On another level, all of creation and all of the realms we can ever reach or think about exist in a reality that is finite and not perfected. In fact, it is a fundamental component of our belief that the central purpose of life is to bring the universe and everything in it to perfection. This must be true, for life to be worth living.

If this universe exists as a dynamic reality, then the life that embodies it needs to be vital and evolving. This world has meaning and purpose because it is part of a great dynamic process that involves every living thing upon the planet, from atoms to celestial beings. We are eternal souls because we are an integral part of the life of God. Our struggles and triumphs have meaning because they are bound up with the evolving manifestation of the Divine in the revealed universe.[1]

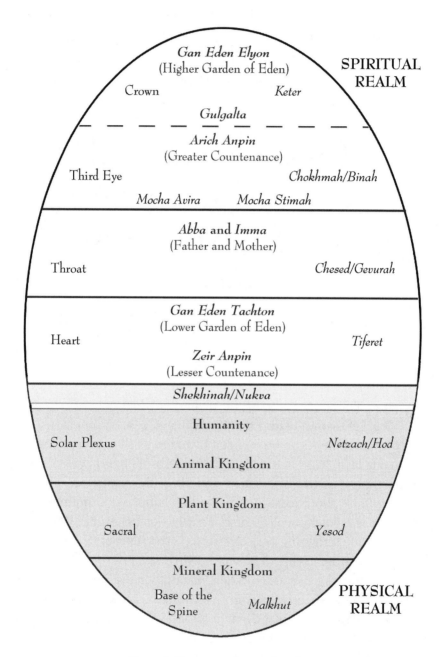

Figure 8. The seven planes of earth

Divine Perfection

The Vedas speak of one year of Brahma as representing more than three trillion earth years.[2] Our recent understanding of time and space, and of the millions of light-years of life that separate us from other galaxies in the universe, has given a certain reality to these enormous numbers. The life of a solar system is forty or fifty billion years. The Divine Being that oversees and vitalizes the life of our system works in dimensions of life, space, and time that we can hardly begin to comprehend. What does the end product of forty billion years of life look like on the physical, mental, and spiritual levels? What do perfection and imperfection mean on such a time scale? Does anyone doubt that life will have evolved in unimaginable ways during that timeframe? Who can even conceive of the purposes and methods of the Being that guides such a process?

The divine beings incarnate in great cycles of alternating activity and contemplation. The periods of contemplation are dedicated to the formulation of their eternal purpose. Once this formulation has been achieved, the thought is sent out into the universe. This creative impulse then gathers life and energy as it passes down through the planes. An impulse from the mind of God animates the whole of life in our solar system.

Creation

We can understand the process of divine activity through the description of the creation of the world in the Hebrew Bible. The first line of Genesis tells us, "In the beginning, God created the heavens and the earth." From the beginning of the Creation process, God created the different planes of existence for the life that was to evolve on this planet. At the same time, it is a fundamental truth of the science of the spirit that any physical creation will be preceded by a spiritual creation. Both are needed as part of the formation of any world or life.[3]

As in the creation of human life, where the husband and wife join together to create new life, the Father aspect (the Holy One, blessed be He) joins together with the Mother aspect (the *Shekhinah*) to create new worlds. They unite on each level of creation to form the basis of that plane.

First, the energy of the lowest center, *malkhut* (kingship), was taken up to create the mineral life of the planet. With this energy, God produced the physical form of our world. The land with all of its topography was fashioned, and then the seas with their depths were carved out.

God then gathered in the energy of the second center, *yesod* (foundation). From the union of God and the *Shekhinah* in this *sefirah*, the plant kingdom was created. All of the wonderful diversity of plant life emerged at this time. This profusion of different lifeforms is a reflection of *yesod's* great fecundity.

The energy of the next center, *netzach/hod* (eternity/splendor), was then stimulated. The divine union in this *sefirah* produced the animal kingdom on all of its various levels. Over hundreds of millions of years, this kingdom grew and developed until it had created highly evolved and complex animals. The advanced forms of this kingdom are endowed with the feelings and passions of the solar plexus center. These feelings embody its spiritual potential.

The heavens were then formed with the embryonic elements of the heart center, *tiferet* (beauty). This was to be the Garden of Eden and the abode of humankind. Here the planes of earth and the evolution of the planet were intended to express themselves in a new and more sublime way of life. This heaven and humanity, the creation that inhabited it, were to be the intermediary between the physical planes and the higher spiritual realms.

The holy scriptures tell us that the Creation process lasted seven days. What is a day in the life of God? In the Hindu scriptures, each day of Brahma is approximately four billion years long. If we imagine the Creation occurring over seven days of similar duration, then we are speaking of a process that took many billions of years. Such a timeframe for Creation makes sense to us today.

At the end of "seven days" the Creation was completed, and the creative energies of the Deity were focused elsewhere. In the biblical narrative, we are told that God rested on the seventh day. This can be understood in terms of a period of withdrawal from action into deep contemplation.

What happens when God rests? In the Kabbalah, we are given an explanation. The word used in the scripture for "rested" is *vayi-nafash*. This word is close in spelling to the Hebrew word for the lowest aspect of the soul, the *nefesh*. On the seventh day, the Kabbalah elucidates, after God ceased creative activity, the divine spirit was breathed into the whole of creation. The Essence of All Goodness gave the world a purpose and the will to evolve and grow. The eternal consciousness was implanted in the outer physical form.[4]

The Ten Creative Utterances

The tradition also provides us with an explanation of how this creative process unfolded. Genesis 1:3 states, "And God said, 'Let there be light,' and there was light." In the beginning, the desire to create the earth entered into the Mind of God. This desire became a sacred thoughtform. This thoughtform was then manifested as sound, a divine utterance. This sound emanated out through all of the planes of earth.

The Ethics of the Fathers (*Pirkei Avot* 5:1) speaks of ten divine utterances through which God established the world. These are the ten *sefirot* or energies that pervade all life. As was mentioned earlier, the ten *sefirot* are, in fact, an expansion of the initial seven centers. These seven centers correspond to the seven basic harmonic sounds or notes. Each *sefirah*, then, has its own sound that expresses its essential nature. The ten utterances that created the world are ten energetic vibrations that set all of life on this planet into motion.

Vibration is a fundamental component of all of existence. Wherever there is life there is energy in movement. From the electrons in an atom to the immense galaxies in the heavens, all of creation is in perpetual motion. At the same time, we know that sound is a wave, a vibration of energy. Sound and the Creation process are intimately intertwined. The "Word of God" is the manifestation of the changeless and ever-present Reality in the physical universe as energy.

The divine utterance, or energy vibration, emanated out through the planes, gathering life and force. Along the way, angelic matter of varying degrees was drawn into the growing vortex of energy. The sound descended into the physical plane and began to take concrete shape and substance. Finally, the Word was transformed into the myriads of different lifeforms that inhabit our planet today.

The creation of this world was an outpouring of divine speech. The ten utterances initiated a cacophony of "living sound" in all different shapes and forms. That sound and music is ever evolving and maturing. One day it will produce a planetary symphony of exquisite harmony and beauty.

The Evolution of *Zeir Anpin* and *Gan Eden Tachton*

The Lurianic teachings describe the spiritual evolution of *Zeir Anpin*, the Lesser Countenance, and *Gan Eden Tachton*, his body of manifestation, through the symbolism of a child's conception and physical development. This process is divided into four stages. The first stage is the union of *Abba* and *Imma* (*zivug yesod beyesod*) and the resulting creation of new life. The second stage is a period of gestation in the divine womb (*ibbur*) and the subsequent birth. Next, there is a phase where the newborn is nurtured as an infant (*yenikah*, or breast-feeding). And finally, there is the stage where the child grows into full consciousness as an adult (*gidul hamochin*, or the development of the brain and mind).[5]

This mystical symbolism expresses a great spiritual truth about the relationship between the Higher Garden of Eden and the Lower Garden of Eden and the relationship of these two tremendous centers of spiritual power to humanity. The relationship between these three spiritual entities has been in a state of constant change and growth ever since the creation of the planet. First, there was a time when *Zeir Anpin* had not yet been created and the Lower Garden of Eden was still unformed. During this period, the Higher Garden of Eden and humanity were the only major centers of consciousness on the planet. A strong impulse descended from the Higher Garden of Eden to the human beings in physical incarnation, but they were unequipped to absorb its force. As a result, this superior stimulus had little impact on their forward evolution.

As humanity developed a greater capacity for reaching into the spiritual realm, a new nexus of life and power began to take shape on the plane of the heart. This extra center, the Lower Garden of Eden, acted as a bridge between humanity and the Higher Garden of Eden. The divine being whom we call *Zeir Anpin* was given the task of overseeing this spiritual work.

The emerging manifestation of *Zeir Anpin* and the development of *Gan Eden Tachton* is analogous to the creation of the *ruach*, or individual soul, and the formation of the *tzelem*, or soul-body. In the process of spiritual development, the *ruach* (individual soul) acts as a step-down transformer for the energies of the *neshama*, or greater oversoul. The *ruach* absorbs and digests these powerful emanations, converting them into a more palatable form that can then be passed on to the *nefesh*, the individual human being in incarnation on the physical plane.

In a similar manner, the Lesser Countenance and the Lower Garden of Eden were created to act as a mid-station between the Higher Garden of Eden and humanity on the physical plane. *Gan Eden Tachton* transmits the will, love, and light of God to the lower worlds. It enables humankind to have direct and potent contact with the Kingdom of Heaven.

The formation and development of the Lower Garden of Eden was an important step in the evolution of *Atik Yamin*, the Sovereign of the world. Just as a human being aspires to join with his soul consciousness, so *Atik Yamin* strives toward cosmic union. The development of a fully flowing heart center in a human being is an expression of the fact that a powerful link with the soul has been achieved. Similarly, the creation of the Lower Garden of Eden was an expression of the establishment of a powerful link between the Sovereign of the world and His spiritual source on cosmic

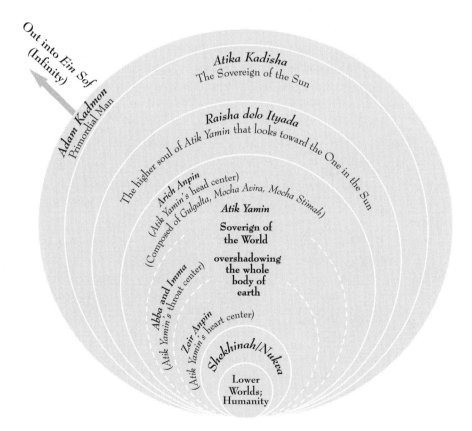

Figure 9. The *partzufim* or divine countenances

levels. It enabled *Atik* and the planet to receive new energies and attain additional states of consciousness that were previously inaccessible to Him and the planet as a whole.

The Lower Garden of Eden began as a small nucleus of evolved souls. Over millions of years, it has grown into the major energy center of the planet. *Gan Eden Tachton* takes in energies not only from the Higher Garden of Eden and the Sovereign of the world but also from sources outside the planetary system. These spiritual centers pour cosmic energies into the earth's heart center, which is then passed onward to humanity and the rest of the planet.

Beyond Our World

The dramatic passages at the beginning of the Hebrew Bible describe the creation of our planet and everything upon it. This archetypal account concerns the life of *Atik Yamin*, the Sovereign of the world. Just as we have a lower self and a higher self, so too the Sovereign of the world has a lower self and a higher self. These two parts of the Divine Being correspond to the *nefesh*, or personality, and the *ruach*, or individual soul. Each of these aspects has its own independent identity and role in the life of the planet.

The *nefesh* of *Atik Yamin* has taken on the job of direct involvement in the planes of earth. This part of the soul is responsible for the guidance and care of all life on this world. In most cases where the Kabbalah speaks of *Atik Yamin*, the Ancient of Days, this is the One to whom it is referring.[6]

The *ruach* of *Atik Yamin* was active at the time of the formation of our world. During the Creation process, this Great Being channeled toward the earth all of the energies needed from outside the system to build the physical planet and its body of spiritual centers. Though still present in the planes of earth, the *ruach* of *Atik Yamin* is now focused on the greater reality of the wider solar system and the cosmos. For this reason, this One has been given the name of *Raisha delo Ityada*, the unknown or hidden Face of God. In esoteric literature, *Raisha delo Ityada* is depicted in profile to symbolize the fact that the consciousness of this Being is turned away from our world and is looking toward the Sovereign of the sun with whom *Raisha* now identifies.[7]

The *nefesh* of *Atik Yamin* overshadows the seven planes of our planet. This "personality" is part of the *partzufim* of the realm of *Asiyah* (the world of Making), with an awareness confined within the limits of our planetary consciousness. The awareness of *Raisha delo Ityada*, the *ruach* of *Atik Yamin*, is not part of the *partzufim* of *Asiyah*. This mind can reach past the boundaries of the planes of earth. And the consciousness of the *neshama* of *Atik Yamin*, the greater soul of which *Atik Yamin* is only a tiny spark, reaches even farther out into the expanses of the wider cosmos.

When we move beyond our earth-centric perspective, our planet takes its place as part of the body of the great One who is the Sovereign of our solar system, *Atika Kadisha*—the Holy Ancient One.[8] The entire solar system forms the body of manifestation for this exalted life. Each of the planets represents a different center in this spiritual body. Everything that happens on all of the planets is part of solar life.

Just as a physical human being in incarnation is linked to a soul on higher planes, similarly the sovereigns of our planet and solar system are linked to beings who are their source or soul on the cosmic planes. They receive guidance and energy from their souls that empowers them to fulfill their planetary and solar incarnations.

In the same way that each human life is only one incarnation of perhaps hundreds of incarnations that his or her individual soul will undergo, similarly this planetary and solar manifestation is only one incarnation out of many that the soul of the planet and the soul of the solar system will experience.

The results of the past incarnations of earth and the solar system will determine the basic components that make up the reality of the next one. Qualities developed in earlier systems will permeate the planetary and solar life of the later incarnations. The further development of these and other spiritual attributes will decide the evolutionary circumstances for each new divine manifestation.

Just as the gains of each human incarnation adds to the overall wisdom and experience of her soul, similarly this incarnation of *Atik Yamin* and *Atika Kadisha* will bring new energy and awareness to the overall consciousness of their cosmic souls. This growth will lead their souls toward liberation on the higher realms of the galactic reality. As a result of this process, billions of lesser lives, including the sovereigns of the

Yechidah (Soul Root) and *Chayah* (*Neshama* of the *Neshama*) of Planetary Sovereigns and *Neshama* (Group Soul) of Solar Sovereigns	**Atzilut** Adam Kadmon (Primordial Man) Greater Galactic Consciousness
Neshama (Group Soul) of Planetary Sovereigns and *Ruach* (Individual Soul) of Solar Sovereigns	**Briah** Greater Constellations

12 Constellations

Yetzirah

Solar Personality	*Atika Kadisha*
Planetary *Ruach* (Individual Soul)	*Raisha delo Ityada*

Asiyah

Nefesh (Personality) and Body of *Atik Yamin*	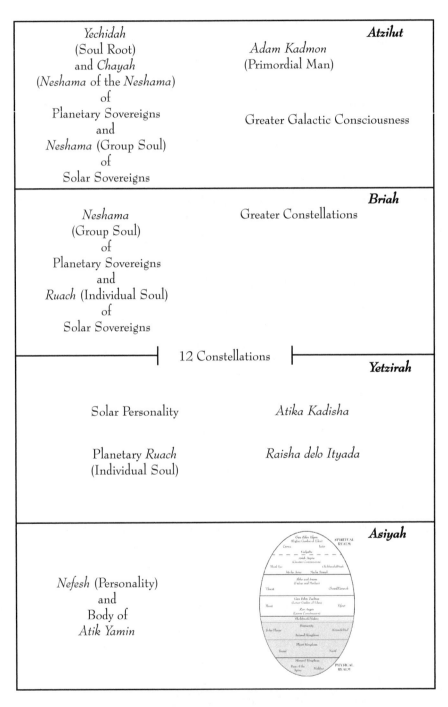

Figure 10. Our wider reality

individual planets as well as the lives of all of humankind, will be raised up and pushed forward in their spiritual evolution, leading the whole of the universe one step closer toward its ultimate objective.

Partners in Creation

Through the concept of divine evolution, we are transformed from powerless spectators into God's partners in creation. When we bind ourselves to God, we are adding to the unity and perfection of creation. By our every act, we bring the ultimate goal either closer or push it farther away. When we make new scientific discoveries or inspirational creations of art and music, we are adding to the beauty and richness of the universal life. When we perform mitzvot, spiritually potent acts, we are strengthening the link between heaven and earth.

If we look at the advancement of the Godhead from this point of view, it becomes something noble and sublime. It is not an attempt to limit God, but rather an expression of the complexity of creation and the beauty that is the unfolding divine process. This idea does not conflict with the notion of the perfection of God in the Absolute. Ultimately, we are striving to reach a reality that is an expression of God's intrinsic perfection. However, this is the aim of existence, not its starting point. Over billions of years we will reach that goal.

Fundamental Forces at Work in Human and Divine Evolution

Influence and Interaction on the Micro- and Macrocosm

There are many factors at work in the unfolding of the cosmos. Three key concepts stand out as crucial to our understanding of the processes taking place in the lives of both humanity and the divine beings who manifest through our wider reality. These ideas encompass powerful spiritual forces that underlie everything that is occurring, as part of the growth and development of our universal reality.

The Breath of God

By the word of God the heavens were formed
and by the the breath of His mouth (ruach piv)
all their hosts. (Psalm 33:6)

As we discovered in the section on Creation in chapter 11, sound is vibration; it is the underlying structure of all living things. What we see as a solid table is really a collection of atoms vibrating in constant motion.

The Word of God creates the outer form. The Word gives each object its specific appearance and shape.

The breath of God, the *ruach*, does not refer here to the individual soul, as in previous chapters. It is the universal life force that flows through all creatures. The *ruach* (literally "wind" or "spirit") is what animates the form. The *ruach* transforms the form from an empty vessel into a living being. As the Baal Shem teaches:

> From the breath, which precedes saying and speech, was drawn life to all of the worlds and to the lower man. And this is called *ruach* (spirit or life force), "and He breathed into his nostrils the breath of life" [Genesis 2:7], because whoever breathes, of his very self he breathes.[1]

Psalm 150:6 exhorts, "Let everything that has breath praise the Lord." The Midrash *Bereshit Rabbah* 14:9 gives this phrase an alternative interpretation: "For every breath a person breathes he should praise the Creator." This midrash plays on the strong similarity between the Hebrew word for "breath," *neshima*, and the word for "soul," *neshama*. There is a profound connection between the breath and the life force that animates all human beings.

The Hasidic master Dov Baer of Mezeritch expands on this interpretation. The life force, he explains, goes in and out through the breath. It descends into the body and then out and up into the higher worlds. Recorded within the breath is every aspect of our condition at that specific moment: what we are thinking, what we are saying, and what we are doing. Our breath reveals to God our exact spiritual condition.

Rebbe Dov Baer compares this process to a goldsmith who inspects and analyzes gold and silver by scraping its surface with a stone. Similarly, God determines the state of our soul by looking at the composition of our breath, the life force from our heart, when it ascends before the Throne of Glory.[2]

The *Sefirot*, *Prana*, and the Breath

This teaching of Rebbe Dov Baer is a good description of the relationship between the breath and the centers, or *sefirot*, in our spiritual body. Our every thought, word, and deed is reflected in the state of our centers, our spiritual "breath." Our centers create an energy signature that provides a clear indication of our spiritual evolution. It details the state of refinement of our character and the development of our consciousness. This spiritual breath or energy signature determines how high we can reach into the heavenly realm and the type of awareness that we can contact.

In Yoga, this combination of breath and energy is called *prana*. Yogis consider the level of our *prana* to be the key to both our physical as well as our spiritual well-being. The twentieth-century Indian spiritual teacher Swami Sivananda was the dynamic founder of the Divine Life Society. He was known for his universal teaching and his Yoga of Synthesis, which combines yogic postures, devotion, service, and meditation. In one of his many books, Swami Sivananda explains:

> A healthy, strong man has abundance of Prana or nerve-force or vitality. The Prana is supplied by food, water, air, solar energy, etc. The supply of Prana is taken up by the nervous system. The Prana is absorbed by breathing. The excess of Prana is stored in the brain and nerve [spiritual] centres....
>
> The Yogin stores an abundance of Prana ... just as a storage battery can be made to store electricity. That Yogin who has stored up a large supply of Prana radiates strength and vitality all around.[3]

Prana is the vehicle for the energy of our system. It carries the energies that run through the planets and constellations. *Prana* provides the spiritual skeleton, the framework on which everything else is built. *Prana* is taken in with every breath. The breath sustains our physical systems, and the *prana* feeds and maintains the centers that make up our spiritual body.

> *And He breathed into his nostrils the breath*
> *of life. (Genesis 2:7)*

There is a higher breath and a lower breath; there is the breath of God and the breath of a human being. Humanity draws on the breath of God, the *prana* of the entire planet and the *prana* of the entire solar system. This *prana* nurtures and sustains our collective soul. Humanity's spiritual state is reflected in the condition of this group *prana*, or spiritual breath. And the quality of this "communal breathing" will affect the spiritual and physical well-being of the planet as a whole.

Just as the physical sun is the source for all forms of physical energy in the solar system, the One who is the life of the solar system gives spiritual energy and divine livingness to all that is within the orbit of the solar emanation. When humanity does the will of God, the planet breathes freely and deeply. Then God's breath, the life force, can flow unobstructed throughout all of the worlds. However, when humanity goes against the will of God, the spiritual breath of the planet becomes laborious and uneven. Then the spiritual body of the planet is not in balance and harmony, and the divine breath, or life force, cannot flow with proper strength and abundance.

The Baal Shem Tov teaches that this is what the Hebrew Bible means in Genesis 6:3, when God declares regarding the generation of the flood, "My spirit (*ruchi*) shall not abide in man forever, for he also is flesh." This verse refers to the breath of God, the divine life force drawn down into the world for the use of humankind. As part of the flood, the full force of God's breath was withdrawn from the world, decreasing the planet's ability to sustain and nurture life. Only after the Children of Israel received the revelation on Mount Sinai was the full force of the divine *prana* returned to the world, filling the Children of Israel with the power of God's living presence.[4]

The *prana* not only holds the basic energies of our system; it also carries the creative power of the *Shekhinah*, the feminine Divine Presence. The *Shekhinah* energy is the subtle expression of the atomic energy of the sun, the force at the heart of the universe. It joins spirit and matter together to create all that exists. The *Shekhinah* energy uses *prana* as its vehicle. It spreads throughout the entire solar system, riding on the *prana* or *ruach piv*, the breath from the mouth of God. The nature of the *Shekhinah* energy will be discussed in greater detail in chapter 13.

Breathing is the most natural movement in the universe. In the Hindu scripture, the creation and dissolution of the universe are compared to the cyclic inhalation and exhalation of a great divine being in deep meditation. Breathing in represents a period of inactivity and meditation, what is called *pralaya*; and breathing out represents a period of outward activity and creation, which expresses itself as the manifest universe.

We are caught up in the breath of God, transported along the path of exhalation. We are part of the unfolding manifestation of Spirit through the myriad of forms and activities of the created universe. The more we refine our personality and character, the better a vessel we will become for the flow of the divine breath. As we learn to live together in harmony and balance, the boundless livingness of the *Ein Sof* will become manifest in humankind.

The World Crises and the Evolution of the Sovereign of the World

The story of the evolution of the earth is the story of the evolution of *Atik Yamin* (the Ancient of Days), the Sovereign of the world. The physical planet is the body of manifestation for this great being. The life of *Atik Yamin* encompasses everything that happens in our world. Just as we go through our difficulties and struggles as we strive to grow and progress, so too the Sovereign of the world confronts and overcomes obstacles and impediments during the process of evolving.

From the divine point of view, it is our spiritual well-being that matters and not our physical happiness. The body is only a temporary entity—a garment that the soul dons in order to experience life on this plane of existence. Just as we would not hesitate to soil or even ruin our clothing if an emergency were to suddenly arise, similarly God does not recoil from placing our bodies under tremendous strain when the need arises. Because of this perspective, we are put through all sorts of difficulties in our personal lives in order to enable us to grow and evolve as human beings.

If we look at the planet from a cosmic perspective, we see the same principle at work. The awe-inspiring Life whose consciousness overshadows our galaxy looks at the One overshadowing the earth much in the same way that *Atik Yamin* looks at us. If creating a serious crisis in the global body of manifestation will galvanize the One overseeing the earth to take another evolutionary step, then the Sovereign of the galaxy will not hesitate to initiate such a crisis. Confronting this wide-scale disaster will bring out planetary strengths and qualities that have not been tapped until now; it will reveal hidden attributes that are important assets for the future evolution of *Atik Yamin*.

Such a world plight will call forth help and energy not only from the physical lives on earth, but also from the spiritual planes of the planet. All the souls in the Kingdom of Heaven and all the great angelic lives will be drawn into the work of responding to the planetary need. Everyone will be thrown into action to help overcome the challenge that the Sovereign of the world faces. These crises will be coordinated within the universal mind of God, so that they conform to the eternal plan for the lives that inhabit our universe on its countless planes.

Our Ecological Crisis Is Also a Spiritual Opportunity

The present ecological condition of the planet represents such a moment of crisis in the life of the Sovereign of the world. Yet this potentially disastrous situation is also a spiritual opportunity. We cannot know what spiritual possibilities this crisis opens up for *Atik Yamin*—such knowledge is beyond our comprehension. We can, however, see the challenge and the spiritual opening that it presents to the human race.

The problems with the environment provide humanity with an opportunity to recognize the underlying unity of all existence. They offer us the chance to discover the interdependence of all life and the profound need for balance and harmony in our world.

This global predicament teaches us to respect and revere all living creatures, just as we should respect and revere all human beings. It demonstrates that we need to learn to work together as a species. It makes clear that we need to find a way to play a constructive role within the overall ecosystem of the planet if our world is to survive.

The spiritual dimension of this planetary emergency also needs to be understood. What is happening is not just a mistake; it is the reflection of an inner process that is taking place in the consciousness of *Atik Yamin*. We are part of the global body; our evolution is part of the planetary evolution. Our struggles and the expansion of our awareness are a part of the expansion in awareness of the planetary Life.

God has given humanity the task of "tending and safeguarding" the Garden (Genesis 2:15). We have a part to play in the well-being of the planet, and we are the only species with a conscious awareness of our role. This is a unique gift and a huge responsibility. We have demonstrated that we can have a powerful impact on the ecosystem of the planet. It is time for us to prove that we can learn how to care for and repair our world as well.

This transformation can occur only if we begin to see ourselves and our relationship with our home in a completely different light. We need to reassess our values and shift the priorities in our lives. We need to change our ambitions and our perception of the adequate fulfillment of our material needs.

A Spiritual Revolution

This human revolution is essentially a spiritual revolution, because it is on the level of consciousness that the desired transformation needs to take place. To be truly effective, change cannot be enforced by law or fear; it needs to be awakened from within.

A global calamity is not just a crisis of form; it is also a crisis of the spirit. In our present situation, part of the challenge is manifesting as a looming ecological disaster, and part is manifesting as the many conflicts raging worldwide. There is a pitched battle taking place between those who value openness and freedom, those who recognize the unity of all of the world's different peoples and religions, and those who reject openness and freedom and believe in the supremacy of a particular doctrine, religion, or race. Surmounting this aspect of the crisis is as much a part of the world's growth and evolution as overcoming the ecological dangers that the planet confronts.

This global crisis is also a spiritual opportunity. It is an opening for us as a race and for the earth as a whole. We are facing a moment of destiny for all of humanity, a crucial crossroads in the life of *Atik Yamin*, the Sovereign of the world.

Fire and Water: Two Paths of Purification

For He is like a refiner's fire. (Malachi 3:2)

I will pour pure water on you and you will be purified. (Ezekiel 36:25)

For the Lord, your God, is a consuming fire. (Deuteronomy 4:24)

God is a purifying pool (mikveh) *for Israel. (Jeremiah 17:13)*

We went through fire and through water, but You did bring us out into abundance. (Psalm 66:12)

There are two methods of purification in the spiritual life: the path of fire and the path of water. Each of these approaches has a higher and a lower level. In each of these processes, the purification can come from within or from without.

Individual Purification

The path of fire is about burning away our imperfections. On the lower level, this mode of purification is called the refiner's fire.[5] The refiner's fire uses the circumstances of our life to manipulate our mind and emotions in a manner that will force us to see ourselves with honesty and accuracy. Once we can see ourselves clearly, we then go through a period of remorse and mental suffering that acts as a purging fire to burn away our faults.

This approach is the normal route that humankind has walked for millions of years. It is a journey that comes to realization over lifetimes, with the incomplete work of one incarnation carrying over into the next life, until union with the higher self is finally achieved.

Water is the second means of purification, where the energy of love washes away our sins. This approach is called the purifying waters.[6] This method can proceed either from without or from within. It comes from without when another human being waters us with love. This love acts like a gentle stream to soothe the pain inside us, sweeping away all bitterness and sorrow and paving the way for inner transformation. The process of cleansing comes from within when the suffering of someone we love unlocks our heart. This heart awakening clears the anger and pettiness built up inside us, removing the barrier to our higher self.

These are the two lower paths. Let us now investigate the two higher evolutionary avenues. The higher path of fire is called God's consuming fire. This blaze burns up our personality flaws and all the inherent tendencies that have accumulated over many lives.[7] Fueled by the energy of our Soul Mother, we are empowered to transcend our lower self and join with the mind of our Soul Father. With this union, the goal of our individual spiritual evolution has been reached and we are reborn into the awareness of the supernal realms.

The higher road of love is called the purifying pool, or *mikveh*. In this spiritual *mikveh*, we are immersed in God's infinite love. The power of that love submerges our individual personality in the waters of divine

Oneness. Our separate consciousness dissolves into the Boundless Ocean of the Absolute.[8]

Planetary Purification

These two methods of purification can also be applied on the planetary level. Up until now, the normal trajectory on this planet has been to grow through struggle and suffering—the refiner's fire. Today, however, we are entering into a new phase in our spiritual evolution. Just like a human being needs to develop the centers in the *Etz haChayim* by raising the consciousness from one *sefirah* to the next, similarly, *Atik Yamin* needs to advance through the planetary centers, raising the global awareness from *sefirah* to *sefirah*.

At this stage in *Atik Yamin's* progress, the heart center, the *sefirah* of *tiferet*, is in the process of opening. As the planetary consciousness is increasingly focused in this *sefirah*, the energy of love will become the dominant energy of our world. Tremendous changes will then start to take place in human relations, as a whole new consciousness spreads across the globe.[9]

Though this process of change has already begun, it will take thousands of years to come to full fruition. Yet from the wider perspective, this is not a large amount of time. Psalm 90:4 states, "A thousand years in Your eyes are like a yesterday that has passed, like a watch in the night." In another divine day or two, we will complete our transition into the consciousness of *tiferet*—a mere "watch in the night" in the planet's lengthy existence.

The process of vitalizing the divine heart center, however, is only the lower station along the route of purification by water, where the water soothes the suffering of the planet. At this point, some of the pain in this world will be washed away, but our suffering will not yet be ended forever. Disease, old age, and death will still be with us for a long time—until the One who envelops and vitalizes the earth unites with the planetary Soul Father, and that is a process that will take eons to achieve.

At that point, the question will be: is this still the same earth anymore? For if the planetary "personality" is transcended, what is it that remains?

Revealing the Kingdom of Heaven on Earth

Since the beginning of time, humanity has been aware that there is another type of life or reality beyond our material plane of existence. Over the millennia, countless mystics, prophets, and seers have entered that supernal realm and returned, imbued with its inspiration and power. This last part of the book looks at the methods whereby we, as individuals and as a species, break through the barrier between these two realms. It explores how the Kingdom of Heaven is revealed on earth.

13

The *Shekhinah*—
the Feminine Divine
Presence

Approaching the Universal Mother
and Her Power

T he *Shekhinah* is the name given in Judaism to the feminine aspect of God. The description of the *Shekhinah* first appears in Rabbinic teaching. The identity of the *Shekhinah* as the feminine aspect of God is then elaborated upon and fully developed in the writings of the Kabbalah. In this chapter, we will explore the nature of the *Shekinah*'s identity, the power that She wields, and the role that She plays in the life of Israel and the planet.

The *Shekhinah* Energy

There are three energy pathways that run through our spiritual body. The Kabbalah speaks of them as three columns. The left-hand pathway is called the column of *din*, or judgment. The right-hand is the column of *chesed*, or mercy. The middle path designates the column of *rachamim*, or compassion. It is also called the path of the *Shekhinah*, the Divine Presence.[1]

As I stated in chapter 1, Yogic teaching identifies three subtle nerves, or *nadis*. Along the left-hand side runs the *nadi* of *ida*, the subtle nerve associated with cooling and the moon. On the right side is the *nadi* of *pingala*, the subtle nerve associated with heating and the sun. Up the middle passage ascends the *sushumna nadi*, the subtle nerve associated with the *kundalini* or serpent power.[2] Esoteric wisdom defines three vehicles for the spiritual energies. The left side is the vehicle for the psychic energy. The divine energy passes on the right side. The creative energy flows up through the central channel.[3]

The energy of the middle pathway, the *Shekhinah* or *kundalini*, is the most powerful force in the universe. The Kabbalah likens its splendor to the light of sixty-five thousand suns.[4] It is the energy that is unleashed with the splitting of an atom. The creative force of the *Shekhinah* binds spirit and matter together.[5] It transports us into union with God.[6]

The *Shekhinah* resides in the lowest center of *malkhut* (kingship). Hindu teaching compares this energy to a serpent coiled up at the base of the spine. Except when it is aroused during the act of sexual union, this spiritual force normally lies dormant. The science of Yoga and meditation are the tools that are used to awaken the *kundalini*. Through intense spiritual practice, the *Shekhinah* is raised up the central channel of the body until it reaches the highest center in the crown. When this occurs, the individual breaks through the barrier between the physical and the higher planes and merges with the Spiritual Father, or *neshama*.

The Nature of the *Shekhinah*

The *Shekhinah* has a number of components to Her nature, each indicating another facet of Her spiritual work. At the most basic level, the *Shekhinah* energy is a stimulating force. Like yeast, She brings alive the spiritual life of those around Her, intensifying their inner growth. The introduction of the power of the *Shekhinah* into a center, or *sefirah*, dramatically boosts the flow of its energy.

The presence of the *Shekhinah* creates profound changes in the nature of the spiritual environment. When a carrier or wielder of this energy is nearby, things start to happen. There is an awakening of the centers and a consequent manifestation of supernatural phenomena. The *Shekhinah* brings our inner world to life. Where God's existence has previously been only an abstraction, it will suddenly become an experience that is tangible and real.[7]

The *Shekhinah* is also a protective energy. She is likened to an eagle that carries her young upon her wings to guard them from predators (Deuteronomy 32:11). The energy of the *Shekhinah* radiates out to the whole area surrounding Her abode. She was the force guarding the Temple in ancient Jerusalem. Her presence shielded the land and the people throughout biblical times. Once Her shelter was withdrawn, the Temple and the land were destroyed. In modern times, the *Shekhinah* was present to defend Israel as the people fought to reestablish their statehood.[8]

The *Shekhinah* can also be a force for destruction. The energy of the *Shekhinah* was used to defeat the Egyptians at the time of Moses and Israel's slavery in Egypt. Her power manifested as sound and vibration to crumble the walls of Jericho for Joshua and the armies of Israel. In the future, She will set in motion the earth-shaking events that herald the Final Days.[9]

The *Shekhinah* is also the great mediator. The *Zohar* is filled with descriptions of the *Matrona*, the royal consort, mediating between the people and the King. The *Shekhinah* is more receptive to our supplications. She shields us from the King's fearsome power. She knows best how to approach the King and gain His favor.[10]

These portrayals are a symbolic expression of the spiritual role that the *Shekhinah* plays in creation. Without Her, nothing could be created. She provides the vehicle for the power of the unmanifest God to become manifest. The *Shekhinah* mediates between the divine and the angelic kingdoms. She builds the bridge between heaven and earth. The Universal Mother supplies us with the creative force to transcend physical consciousness and unite with our spiritual source.[11]

The Soul of the *Shekhinah*

The *Shekhinah* is also a soul in the Kingdom of Heaven. For the *Shekhinah* energy to be developed, there needs to be a physical instrument. The spiritual mission of those who belong to this collective soul is to serve as carriers of the *Shekhinah* energy. These souls work as the embodiment of this force on earth and also in the spiritual realms. Their lives are focused on raising and refining the creative energy, so it can be used to further the implementation of the divine plan.

There are many levels to the soul of the *Shekhinah*. The part of the soul that incarnates will determine the extent and nature of Her influence. The energy needs to be developed and purified to be effective; the greater the purity, the more potent and rarified it will be.

When someone from this soul raises the *Shekhinah* energy to the crown, the tremendous force of the *Shekhinah* is joined to the will of God. The will of God can then be directed with great effect anywhere in the world. Such a person is a divine instrument of extraordinary dimensions. Wherever her consciousness is focused, the will of God will pour in to overshadow the situation with tremendous spiritual force. It will penetrate the divine purpose into the inner chambers of the hearts of people everywhere.

The *Shekhinah* in Ancient Israel

The *Shekhinah* played a central role in the religion of Israel in ancient times. The entire structure and ritual of the Temple were designed to harness the energy. Many of the details of the organization and discipline of life within the Temple area can be attributed to this overriding spiritual fact.[12]

Once a reservoir of *Shekhinah* energy has been established, there needs to be a group of individuals who are trained to wield its dynamic power. Forging such an instrument is not easy to accomplish. Not every individual has the qualities that are necessary to be a vehicle for the *Shekhinah*; only a still rarer few can learn to utilize the energy in its higher aspects. This is the reason why an entire section of the people was separated out from the rest of Israel and consecrated as priests. This select group was trained to protect and work with the *Shekhinah* energy.[13]

Because of the enormous power of the *Shekhinah*, much effort was invested in trying to prevent the misuse of Her energy. If this great spiritual force were directed to evil purposes, it could cause untold harm. Allowing the might of the *Shekhinah* to fall into the wrong hands would be akin to giving an atom bomb to a group of terrorists. The consequences of such an act of folly could be devastating.

At the same time, as noted earlier, this energy is a great stimulator. She stimulates whatever is present in the people in Her proximity—both the good and the bad. For example, if individuals have spent their time in unbridled sexual activity, then contact with the *Shekhinah* energy would stimulate the *yesod* center, arousing strong sexual sensations in those individuals. On the other hand, if they had spent their time engaging in acts of selfless service, then the *sefirah* of *tiferet* would begin flowing, and a torrential downpour of love would flood into their hearts.

For these two reasons, the *Shekhinah* energy was carefully guarded within the Temple compound. The number and nature of the individuals who came into contact with the energy was meticulously controlled. This shielding was accomplished in a number of ways.

On the physical level, the Temple itself was divided into different courts, with access being increasingly limited as one entered deeper into the inner domain. This sanctification process reached its peak in the Holy of Holies, where only the High Priest was allowed to penetrate. Here, in the inner sanctum of the Temple, the *Shekhinah* could be kept in pristine condition, a puissant reservoir of pure energy.

On a human level, the priests and the Levites who worked in the inner courtyards all had to maintain a high level of purity in thought, word, and deed. This purity allowed them to be around the energy without harming themselves or the quality of the source. If they did not maintain a strictly disciplined life, they would become ineffective instruments for the power of the *Shekhinah*. The reservoir of energy in the Temple would then become polluted and all of their work would be in vain.

The most dramatic expression of the use of the *Shekhinah* energy came on Yom Kippur, the Day of Atonement. The whole nation spent this day in prayer and fasting. Hundreds of thousands of pilgrims were crowded into the Temple area on this sacred occasion. The High Priest followed an elaborate ritual throughout this solemn and sacred day that included fasting, ritual immersions, five changes of clothing, and numerous sacrificial offerings. At the climax of the worship, the High Priest entered into the Holy of Holies with an incense offering. When he reemerged, he blessed the people using the Sacred Name of God. When the High Priest pronounced the Divine Name, he emanated such tremendous power that all those in the Temple area were thrown on their faces in awe. On this day, at this moment, the purity of the High Priest and the aspirations of the people in prayer and fasting combined together with the potency of the Name and the *Shekhinah* energy to bring through an extraordinary spiritual force. This force cleansed the people of all of their spiritual impurities and wiped away their sins. It was in the most glorious sense of the phrase a day of atonement and forgiveness.

The *Shekhinah* was a potent spiritual catalyst for anyone who came to visit the Temple. Her rays of blessing shone forth upon all throughout the entire year. Whoever came before God with sincere devotion would have their awareness awakened. They would attain sublime levels of inner experience through Her grace.

The emanations of the *Shekhinah* were not restricted to the Temple area. Her energy field radiated out across the entire country and the world beyond. The *Shekhinah* energy enabled the prophets to prophesy and to perform their many miracles. Its development was a science that was learned in the School of the Prophets. In these nurseries or laboratories of holiness, the prophetic disciples lived in conditions of sanctity and purity while they trained in the methods of raising the *Shekhinah*. Yet the focal point of the energy was the Temple in Jerusalem and the sacred presence that dwelt there.[14]

The *Shekhinah* energy is everywhere. However, it is more potent in certain locations and more prevalent in particular nations. The land and the people of Israel are one such place and nation. If the people are sufficiently evolved and the land has been sanctified, then the *Shekhinah* will once again be raised up in the Land of Israel. If not, then She will lay forever in the dust, and the Divine Presence will not be awoken again in Israel.

The Mystical Tradition

In the mystical literature, the *Shekhinah* is called by many names: the moon, the mother, the bride, and the daughter. The representation of the *Shekhinah* by these female images is more than just symbolism. The *Shekhinah* energy is bound to the feminine in its very essence: a man may take up and use this energy, but it will be a female that embodies the soul. This is the explanation for the priestesses and oracles of ancient times. It is also the reason for the goddess worship of the ancients.

The relationship between the *Shekhinah* and the female gender is an idea that is understood in the Eastern religions. In Hinduism, the goddesses embody the *Shakti*, or power of the gods. In India, it is not uncommon to see a young girl worshipped as a manifestation of the Divine

Mother. In Tibetan Buddhism, a lama is instructed to marry a *dakini*, or female spirit—someone who carries this energy.[15]

Devotion to the *Shekhinah* as the Mother aspect of God also plays an important role in Christian worship. The cult of Mary is a powerful force in the church and was the special devotion of Pope John Paul II. He credited the "Holy Mother" with saving him from an assassin's bullet. He also believed that it was Mary who made possible his triumph in the struggle to bring down the Communist regime of the Soviet Union.

Judaism also has special prayers that turn to the *Shekhinah*. She assumes a central role in the Ari's *kavanot* (contemplations) for the prayers. Our relationship with the *Shekhinah* plays an important part in the teachings of Hasidism as well. The Baal Shem Tov emphasized the importance of reciting our prayers and fulfilling the mitzvot (spiritual acts) for the sake of the *Shekhinah*.[16] Waking up at midnight and reciting prayers of lamentation over the exile of the *Shekhinah* is a common practice for both Kabbalists and Hasidim.

In the mystical tradition, the Sabbath is deeply connected with the *Shekhinah*. Her power was fundamental to the process of Creation, and She also played an important role in the Exodus from Egypt—both key elements of Sabbath remembrance.

According to the tradition, the Sabbath day is divided into three periods: Sabbath eve, Sabbath morning, and Sabbath afternoon. Each period has its own particular spiritual quality that is linked to one of the three major divine countenances: *Atika Kadisha* (the Holy Ancient One), *Zeir Anpin* (the Lesser Countenance), and the *Shekhinah*. Friday night is devoted to the *Shekhinah*.

The traditional prayers for Friday night provide us with a good indication of the conception of the Divine Mother in Judaism. Foremost among these is the prayer *Lecha Dodi*, "Come My Beloved," by the sixteenth-century Kabbalist Shlomo Alkabetz. In this plaintive supplication, the *Shekhinah* is depicted in a number of forms that reflect the varying facets of Her nature.

Shekhinah as Bride

Three main images of the *Shekhinah* adorn the *Lecha Dodi* prayer. The first is the *Shekhinah* as the bride or loved one of God. This is a metaphor for when She is in Her full glory. In this exalted state, She is radiant and beautiful. Her appearance as the bride of God is described for us in the Kabbalah.[17]

As the *Shekhinah* approaches the Holy Blessed One, She is wearing a magnificent gown. The gown is white, to signify Her purity. She is also bedecked in jewels, as an expression of the potent energies that She wields. The *Shekhinah* is escorted by scores of divine maidens and angelic beings, to symbolize the strong protection that surrounds Her and the profound devotion that She elicits. Her face is full of joy and light; Her splendor is indescribable. She has come to spiritual fulfillment; all of Her centers are flowing, and She is united with Her heavenly Spouse.

The identification of the *Shekhinah* as God's bride is constantly referred to in the refrain of the *Lecha Dodi*: "Come my beloved to greet the bride, let us welcome the presence of the Sabbath." It is also alluded to in a number of other verses of the prayer. In one verse, we are told that God will rejoice over the *Shekhinah* just like a bridegroom rejoices with his bride. And in the last stanza of the *Lecha Dodi*, She is called the "crown of Her Husband," evoking the moment of climax in the spiritual ascent, when the energy of the *Shekhinah* is raised to *keter*, the crown center, and the individual unites with his or her Soul Father. This image evokes not just the mystical union of the individual with the soul, but also the union of God and Israel and the merging of the spiritual and physical realms. It is the final consummation of the divine marriage.

Shekhinah as the Royal Sanctuary

The second portrayal of the *Shekhinah* in the *Lecha Dodi* is as the Royal Sanctuary. She is called the Temple, because the life of pure spirit is revealed through Her mediation. The *Shekhinah* makes possible the concrete experience of God. She embodies the Divine in form. She fills the Temple with Her being. Like the mother who cares for the child growing in her womb, the *Shekhinah* is the finite vessel that holds the infinite light of God.[18]

The return of the *Shekhinah* and the rebuilding of the Temple are intimately linked in the Jewish tradition. A prayer for Her return is also an aspiration for the creation of a House of Prayer for all nations. It is a plea for the coming of the Great One, the Messiah who will lead humanity toward God.

Shekhinah in Exile

The *Shekhinah* in exile is the third picture painted of the *Shekhinah* in the *Lecha Dodi*. This is Her lowest state of being, where She is separated from Her spiritual Spouse. In this state, all radiance and joy have left Her. In one verse, the *Shekhinah* is described as dwelling amid the ruins in the vale of tears. In another verse, She is depicted as cast in the dust. Both of these images are metaphors for the debasing of the *Shekhinah* where Her energy is drawn downward until She can emanate out only through the lowest of the centers, *malkhut*, the center of the physical earth.[19]

In other verses, the *Shekhinah* is described as ashamed, confounded, downcast, and agitated. All these depictions express the fact that the *Shekhinah* is not in Her rightful "place." As a result, the world is out of kilter and life seems flat, meaningless, and devoid of energy. There is an imbalance in creation and a separation of humanity from God. This is what it means for the *Shekhinah* to be in exile.

Raising the *Shekhinah*

These three graphic and dynamic images are bound together in the *Lecha Dodi* prayer by our aspiration to raise Her from the dust and restore the *Shekhinah* to Her natural abode with God. This collective yearning is constantly referred to in the different stanzas of the prayer. In one verse, we cry out, "Shake the dust off Yourself, arise, don Your glorious garments." In another, we exclaim, "Arouse Yourself, for Your light has come, arise, shine." And again we plead, "Awake, awake, utter a song."

The task of raising the *Shekhinah* is vital for Israel. In Judaism, the relationship between God and Israel is closely tied to the state of the *Shekhinah*. On a certain level, the condition of the *Shekhinah* reflects the spiritual condition of the people. We are intimately linked with the feminine aspect of God.

In the Kabbalah, the sun is symbolic of God as the Father; the moon is symbolic of God as the Mother. The Jewish calendar revolves around the moon, as do all of our holy days. We are very conscious of the phases of the moon, and we celebrate each new moon and bless its arrival. There is a midrash that states that at the beginning of Creation the light of the moon was equal in brightness to the light of the sun.[20] During the ceremony for blessing the new moon, there is a prayer that asks God to make the light of the moon like the light of the sun, as it was at the beginning of Creation. This blessing expresses our wish that the *Shekhinah* be raised up again to unite with the Holy Blessed One. Underlying this request is our fervent hope that the living presence of God will be returned in fullness to Israel, and the radiant glory of the Divine Mother will be manifest throughout the entire world.

14

The Evolution of the Concept of the Temple

Creating a Dwelling Place for the Divine

Build Me a sanctuary and I will dwell in your midst.

Exodus 25:8

In Exodus 25:8 God commands the Children of Israel to build a dwelling place for the Divine Presence in the world. The Midrash tells us that the Sanctuary they built in the desert was constructed according to the blueprint of the supernal *Mikdash*, or Temple, in the higher realms.[1] The Baal Shem Tov explains that as the Israelites fashioned a physical structure, they continually strove to keep their minds connected to its spiritual counterpart in the heavens.[2]

The Work of Self-Transformation

There are two components to the process by which we link with the heavenly Temple. The first component is the work of self-transformation. By laboring to perfect ourselves, we remove the rough edges and dirt from our character, thereby transforming ourselves into worthy dwellings for the Eternal One.

This, the Baal Shem teaches, is the inner meaning of Exodus 21:24, "an eye for an eye and a tooth for a tooth." There is a divine eye that watches over humanity. When we sanctify our vision, we become a vehicle for that supernal eye. There is a divine ear that listens to our prayers and supplications. When we purify our hearing with words of inspiration and holiness, we become a vehicle for that divine ear. When we sanctify our lives, the supernal energies pour into us from the higher worlds and then flow out from us into this physical plane of existence. In this way, we become a vital part of God's body of manifestation—a living *mikdash*, or temple.[3]

The Power of a Consecrated Life

The struggle to transcend our natural limitations constitutes the second component of the process of higher contact. The Baal Shem elucidates: When we first conceive of an object, the image in our mind is sublime and complete. However, no matter how noble our intentions may be when we begin our project, what appears in the real world will never conform to the beauty and precision of the picture in our thoughts. It can only be a mere shadow of this magnificent vision.

It is here, the Baal Shem comments, that the unique awareness of those who built the Sanctuary in the desert can be seen. Because the Israelites who toiled on this structure were overshadowed by the *Shekhinah*, they worked according to the inspiration of a higher vision. As a result, they were able to replicate the heavenly Sanctuary in all of its beauty and glory.

The building of the desert Sanctuary reveals the power of people who have consecrated their lives and made themselves into divine instruments. It illustrates the gap between work that we can achieve as solitary individuals and what can be accomplished when we function as part of the body of God. Through divine inspiration, the imperfect hands of a human being can create perfection. Through sanctifying our lives and raising our consciousness, the Kingdom of Heaven can be revealed on earth.

The Creation and Growth of a Divine Thoughtform

The whole notion of the *Mikdash*, or Temple, can also be understood in a completely different manner.

God begins the creative process by encasing the divine idea in a finite thoughtform. This thoughtform then descends through the worlds, sending out a distinctive energy vibration that expresses its spiritual essence. Spirit, matter, and consciousness respond to this expression of the will of God at all levels of the manifest universe, taking up its message and striving to bring its purpose to culmination in concrete form.

The divine impetus continues to gain strength and vitality, spreading its influence throughout all of the worlds for eons of time, building a body of manifestation composed of all those who have aligned themselves with its mission. This thoughtform persists in sending out its sacred message until the will of God is withdrawn. Then the process of dissolution begins, as the great structure that has been built to support its materialization starts to dissipate, while a new divine thoughtform begins taking shape on the countless planes of the universe.

The *Mikdash*, or Temple, is the name given to one such thoughtform. Over the millennia, it has taken on a variety of forms. A story from the life of Francis of Assisi, the thirteenth-century Christian saint known for his life of poverty and devotion, explains how this process unfolds.

Saint Francis's spiritual mission began when he was praying one day in his favorite church in Assisi. In the middle of his prayers, he looked up at the crucifix hanging over the altar and saw the figure on the cross come alive. The figure looked at Francis and in a powerful voice commanded him, "Build my church!"

Francis took the command literally and started to repair the ruined churches on the hillsides around Assisi. In this way, he began to serve God and gradually gathered a group of spiritual seekers around him. When the numbers of his followers began to swell, Francis realized that he had to create a rule and structure for his disciples, so he went to Rome to ask the pope for permission to form a monastic order of his own.

When the pope heard Francis's request, he did not know what to do; he was impressed by the sincerity and simplicity of the young mendicant, but new orders were not formed every day. Also, Francis wanted to live a life of utter poverty without possessions of any sort, like Jesus and his disciples, and this seemed rather impractical and naïve to the pope and his advisors.

The night after his audience with Francis, the pope had a powerful dream. In the dream, he was looking leisurely over Rome, when he suddenly saw one of the great churches of the city start to crumble. Horrified, he tried to shout for help, but his tongue clung to the roof of his mouth.

Approaching from a distant corner, a small figure in a brown robe appeared in the piazza and walked over to the church. The figure leaned the whole of his body against the church. As he braced his shoulder to support the building, he grew in size until all alone he was able to restore the church to its proper position. The little man then turned around to face the pope, and he saw that the man was none other than Francis from Assisi. The pope then understood that Francis would repair and uphold the collapsing church of Christian faith. Francis's original vision had come full circle and taken on a new level of meaning.[4]

The Evolution of the Thoughtform of the Temple

In the same way that Saint Francis's calling to "build the church" evolved over time to express a more symbolic, but no less dynamic and powerful, manifestation of the original command, the divine idea that we call the Temple has also changed over the millennia to be fulfilled in a number of different forms.

Thirty-five hundred years ago, the Children of Israel received the divine command to construct a *Mikdash* from Moses, and they erected a physical edifice dedicated to the God of Israel in response. This vision of the *Mikdash* lasted until 70 CE, when the Second Temple was destroyed by the Romans.

A thousand years later, the Kabbalists understood the Temple as a mystical edifice that receives the potent spiritual energies that descend from the heavens. Seven hundred years after that, the Baal Shem Tov raised the ideal of the *Mikdash* to yet another level. He understood the Temple as a place within each of us that can serve as a dwelling place for God. This sacred place is created by sanctifying all aspects of our life and by infusing all of our actions with divine virtues. In this way, each of us becomes a little *mikdash* where the living presence resides.[5]

This teaching of the Baal Shem Tov prepares the way for the next step in the progression of the divine ideal called the *Mikdash*. It sets the stage for a new conception of the Temple that combines the teaching of the Baal Shem Tov with the Kabbalistic knowledge of the inner reality underlying this ancient structure.

This new paradigm is hinted at in a teaching from another Hasidic master, Shmuel Bornstein of Sochatchov, who lived two centuries after the Baal Shem. His teaching addresses the argument between the biblical commentators as to whether the command to assemble the Sanctuary in the desert was given before or after the sin of the Golden Calf. In a novel interpretation, Rebbe Shmuel suggests that there is, in fact, no real argument between the commentators, because the command to build the Sanctuary came both before and after the Golden Calf.

Before the sin of the Golden Calf, the Sanctuary was intended to be an ethereal temple composed of light and energy. Afterward, however, God decided that the Children of Israel required a physical temple as a channel for their desire to have a concrete form of worship. Therefore, the Almighty commanded them to construct the physical structure that is described in the Hebrew Bible.[6]

Today, we can envision the Temple as a supernal network of light and energy constructed through the inner work of prayer and meditation. The love and will of God pour into our world through the structure of this *Mikdash*, helping to bring the plan of God to culmination on earth. Building this Temple is the great undertaking before the people of Israel. It is the goal of all those who care about the well-being of humanity and the evolution of our planet, wherever they may live.

Thirty-five hundred years after the Israelites constructed the original Sanctuary in the desert, the divine thoughtform of the *Mikdash* is still very much alive. Each of us has a part to play in its revelation. Each of us draws forth one small portion of its awesome spiritual power. Together we are working to fulfill its thousands-of-years mission to anchor the sacred presence of the Infinite and Eternal in our finite material world.

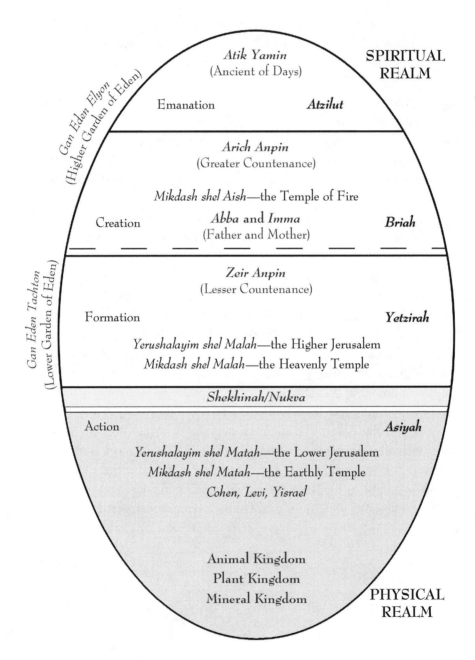

Figure 11. The divine thoughtform of the Temple in the four realms

15

The Manifestation of the Divine Thoughtform in the Four Realms

The Journey from the Mind of God to Concrete Reality

For My thoughts are not your thoughts,
and My ways are not your ways.

Isaiah 55:8

Endless thoughts run through our minds every day without creating any tangible effect upon the world around us. God's "thoughts" are of an entirely different order. A divine thought is an extraordinarily potent force; it can create and destroy worlds in a moment. In the morning prayers, we affirm, "In His goodness He renews each day, continuously, the work of Creation." It is a thought in the mind of God that sustains and vitalizes the whole world.

The manner in which a divine thoughtform becomes fully manifest and developed is complex and multistaged. We have already taken a look at the general concept of a sacred thoughtform in our discussion of the Creation. We will now explore how a thought in the mind of *Atik Yamin*, the great being who overshadows our planet, manifests on the seven planes of earth consciousness, in the four stages of *Atzilut* (Emanation), *Briah* (Creation), *Yetzirah* (Formation), and *Asiyah* (Action).[1] In order to get a clearer idea of how this process works, we will apply these ideas to the *Mikdash* (Temple) and show how it might be expressed in our time.

Atzilut—the Realm of Energies

We begin with the stage of *Atzilut*, or Emanation, the realm of pure energies. The whole process of manifestation starts when a desire arises in the inner depths of the Sovereign of the world—the One we call *Atik Yamin*, or the Ancient of Days. This desire is in actuality the impression of the will of God in the Absolute upon the consciousness of *Atik Yamin*. This mind impression is coming to *Atik* from the One who is his Soul Father. The Temple is not just a concept of this world; it is an eternal entity that exists on all levels of reality. This thoughtform embodies the structure for revealing the infinite light, being, and consciousness of God in the Absolute throughout all the planes of the manifest universe.

The awakening of this desire, or impression of will, in the heart of the Ancient of Days throws *Atik Yamin* into deep contemplation. This contemplation causes energy to come pouring into the planetary centers from the *neshama*, or group soul. These energies provide the building blocks for the conversion of this desire into a reality.

To bring a divine thoughtform to fruition, a complete *Etz haChayim* is needed—a full body of spiritual centers. Each Tree of Life has seven major centers, but the quantity and quality of the energies in those *sefirot* will vary for each new celestial impetus. Each conception requires a unique combination of energies to manifest its form in fullness and harmony.

What balance of energies will materialize the divine thoughtform called the Temple?

First and foremost, a concentrated dose of *Shekhinah* energy is needed to provide the creative impulse for this work. Next, a commanding influx of the energy of *chokhmah/binah* (wisdom/understanding) is needed to endow those fashioning the divine thoughtform with guidance and inspiration. King Solomon was a temple builder, and he was esteemed for his wisdom.

The energy of *yesod* (foundation) is supplied in abundance to bestow the cohesive force to order and bind together all the different facets of this undertaking. And a strong emanation of the energy of *tiferet* (beauty) from the heart center is required to impart the power and magnetic pull of the attribute of love. If we want to inspire people to dedicate their lives to the undertaking of the Temple, then love is an essential ingredient.

This truth became evident during the building of the Sanctuary, or Tabernacle, in the desert. God commanded Moses to ask the Children of Israel for the materials needed to build the Sanctuary and told him that each person should donate toward the work "according to the prompting of his heart" (Exodus 25:2). Only the prompting of the heart can provide the spiritual materials for the Temple. A vessel for the Divine Presence is created through a gift freely given from the place of love and devotion inside us.

Finally, we need a steady flow of the energy of *keter* (the will of God) to animate the new creation with life and dynamism—the will to be and manifest.

Briah—the Realm of Pure Thought

The deep contemplation of *Atik Yamin* arouses into outer activity the exalted being called *Arich Anpin*, the Greater Countenance—the One who embodies the mind of God. In *Briah*, the energies gathered in *Atzilut* begin to form into a tangible thought as the *Mikdash*, or Temple, takes definite shape as a structure composed of pure consciousness.

Diverse aspects of the supernal mind are applied to this demanding task. The energy of the higher mind is brought in to infuse the thought with the breadth and depth of God's original vision. The energy of the lower mind confers a more solid dimension in the form of intuitive symbolism and energy relationships.

What began as an abstract desire is now a vital and vibrant thoughtform in the mind of *Atik Yamin*. This embodied inspiration is known in the tradition as the *mikdash shel aish*—the temple of fire. The *mikdash shel aish* contains the divine purpose behind the temple's creation, the impression from God in the Absolute that gave birth to this ideal.

The *mikdash shel aish* cannot be comprehended using our human brain. It can only be accessed by our higher intuition through direct contact and experience. This truth is portrayed in a story from the Talmud, *Menachot* 29a. This passage recounts how God instructed Moses to build the ritual objects for the Sanctuary in the desert. When it came to the construction of the menorah, the sacred candelabra, Moses had difficulty visualizing the menorah. God then showed him the image of a menorah composed of fire, and Moses was able to make out its appearance.

The Baal Shem Tov explains that the menorah that God displayed to Moses was not an ordinary image like the pictures we visualize in our imagination. The eternal ideal of the menorah was revealed to Moses, as it exists in the universal mind of God. Moses then absorbed this ideal into his consciousness and created an earthly menorah made from physical materials.[2]

There are luminous beings in the body of *Arich Anpin* who are charged with the task of keeping the defined purpose of *Atik Yamin* a clear and vibrant thoughtform that is impregnated with the energy of the will of God and alive with divine livingness. These elevated ones are in a state of constant deep meditation, holding the ideal of the temple of fire "steady in the light." Their constant meditation ensures that the *mikdash shel aish* is always fully energized and available to those dwelling in the lower worlds, to contact and draw on its power.

Other noble beings in the body of *Arich Anpin* transmit this vitalized thought to *Zeir Anpin*, the Lesser Countenance, and all those living in *Gan Eden Tachton*, the plane of the heart. The divine countenances called *Abba* and *Imma* are part of this aspect of the creative process. And then there are the fervent builders who construct the divine thoughtform out of their own being—who provide the mental matter and energy for the other aspects of this holy enterprise. Together, these three groups make up the center of light and energy in the planetary body called *Gan Eden Elyon*, where the work of creation in mental matter (*Briah*) proceeds.

Yetzirah—the Realm of Formation

In the next phase of manifestation, *Yetzirah*, or Formation, the pure thoughtform that was created in *Briah* takes on a distinct shape. Here the thought in the mind of God becomes a living reality.

This operation takes place on the plane of the lower Garden of Eden (*Gan Eden Tachton*)—the heart center of the planet—which is overseen by the consciousness of the Lesser Countenance (*Zeir Anpin*). *Gan Eden Tachton* is where the mental image made of pure thought is molded into an idea composed of sound and words. In *Yetzirah*, the divine purpose is transformed into a tangible plan.

The supernal workers of *Yetzirah* turn the mind impressions of the divine thought into a concrete blueprint that can be implemented on the physical plane. These souls beyond the bounds of time gaze into the multiple possibilities that form the future and set out a plan to fulfill God's purpose on earth. The plan is constantly adjusted to take into account our ever-changing reality and the choices that humans make in the sphere of free will.

Once a plan has been constructed, the dwellers in the realm of *Yetzirah* function on the inner side to inspire, guide, and energize humanity in the direction of the divine plan. Through the mental impression of hearts and minds, they act to stimulate the consciousness of those who inhabit the material world. The further human beings have evolved, the easier it is for those on higher planes to contact and influence them.

At the center of *Gan Eden Tachton* is the higher Jerusalem—*Yerushalayim shel malah*. And at the center of the higher Jerusalem is the heavenly Temple—*Mikdash shel malah*—a radiant locus of power that anchors the light, consciousness, and energy of the *Ein Sof* (Absolute) at the heart of the Kingdom of Heaven.[3] When the stone Temple stood in Jerusalem, there was an integral connection between this supernal center and its physical counterpart in the lower world.[4]

The heavenly Temple is a nucleus of souls that pour love, guidance, and energy into our material reality. The earthly Temple was a dedicated space where this tremendous spiritual power was made accessible to humanity. The more people came to the ancient Temple, the more the number of celestial workers expanded and grew. Gradually, a strong spiritual atmosphere built up, and a partial overlapping was formed between the planes. This process of vivification and alignment continued to grow and strengthen until the earthly Temple was transformed into a vibrant and dynamic outpost of the Kingdom of Heaven.

The angelic kingdom plays an important role in the *Yetzirah* phase of a thoughtform's manifestation. They embody the energies of the planet and wield these energies to create the varied lifeforms. There are hosts of angels that toil on the planes of *Yetzirah*. Both the Talmud and the *Zohar* are filled with descriptions of these angelic laborers and their overseers.[5]

The angelic beings who are active during this stage have their principal dwellings in *Gan Eden Tachton* on the planes of the heart center, and on the higher sub-planes of the solar plexus center. The archangels Michael, Gabriel, Uriel, and Raphael, however, have their abode on the highest planes of planetary consciousness. They contribute the major elements of their work during the stage of *Briah*. Nonetheless, the archangels are responsible for overseeing all of the efforts dealing with the form side of life on the seven planes of earth.

The archangel Michael is the High Priest of the heavenly Temple. He offers up the souls of the righteous as sacrifices on the altar of the *Mikdash shel malah*. These saintly individuals have dedicated their lives to the work of building the Temple. They incarnate upon earth to help bring this divine mission to realization.[6]

Asiyah—the Realm of Concrete Action

Finally, we enter the phase of action where the divine thoughtform of the Temple is manifest in our world. Today, many people no longer think in terms of a physical temple. However, we can still use the traditional division of Israel into *cohen, levi,* and *yisrael* as a basis for explaining how this spiritual endeavor might be fulfilled.[7]

There are three groups of workers who take up this objective. The first group, what we will call the *cohanim*, or priests, is made up of individuals who operate in the realm of meditation and prayer. Their task is to hold the energies that are needed to bring God's plan to completion. This inner work affects every aspect of their lives. Their lifestyle, living situation, and activity all need to be carefully regulated to facilitate the passage of the powerful energies they receive through their bodies. This is the primary function of the *cohanim*, the centerpoint of their lives. It is a task that is performed in solitude and seclusion in conjunction with the souls on higher worlds. Their combined efforts make possible all the other physical plane activities of this spiritual enterprise.

The second dimension of the vocation of revealing the Kingdom of Heaven on earth is to access the thoughtform on the plane of the planetary heart using the higher intuition. The received inspiration is then transformed into ideas and ideals to uplift humanity. This is the role of the second group, the *leviim*, or Levites. The *leviim* use their creative and intellectual talents to awaken the hearts and minds of their fellow human beings to the new and more expansive ways of thinking and living that form the foundation for the future Temple. These individuals play a more public and outward role in the plan of God than the first group. They serve as a crucial intermediary between the contemplatives and the last group, who establish the divine design in tangible form.

The last group takes up these inspirational teachings and sets them into motion in the day-to-day life of ordinary human beings. *Yisrael*, or Israel, as they are called, concentrates on self-transformation through selfless service. They labor for the physical, social, psychological, and spiritual well-being of their brothers and sisters in the world. This service awakens within them the virtues of love, compassion, and generosity and destroys the negative traits of prejudice, selfishness, and hate.

Yisrael draws on the energies made available by the first group, the *cohanim*, focused on the inner plane. They are inspired in their efforts by the ideals of the *leviim*, who access the sacred thought on the heart plane. And they themselves provide the human power for the other groups to manifest the Temple on the physical plane.

This complex multidimensional process demonstrates how a thought in the mind of God descends through the planes and is birthed into our world. A divine thoughtform brings new energies into our consciousness, creates innovative teachings, introduces fresh ways of living, and reveals as yet unknown pathways in the Kingdom of Heaven and the supernal realms. These exalted ideals lie at the heart of our collective evolution. They propel humanity forward on its journey of the spirit.

16

The Messianic Soul

*The Great Ones Who Answer
Our Cry for Help*

All the major religions of the world are waiting for the coming of the Messiah. The Messiah, however, is not a single individual. It is a collective soul of highly evolved beings who dwell in the spiritual realm. All the great teachers of humankind have come from this group soul.

The Soul of the Messiahs

The Soul of the Messiahs is a vast soul with many different aspects and dimensions. Buddhist tradition teaches that the bodhisattva Avalokiteshvara split his soul into a thousand different pieces, and each of these sparks grew into a bodhisattva to incarnate over the ages for the benefit and liberation of humankind.[1] Rabbinic teaching tells us that there will be two eminent ones from the Soul of the Messiahs who will come into incarnation: the Messiah the son of Joseph and the Messiah the son of David. In the *Tikunei Zohar*, we are informed that the soul of the Messiah the son of Joseph is composed of thousands of divine sparks.[2]

Different parts of the Soul of the Messiahs will manifest at different times in history. The Buddha may appear in India and Moses in Israel, but they both work together. The Anointed Ones all come from one majestic

Soul. They have incarnated on this physical plane of existence for the sake of people everywhere.

Whenever humanity reaches a point of dire need, a heart-wrenching cry goes out from the inhabitants of earth that reaches up into the higher planes of the Kingdom of Heaven. This plea for help evokes a divine response from those who dwell upon the plane of the Messiahs. The Messiahs have taken upon themselves the spiritual task of aiding humanity at appointed times in the plan of God. They have spent many eons preparing for the moment when they will be called upon. Whenever they take physical incarnation, they bring with them the tremendous spiritual power of the supernal source from which they have come.

The Characteristics of the Messiah

What qualities will the Messiah possess?

The Messiah will be the bearer of profound wisdom and compassion. The Compassionate One will exhibit deep understanding of the human condition, of the joys and sorrows of this earthly life. The Savior will radiate out a powerful force of love, magnetically drawing young and old into the presence. The Divine Defender will come to help the righteous and also the lowly. The fallen and the downtrodden hold a special place in the heart of the Messiah.

One of the powers that the Redeemer will demonstrate is the ability to heal spiritually. This gift will be a sign that the Anointed One carries the energy of divine grace. This energy is wielded by enlightened souls who have raised the *Shekhinah* to the highest center in the crown. Through the healing force of God's grace they can bring about miraculous cures.

The source of all illness lies in the body of the *sefirot*. Due to wrong living, an energy blockage builds up in the spiritual centers. This results in the formation of disease in the physical body and mind. However, when the power of divine grace passes through the centers, it burns up the dross that has accumulated there. This clears the blockages in the *Etz haChayim* and restores the individual to health.

The application of the spiritual force of God's grace can also bring about sudden conversions. Individuals whose impurities have been removed are catapulted into a higher state of awareness and a completely different view of life. In this new mind-set, all of their old ways of living seem totally irrelevant.

Such personal transformations need not be the radical movement of a sinner becoming a saint; there are many levels on which a change can occur. Contact with an Awakened One can transform a narrow-minded and parochial person into an open and universal thinker, or it can take an individual who has a raging temper and wipe away this crippling personality defect.

The Messiah will also have the blessing of prophecy. This is the proof of union with God. To prophesy one must merge with the mind of the Most High. This fusion occurs when the *Shekhinah* energy is raised to the *sefirah* of *chokhmah/binah*, the third eye, to meet with the divine energy that is descending from the crown. The whole head then becomes fused into a single center of light and energy, as the *sefirot* of *keter* (crown) and *chokhmah/binah* (wisdom/understanding) bind together and the gap between the physical and spiritual planes is bridged. The individual identity of the prophet then falls away as union with the larger soul, or *neshama*, takes place.

In this state of being, the plan of God is seen in a timeless whole. The divine thoughts are directly impressed upon the prophet's consciousness. A prophet sees beyond all external images and details to the core reality. The eternal essence infuses the vision of the prophet, who then has to translate this transcendent revelation into the realm of ideas and words.

God can also communicate directly with the prophet, where the words pass from one to the other as straight dictation. The prophet then becomes the mouthpiece of the soul. The prophet's very will is bound up with God; no thought or action enters the mind but that which God imposes. The personality is but a shell that remains to allow the appearance of a normal existence. But there is no one in that shell—no personal desires or free will.

God can overshadow this perfected vehicle at any time, even speak through the prophet's physical personality without his or her conscious awareness. In fact, there may be no recollection by the prophet of the message that was conveyed after the overshadowing has ended. Unlike hypnosis and possession, which are a function of contact with the lower psychic, the prophetic experience takes place through union with the Divine. The prophet has been completely absorbed into the Cosmic Vastness.

The Work of a Messiah

Many people have come to expect the time of the Messiah to be a kind of utopia where all suffering and difficulty will disappear. There will be no more sickness and no more death. The lamb will lie down with the lion, and each person will sit under his or her vine in peace and tranquility.

It is true that when a Great One comes a new reality emerges. However, the transformation that takes place occurs mainly in our inner, not our outer, reality. The mission of a Messiah is to take humanity forward in its spiritual evolution. A revitalized way of thinking is taught, a different approach to life is demonstrated, and more refined energies are anchored on the earth plane that carry us into higher and more exalted states of being. Over time, the work spreads as increasing numbers of people take up the new energy and awareness and change their manner of living. Finally, the whole world becomes permeated with its spiritual vibration and the messianic era is born.

The incarnation of a messianic soul is a pivotal moment in the history of humankind. An Illumined One initiates a transformation in the very essence of our being. The fabric of our day-to-day reality is shattered, and we are lifted into a completely different awareness. A Messiah propels humanity forward—thrusts us into the next stage of the unfolding of human consciousness.

It is a paradox: on the one hand, a Messiah's mission is to fulfill the prophecies and the teachings of the past; on the other hand, the Noble One comes to shake up all of the existing beliefs. Ironically, those who have waited most loyally for the Messiah are the ones who are most likely to be disturbed by the ideas they hear, while those who have rejected the old ways and teachings will enthusiastically receive the ideas that are revealed.

The One Who Comes

It is known long before the time of arrival when a Redeemer will incarnate. The life is planned far in advance of the moment of birth.

Enormous organization goes into preparing the way for such a soul. Yet in the end, it is the actual world conditions at the moment of incarnation that will determine which part of the Soul of the Messiahs will respond to humanity's call.

Like any other *neshama*, or group soul, the Soul of the Messiahs is composed of many individual souls who embody the energies and consciousness of the different divine attributes, or *sefirot*. The individual that incarnates as the Messiah can potentially come from any part of the larger group soul.

For an Anointed One to work on the physical plane, however, there need to be individuals who are prepared to take on the energy and mission. These souls need to have done the work of refining their personalities. They need to have a profound yearning for a new revelation and a change in direction. Only someone who is open and seeking will be capable of receiving the higher vision that the Messiah will impart. Others will simply treat both the messenger and the message with disbelief and scorn.[3]

Humanity has free choice. With each step in our evolution, we can achieve our goal either in the highest or the lowest. The plan of God will shift in accordance with the state of humanity's development. When the predestined moment for an incarnation arrives, we will receive the Messiah for whom we are prepared.

An invoking call will arise from humanity and a Messiah will be born upon earth in response. The strength and purity of that outcry will determine the part of the Soul of the Messiahs that incarnates. Will it be one from the solar plexus of the Soul, or will it be one from its crown? It is in our hands to decide.

If the Messiah comes from a higher aspect of the Soul, then amazing work will be accomplished with far-reaching and profound effect worldwide. A tremendous inflow of divine life will pour into the world. New spiritual horizons will open up. The will of God will overshadow all of humanity. There will be additional development in our body of centers and the influx of more refined energies into the body of humankind.

If humanity is behind schedule in its spiritual evolution, if there is no one who is ready to receive such a glorious One, then a lower aspect of the Soul of the Messiahs will incarnate. Such a Messiah will not bring the same energies or have the same impact as a higher manifestation of the Soul. The scope of influence and the changes that are carried out will be much more limited. The requisite miracles will be performed and the appropriate actions executed, but God will not be able to work through this instrument on the same level, nor will humanity be moved to respond with the same energy and enthusiasm. It will be a smaller step that is taken in the evolution of the race.

How will the Messiah manifest? It can happen in a number of different ways. Like the Buddha or Moses, a fully realized teacher may come to a particular people and place. The work will begin from this cultural and geographic location and then spread out to other countries around the world.

On the other hand, there are so many different peoples who are waiting for a Messiah that a different Messiah may come to each nation or religion on its own. We then would have a *Mashiach* for the Jews, a second coming of Jesus for the Christians, a *Mahdi* for the Muslims, a *Mitreya* for the Buddhists, and a *Kalki* for the Hindus. Or perhaps, we may even have them all come at once: a Messiah who comes to advance each religion, as well as another advanced soul who comes to lead the whole of humanity forward onto the next stage in our collective evolution. God can work in many ways. We need to be open to them all.

In whatever manner the Messiah manifests, such a lofty soul will not take physical birth for the benefit of only one nation or religion. An Awakened One incarnates for the sake of all of humankind as part of God's eternal plan. The exact circumstances of the birth are not of crucial importance. All that truly matters is that we are prepared to receive the Messiah when he or she arrives.

Acknowledgments

M any people have helped to bring this book to fruition. I am deeply grateful to all of them.

My father, Earl Glick, and my sister, Rani, and her husband, Jan-Willem, have offered me their generous support. My sons, Adir and Navonel, have helped and encouraged me throughout the conception, writing, and publishing of this book. Adir was a source of constant assistance, reading endless drafts, participating in webinars, and engaging in long hours of discussion and debate. Navonel provided a crucial technical lifeline, offering countless hours of practical help as well as the creative work of designing many of the illustrations for the book. My dear friends Yossi and Sarah Halevi have sustained and upheld me at every stage of this process. Edoe Cohen has been indispensable in a dozen different ways, especially in the creation and maintenance of my website, www.daatelyon.org. Moriah Halevi contributed her beautiful drawing of the *sefirot*. Rabbi Elie Kaplan Spitz supplied the great author picture for the book.

Thanks to Ruthy Abinun, Dr. Norman and Judy Enteen, Reb Mimi Feigelson, Dorothy Sandler-Glick, Sharon Goodman, Rabbi Alon Goshen-Gottstein, Dr. Maria Reis Habito, Michelle Katz, Dalia Landau, Dr. Yehezkel Landau, Sharon Laufer, Dvora Mizrachi, Rabbi Yael Saidoff, Bret Shupak, and Hannah Yannai for their support, care, and friendship. A special thanks to the English lovers of Divine wisdom Hilda Hayward, Gordon Smart, and the late Dave Coppard for their companionship and enthusiasm. Heartfelt thanks to the dedicated seekers of wisdom who spent two years sharing wisdom webinars with me: Minna Amsel, Roxanne Bensaid, Natalia Cediel, Susan Cetlin, Deborah Defilippo, Adir Glick, Sarah Halevi, Hannah Roen, Danielle Saffer, Michael Strum, and, of course, my wife, Nomi.

My gratitude to my publisher, Stuart M. Matlins, who took on this project, enabling me to bring this teaching to a wider audience. Stuart is a publisher of remarkable courage and vision. Many thanks to Rachel Shields, who has been a great project editor, providing helpful input and cheerful encouragement all along the way. Leah Brewer, Barbara Heise, Tim Holtz, Mike Myers, Emily Wichland, Amy Wilson, and all the rest of the friendly and professional staff at Jewish Lights have been a pleasure to work with. I am indebted to Jewish Lights for granting me permission to include excerpts from my book *Living the Life of Jewish Meditation: A Comprehensive Guide to Practice and Experience* in this publication.

And finally, there are no words that can express my gratitude to my wife, Nomi, who once again has been at the center of this project. Without her clarity of thought, wisdom, perseverance, and belief in my work, *Walking the Path of the Jewish Mystic* would never have been written. Her love, vision, and spirit of sacrifice and service are a cherished gift and blessing in my life.

Notes

Introduction: Awakening the Higher Knowledge (*Daat Elyon*)

1. Emmanuel Chai Riki, *Mishnat Chasidim* (*Kitzur Etz haChayim*), with the commentary *Biur Shaar* by Michael Bornstein, *Masekhet Briat Adam Kadmon*, chap. 1, *mishnaot* 4–5; see notes 40, 43, 44.

2. "Once some blind men chanced to come near an animal that someone told them was an elephant. They were asked what the elephant was like. The blind men began to feel its body. One of them said the elephant was like a pillar; he had touched only its leg. Another said it was like a winnowing-fan; he had touched only its ear. In this way the others, having touched its tail or belly, gave their different versions of the elephant." "M," *The Gospel of Sri Ramakrishna*, 7th ed., trans. Swami Nikhilananda (New York: Ramakrishna-Vedanta Center, 1984), p. 191.

3. Nachman of Breslov, *Likutei Maharan Tanina* 2, and *Otzer haYirah*, *Mahadura Batra*, *Shalom* 5 (New York: Breslov Hasidim Publications, 1969).

4. Gedaliah Kenig, lecture at Har Tzion Yeshiva in Jerusalem in the mid-1970s.

5. "M," *The Gospel of Sri Ramakrishna*, trans. Nikhilananda, p. 859.

6. Parts of this section are taken from my book *Living the Life of Jewish Meditation: A Comprehensive Guide to Practice and Experience* (Woodstock, VT: Jewish Lights, 2014), pp. 185–87.

7. Ze'ev Wolf of Zhitomir, *Or haMeir*, Torah portion *Shofetim*, quoted in *Baal Shem Tov al haTorah*, compiled by Natan Nata haCohen Dunner of Kalbiel and Shimon Menachem Mendel Wodnik of Gavorchov (Jerusalem, 1974), Torah portion *Shemot* 14.

8. Levi Yitzchak of Berditchev, *Kedushat Levi*, Torah portion *Shemot*.

The Garden and the Cosmic Vessels

1. Yosef Gikatilla, *Shaarei Orah*, *shaar* 8, name of *binah* (understanding), in the commentary by Matityahu Dalkart, note 3. See also *Zohar* 1:29b, "The secret of all this [the Hebrew letter *bet* in the word *bereshit* at the beginning of the Hebrew Bible] is that there are two worlds." See also *Zohar* 1:47b: "'Thus was finished'

[Genesis 2:1], the higher works were finished and the lower works were finished, the heavens and the earth, both above and below." There are many other similar examples that indicate that heaven and earth were different worlds.

2. Gikatilla, *Shaarei Orah*, shaar 1, name of *Etz haDaat* (Tree of Knowledge); see note 6 in the commentary at beginning of this name, and also the introduction to the book on humanity as the go-between for the higher and lower worlds, in the section beginning: "Because God wanted to reveal the divine unity and attribute of goodness in the creation, the world below was created in the model of the world above."

3. In the teachings of the Ari, he speaks of the supernal Torah (holy scriptures) in the mind of God and how each human is one letter of this Torah, one teaching or spark of the universal mind that it is his or her task to reveal in the world. See, for example, Chayim Vital, *Shaar haGilgulim*, introduction 17. See also chapter 9 of this book, "The Organization of the Heavens," the section called "The Mind of God" and notes 23 and 24 there.

4. Gikatilla, *Shaarei Orah*, shaar 1, under the name of *Etz haDaat* (Tree of Knowledge), speaks about the misuse of the *Shekhinah* energy in a sexual fashion. See also the commentary of Rabbenu Bachya on Genesis 3:6, p. 14a; also Job 4:18; and midrash *Tanchuma Yashan* 2:88; midrash *Tanchuma Chadash*, Torah portion *Mishpatim* 18, cited in Bernard Jacob Bamberger, *Fallen Angels* (Philadelphia: Jewish Publication Society, 1952), p. 171.

5. *Bereshit Rabbah* 20:12. See also *Zohar* 1:36b.

6. Chayim Vital, *Etz haChayim*, Hekhal 2, Hekhal Nikudim, shaar 2, Shaar Shevirat haKelim, shaar 9; Gershon Scholem, *Kabbalah* (Jerusalem: Keter Publishing House, 1974), pp. 135–40.

7. Glick, *Living the Life of Jewish Meditation*, p. 102.

8. Shlomo Efrayim of Luntchitz, *Olelot Efrayim*, article 166, cited in Ya'acov Yosef of Polonnoye, *Toldot Ya'acov Yosef*, Torah portions *Shemot* 6 and *Shofetim* 11.

9. Asher Tzvi of Ostraha, *Ma'ayan haChokhmah*, Torah portions *Ki Tissa* and *Metzora*, quoted in Nachman of Tcherin, *Derekh Chasidim, Yirah veAvodat haShem* 393, 395 (New York: Breslov Hasidim Publications, 1977).

Chapter 1: The Body of Spiritual Centers

1. Vital, *Etz haChayim*, Hekhal 1, Hekhal Adam Kadmon, shaar 1, anaf 2, Drush Egulim veYosher.

2. *Chakra* is the Sanskrit word for "wheel." The term is used in Tantric and Yogic texts to describe the subtle energy centers located along the spine. The *chakras* are first mentioned in the Vedas—the Rig Veda, for example. The Sri Jabala Darshana Upanishad, the Yoga-Shikka Upanishad, and the Shandilya Upanishad are other early Yogic texts that discuss the *chakras*.

3. *Sefer Yetzirah* 1:2. It is unclear where the term *sefirah* comes from. One possibility is that the word *sefirah* comes from the Hebrew word for "sapphire"—*sapir*. The *sefirot*, or spiritual centers, are like brilliant jewels that radiate energy and light. Interestingly, the Torah tells us in Exodus 24:9–10 that Moses, Aaron, and the seventy elders of Israel ascended Mount Sinai, where they beheld the God of Israel, and "under His feet there was a kind of paved work of sapphire stone (*livnat hasapir*)." The *sefirot* are God's footstool ("under His feet"), the medium by which the Infinite Divine Oneness is made manifest in the finite universe of innumerable forms. Another speculation is that the word *sefirah* is related to the word *mispar*, "number." The *sefirot* are the basic building blocks or numbers of the universe.

4. The Baal Shem speaks of the ten *sefirot* in a human being as how we are made in the image of God. See Ya'acov Yosef of Polonnoye, *Toldot Ya'acov Yosef*, Torah portion *Lekh Lekha*, as quoted in Dunner and Wodnik, *Baal Shem Tov al haTorah*, Torah portion *Bereshit* 58, and *Ben Porat Yosef*, p. 17a, also quoted in Dunner and Wodnik, Torah portion *Bereshit* 64. See also note 51 there quoting Yitzchak of Kamarna, *Imrei Peninim*, p. 207.

5. Glick, *Living the Life of Jewish Meditation*, p. xix.

6. Sivananda, *Practical Lessons in Yoga*, 8th ed. (Shivanandanagar, India: Divine Life Trust Society, 1997), pp. 81–87.

7. See, for example, Gikatilla, *Shaarei Orah*, beginning of *shaar* 3/4 on this issue. It explains how the two *sefirot* of *netzach/hod* (eternity/splendor) need to be understood together, that sometimes they work together and sometimes apart. Also, that *netzach* is the channel for bringing down the higher energies of the *chesed* (mercy) line on the right and *hod* is the channel for bringing down the higher energies of the *din* (judgment) line on the left. This section is also quoted in my book *Living the Life of Jewish Meditation*, p. 47.

8. The classic text in the *Zohar* describing the centers as limbs in the body of God is the section called *Petach Eliyahu* that is recited Friday evening in many Hasidic and Kabbalistic communities. It comes from a section in the second introduction to *Tikunei Zohar*.

9. After the destruction of the Temple and the end of prophecy, the science of raising the energies was forgotten, and the body of centers ceased to be a living reality for the Kabbalists. Instead, they were relegated to the celestial realm and became the subject of philosophical and mystical contemplation. Therefore, the highest center, *keter* (crown), instead of being the culmination of the inner meditative awakening, became detached from the rest of the body and sits like a crown on the head. *Chokhmah* (wisdom), instead of being the third eye that enables us to see through the mind of God, became the symbol for the brain. *Chesed/gevurah* (mercy/power) migrated from the throat down to the shoulders to the right and left arms and became symbolic of God meting out mercy with the right hand and

judgment with the left. *Tiferet* (beauty) became the whole torso. And *netzach/hod* (eternity/splendor) moved down from the solar plexus area to become the two legs—the spiritual supports of the divine body. *Binah* (understanding) moves back and forth between its original place in the head as the left eye, and the heart, a reference to the Rabbinic dictum that the heart is the seat of understanding (*halev meyvin*). *Yesod* remains the genitals, but *malkhut* becomes the feet instead of the center at the base of the spine, where the feet are folded during meditation. See the segment on the *Shekhinah* energy at the end of the next section "The Three Energy Pathways" and also chapter 13.

10. *Sefer Yetzirah* 1:1 speaks of the thirty-two paths of wisdom. In Kaplan's commentary on *Sefer Yetzirah* (Kaplan, *Sefer Yetzirah: The Book of Creation* [York Beach, ME: Red Wheel/Weiser Books, 1997], pp. 8–9), he notes that the thirty-two paths are compared by the commentators to the nervous system of the body: thirty-one nerves that emanate from the spinal cord and the thirty-second, highest path, which corresponds to the entire complex of cranial nerves, which are twelve in number. He mentions a variety of sources in this regard. *Ra'avad*, *Tikunei Zohar Chadash* 112c, *Peliya* 213a, *Pardes Rimonim* 12:1, *Mavo Shaarim* 5:2:6, *Etz haChayim, Shaar haTzelem* 2.

11. Dov Baer of Mezeritch, *Lekutim Yekarim* 54. In one of his teachings, Rebbe Dov Baer describes the experience of walking amid these supernal pipelines of energy that emanate into the *sefirot* from the higher and lower worlds.

12. Riki, *Mishnat Chasidim, Hekhal* 1, *Masekhet Briat Adam Kadmon*, chap. 2, *mishnah* 1.

13. Sivananda, *Kundalini Yoga*, 10th ed. (Shivanandanagar, India: Divine Life Trust Society, 1994), p. 20. See Arthur Avalon [John Woodroffe], *The Serpentine Power* (New York: Dover Publications, 1974), pp. 110, 113. See also "M," *The Gospel of Sri Ramakrishna*, trans. Nikhilananda, p. 499.

14. In both Kabbalistic and Indian thought, the right-hand side is associated with God and the left-hand side is associated with the forces of evil. The left-hand or psychic powers, however, are not so much linked to evil, but rather are vulnerable to misuse for evil purposes unless there is the protective power of the divine attributes of the right-hand side. Psychic power is energy that is of a higher vibration than physical energies, while still having a form. The divine energies are formless or pure spirit.

15. *Bereshit Rabbah* on Genesis 2:4. See also Rashi's commentary on Genesis 1:1, where he brings this midrash in the name of the Alshikh, who quotes it in the name of *Bereshit Rabbah* 12.

16. Glick, *Living the Life of Jewish Meditation*, pp. 193–95.

17. Gikatilla, *Shaarei Orah*, shaar 2: name of *El Chai* (the living God); and "M," *The Gospel of Sri Ramakrishna*, trans. Nikhilananda, pp. 499–500.

18. See, for example, 1 Samuel 10:5–6, 19:19–24; 2 Kings 2:1–15. See also the Rambam (Moses Maimonides), *Mishneh Torah, Hilkhot Yesodei haTorah*, chap. 7.
19. This explains the reason for the shift to the traditional positioning of the *sefirot* in the body, as is elaborated in note 9.
20. The widespread consensus in the tradition is that prophecy ended with the prophet Malachi. See, for example, Talmud, *Yoma* 9b and *Sanhedrin* 11a. Also see the commentaries of the Radak, Ibn Ezra, and Abarbanel on Malachi 1:1, as well as the Malbim on Malachi 3:22.
21. See the commentary of the Ramban (Nachmanides) on Leviticus 17:11.
22. See note 10.

Chapter 2: The Centers

1. Gikatilla, *Shaarei Orah*, shaar 1, the *Shekhinah* is called *adamah* (earth) and *karka* (ground).
2. Gikatilla, *Shaarei Orah*, shaar 1, name of *bracha* (blessing), note 1.
3. Gikatilla, *Shaarei Orah*, shaar 2, the name of *El Chai* (the living God).
4. *Malkhut* (kingship) is seen as the receptive aspect of deity, receiving the seed of spiritual life from the other *sefirot* and manifesting it in the world. See Gikatilla, *Shaarei Orah*, shaar 1, the name *yam* (sea). See also *shaar* 8, names of *Shekhinah Ilah* and *Makor Chayim*.
5. According to the Ari, *Arich Anpin* (the Greater Countenance), or *keter* (crown) aspect of the Godhead, is the source of *malkhut* (kingship) or *Nukva* (the feminine aspect in the Godhead). According to R. Moshe Chayim Luzatto, *Nukva* was the beginning point in the divine thought of creation. This is the hidden meaning of the phrase "last in creation, first in thought." See *138 Pitchei haChokhmah, Petach* 104. Also see *Mishnat Chasidim, shaar Arich Anpin*, chap. 4, *mishnah* 1, note 111 in the commentary.
6. Gikatilla, *Shaarei Orah*, shaar 2: name of *El Chai*.
7. Gikatilla, *Shaarei Orah*, shaar 2: the name *brit* (covenant), the section on *brit milah* (circumcision) and how it is the gateway to *tiferet* (beauty), and the relationship between the two.
8. Baal Shem Tov, *Tzava'at haRivash*, p. 10a, quoted in Dunner and Wodnik, *Baal Shem Tov al haTorah*, Torah portion *Bereshit* 36. For a beautiful explanation of *yesod* as the power of *hitkashrut* see Dov Baer of Mezeritch, *Lekutim Yekarim* 156.
9. Gikatilla, *Shaarei Orah*, shaar 2, name of *El Shaddai*—the God that said to the world, "*Dai* (enough)," that is, the aspect of the Godhead that sets limits and borders and organizes the raw material of creation into lifeforms. See also the name of *yesod*; the four elements are called *yesodot* (foundations) because this center organizes and energizes them. And also the name *tov* (good). This center is used (in conjunction with the *Shekhinah* energy) in the Creation process, and that is

why it says each day that God looked at the work and saw that it was good. *Yesod* is what integrates everything together and makes it good.

10. Gikatilla, *Shaarei Orah, shaar* 2, name of *sekhel tov* (a good mind). Through this center, we enter into the *aspeklaria hameirah* (the clear mirror) and are able to understand and contemplate God's truths. This center is also called *uman* (crafts-person)—crafting new life, ideas, and works of art.

11. In the Tantric text *Adhyatmaviveka*, for example, the solar plexus, or *manipura chakra*, is associated with the lower emotions of "shame, treachery, jealousy, desire, supineness, sadness, worldliness, ignorance, aversion (or disgust), fear" (quoted in Avalon, *The Serpentine Power*, p. 139). Swami Prabhavananda of the Ramakrishna Order also linked this center with the lower emotions (Prabhavananda, *Realizing God: Lectures on Vedanta*, ed. Edith Dickinson Tipple [Kolkata, India: Advaita Ashrama, 2010], p. 60). The linkage of the solar plexus with our emotions resonates with our modern understanding of human nature. Emotion is experienced in the stomach area. The physical organ of the stomach is aligned with this *sefirah*, as is the pancreas. There is medical research that points to a linkage between emotional stress and stomach ailments and even diabetes, affirming the connection between this center and the emotions. There is also another reason why this *sefirah* is associated with emotions. As explained a little further on, psychic energy flows powerfully through this center. This energy works through feelings rather than reasoning. When we have an intuitive sense about something, we call it a "gut feeling"; it is really a psychic intuition that we are experiencing.

12. Gikatilla, *Shaarei Orah, shaar* 3/4, near the end, on the name of *netzach* (eternity). Also see Dov Baer of Mezeritch, *Likutei Amarim*, p. 18b, and *Tza'avat haRivash*, p. 10a, quoted in Dunner and Wodnik, *Baal Shem Tov al haTorah*, Torah portion *Bereshit* 36, "*netzach* (victory)—and he shall vanquish a particular attribute [or imperfection]."

13. The solar plexus is a complex network of nerves that groups together nerves from a number of important systems in the body. This physical function is an outer expression of its inner function as a gathering point or bridge between the higher and lower human being—gathering together the energies of the three lower centers and transferring them up into the higher centers. It is called the solar plexus because its appearance is like a central round body with rays going out in all directions. This physical appearance is also a reflection of its inner nature. Like the sun, which bleaches out any stains or blemishes in a cloth, the solar plexus cleanses and clears the lower energies so that they can be used for higher purpose. It lifts a human being out of the lower emotions of lust, jealousy, and anger into the higher emotions of love, generosity, and compassion.

14. See Prabhavananda, *Realizing God*, p. 59: "The next center, the *manipura*, is situated at the root of the navel and has ten petals. It is the seat of psychic power. As

the energy rises to that center through the *sushumna* [the central pathway], psychic visions and experiences and occult powers manifest." In Tibetan Buddhism, this center is the home of the female *kundalini* energy instead of the *chakra* at the base of the spine, which is the home of this energy in both Yoga and the Kabbalah. This is because this center relates to a different aspect of the female energy. In the Kabbalistic and Yogic systems, the left hand or psychic component is identified as female in relation to the energy of the right side, which is considered to be male. This *chakra*, therefore, is the home of this left-hand/psychic female energy.

15. This is why this *sefirah* is associated with lower prophecy, dreams, and visions. It is through the power of the psychic that these revelations occur. See Gikatilla, *Shaarei Orah*, shaar 3/4, the section on the name *etzem hashamayim* (the very heavens). Also the section on *makom ha'etza* (place of counsel). Interestingly, the text speaks about *binah* (understanding) as the beginning of *etza* (counsel or advice) and *netzach/hod* (eternity/splendor) as the end point of *etza*, which to me indicates it is the lower guidance—less reliable and clear. Also see the name *yachin*. The two pillars of *yachin* and *boaz* are the channels through which the three aspects of the soul—the *nefesh*, *ruach*, and *neshama*—ascend and descend through the worlds. Gikatilla also connects the *sefirah* of *netzach/hod* to the three aspects of the soul entering and leaving the body. The souls incarnate by coming down from *binah* and descending through the levels, and when they leave, they ascend in the opposite direction.

16. Vital, *Shaar haGilgulim*, introduction 22, section beginning: "surely this matter of incarnation." Also see Gershon Scholem, *Kabbalot of R. Jacob v R. Isaac haKohen B'nei R. Jacob haKohen*, in *Mada'ae HaYahadut* vol. 2, pp. 254–55, quoted in Bamberger, *Fallen Angels*, pp. 174–75.

17. Glick, *Living the Life of Jewish Meditation*, p. 194.

18. See Deuteronomy 12:29–31 and all of chapter 13. Interestingly, in Gikatilla, *Shaarei Orah*, shaar 3/4, he speaks of twenty-four heavenly courts that work to vanquish all those that stand on the left-hand side, the other side, the side of Satan, to protect Israel. Perhaps this discussion is in *netzach/hod* (eternity/splendor), because this is where the left side's power and influence are greatest and people are most vulnerable.

19. Baal Shem Tov, *Tza'avat Rivash*, p. 4a; Dov Baer of Mezeritch, *Lekutim Yekarim*, pp. 3c and 15b, quoted in Dunner and Wodnik, *Baal Shem al haTorah*, Torah portion *Ekev* 51, 52, and note 40.

20. See Silverio de Santa Teresa, shorter edition of *The Works of Saint Teresa*, Saint Teresa of Avila, *The Foundations*, chap. 7, quoted in Marcelle Auclair, *Saint Teresa of Avila*, trans. Kathleen Pond (Petersham, MA: St. Bede's Publications, 1988), pp. 218–20. Saint Teresa uses the term *melancholia* to describe this condition. Marcelle Auclair refers to it as neurasthenia. I am looking at it from a completely

spiritual perspective as behavior that results from a problem with the psychic. For more detailed information on this subject, see my book *Living the Life of Jewish Meditation*, chapter 14, "The Psychic: The Danger of Delving into the Inner Realm."

21. It is interesting to note, in this context, the Baal Shem Tov's teaching (see Dunner and Wodnik, *Baal Shem Tov al ha Torah*, introduction to *Kuntris Meirat Einayim* 69) that he came to show the path of approaching God through love rather than fear—another possible way to express the movement from the solar plexus to the heart center. In the Ramakrishna Order, they advise people to meditate focusing on the heart center.

22. Gikatilla, *Shaarei Orah*, *shaar* 5, the beginning section on how the name *Yud Heh Vav Heh* is central for the whole Kabbalistic tree; how everything is joined together through this name, just as the trunk of a tree binds the different parts of a tree together. This same idea can also be said of the *sefirah* of *tiferet* (beauty). See *shaar* 5 on the name *tiferet* where it elaborates on this theme and on the different garments of glory that God puts on through this name to bind together and manifest the whole of the Tree of Life. Also, at the end of this *shaar*, see the name *atah* (you), how it includes everything—from *aleph* to *tav* (a–z)—plus the *heh* of the name of God.

23. Love does exist in the animal kingdom, but it is an instinctual love, like the instinct that a mother animal feels to care for her young. Animals care for and fiercely protect their own young and will defend the members of their tribe. They will even care for the young of another species if the instinct is flowing strongly. But it is all at the level of instinct and does not normally reach beyond the level of the physical. Similarly, if an animal from outside the tribe comes, the others will shun or attack it. On the other hand, an animal that spends a lot of time around humans can begin to open its heart center through its interaction with human beings.

24. It is the mastery of the spoken word that makes an effective teacher. The words of a real spiritual teacher are infused with power and authority. This phenomenon occurs through the energy of the throat center.

25. The higher creative power of the throat center is symbolically expressed in the Kabbalah by the descent of the *sefirah* of *binah* (understanding) into the throat. On the one hand, this descent is viewed as a degradation of the energy of *binah*. On the other hand, it is this descent that makes the energy of *binah* accessible to the souls who have not fully awakened their head center and transforms the throat into a center of higher creativity.

26. One could say that the throat is the bridge that joins together the energies of the torso with the higher energies of the head. The physical form of the throat is the outer expression of its inner purpose. In the Kabbalah of the Ari, not only does *binah* descend to the throat, but the consciousness of *Zeir Anpin* (the Lesser

Countenance), which embodies the *sefirah* of *tiferet* (beauty), is lifted up to the throat to be nestled by the *partzuf* (divine countenance) of *Imma* (Mother), which embodies the *sefirah* of *binah*. This is the symbolic expression of the blending of the energies of these two *sefirot* in the throat center. For a further explanation of this process, see the section entitled "The Body of Earth" in chapter 9.

27. The throat is the vehicle for the breath that enters and exits the body through its medium. The breath carries the life force, or what the yogis call *prana*, which is an essential ingredient in any healing process. According to Yoga, it is the proper circulation and balance of the *prana* in the body that maintains the body's health. In Hebrew, the word for "soul," *neshama*, is almost identical with the word for "breath," *neshima*. It is the breath that animates the body with the life force of the soul and keeps it functioning properly. The *Shekhinah* energy is carried through the body on the *prana*. Therefore, it is through the throat center that the energy of the *Shekhinah* is focused in healing. (See the section entitled "The Breath of God" in chapter 12.) See also Rebbe Nachman of Breslov, *Likutei Maharan Tanina* 4:12, where he explains that the *sefirah* of *chesed* is the attribute of a *cohen* (priest), and how through the energy of this *sefirah*, the priest has the power to heal, as in Leviticus 13:31, "And the priest shall close up the wound."

28. Rebbe Nachman of Breslov in *Likutei Maharan* 231 speaks of how the healing power of the planets is channeled into the different herbs and grasses, and this is how all medicinal herbs are formed. However, he says, through the power of prayer, we can draw the healing power of the planets directly to us, without the need for the herbs or medicines. He suggests that we use this thought as a *kavanah* (intention) when we say the verse in the morning prayers "And the hosts of heaven bow down to you" (Nehemiah 9:6). This whole idea is a reference to harnessing the power of the angelic kingdom and its lords.

29. The whole biblical account of Creation is based upon the creative power of the divine word. All the acts of creation begin with the words "and God said." For more on this concept, see the section on creation in chapter 11.

30. In the Kabbalah, the *sefirot* of *chokhmah* (wisdom) and *binah* (understanding) are the vehicles for the energy of *keter*, the energy of the *Ein Sof* (Absolute), to flow into the world or a human being. *Chokhmah/binah*, or the third eye, forms the bridge whereby the consciousness of pure spirit enters into our awareness. See Gikatilla, *Shaarei Orah*, *shaar* 9, the name of *chokhmah*.

31. This center is the seat of the highest level of creativity, where we receive pure inspiration directly from the mind of God. In the Kabbalah, *chokhmah* is pure mind, pure thought—the consciousness of Oneness. Through this center, we tap into this pure mind and then integrate it into our consciousness using the defining power of understanding, or *binah*. See Rabbi Aryeh Kaplan's commentary on the *Sefer Yetzirah*, pp. 11–12. See also Gikatilla, *Shaarei Orah*, *shaar* 9, name of *chokhmah*.

32. Riki, *Mishnat Chasidim: Hekhal* 1: *Masekhet Briat Adam Kadmon*, chap. 2, *mishnah* 9. See note 82 on the power of the tzaddik to emanate spiritual power from his eyes. The Indian sage Sri Ramana Maharshi was renowned for his ability to transmit spiritual power through his look. See, for example, the account about Mastan in David Godman, *The Power of the Presence* (Tiruvannamalai, India: David Godman, 2000), vol. 3, pp. 23–24, and the case of Muruganar in vol. 2, p. 113. A less gentle expression of this power is found in the stories in the Talmud about rabbis who could burn people to ashes with one look, a classic example being the story in *Shabbat* 33b about Rabbi Shimon bar Yochai, who came out of a cave after seven years of meditation. Seeing a laborer in the fields, he became outraged at someone doing normal mundane work and burned him to ashes.

33. "M," *The Gospel of Sri Ramakrishna*, trans. Nikhilananda, p. 500.

34. Aryeh Kaplan, *The Living Torah: The Five Books of Moses and the Haftarot*, trans. Aryeh Kaplan (New York: Maznaim Publishing, 1981), Torah portion *Beha'alotekha*.

35. The link between meditation on the *ajna* and peace is explicit in the Bhagavad Gita 6:13–15 and implicit in the Yoga Sutras of Patanjali as well as other major Hindu scriptures. Also, peace is essentially an attribute of the mind. Therefore, it is linked to the *sefirah* of *chokhmah/binah*, which is the *sefirah* of the mind. Perhaps this is why the rabbis say that *talmidei chakhamim*, the disciples of the sages, increase peace in the world. Through the study of sacred scripture, the consciousness is raised to a higher awareness, which then brings the energy of peace flooding into the mind. In this regard, see Yisrael Yitzchak Dancyger, *Yismach Yisrael*, on Lag B'Omer, the first teaching.

36. Gikatilla, *Shaarei Orah*, *shaar* 10, the name of *Eheye*, at the beginning of the *shaar*. Also see "M," *The Gospel of Sri Ramakrishna*, trans. Nikhilananda, p. 499. See also Sivananda, *Practical Lessons in Yoga*, pp. 85–87.

37. For an example in the Kabbalah, see the Sabbath prayer *Lecha Dodi*, which describes this union in several places. For an example in Hindu teachings, see "M," *The Gospel of Sri Ramakrishna*, p. 500. For an example in the Christian tradition, see Marcelle Auclair, *Saint Teresa of Avila*, pp. 239–41.

38. "M," *The Gospel of Sri Ramakrishna*, pp. 499–500. See also Sivananda, *Practical Lessons in Yoga*, pp. 85–87.

39. Glick, *Living the Life of Jewish Meditation*, pp. 159–60.

40. Gikatilla, *Shaarei Orah*, *shaar* 7, the names of *El* and *rav chesed*, the section beginning: "And know that above all the camps."

41. Riki, *Mishnat Chasidim, Shaar Zivug Abba v'Imma*, chap. 1:3, see note 167; also, Shar'abi, *Nahar Shalom* on the *Etz haChayim* of Vital, p. 41d, chap. 9.

42. See Gikatilla, *Shaarei Orah*, *shaar* 5, on the name *daat* (knowledge) and *Etz haDaat* (Tree of Knowledge) as the pathway to *keter* (crown). Through *daat*, the

middle column reaches up to *keter*; without *daat*, we cannot make the jump from *chokhmah* to *keter*. *Daat* joins with *chokhmah* (wisdom) and *binah* (understanding) and draws all the three centers into close contact with *keter*, essentially becoming one with it.

43. See Vital, *Shaar haGilgulim*, introduction 28. Also *Mishnat Hasidim, Shaar Arich Anpin*, chap. 2, explanation of *mishnah* 3.

Chapter 3: The Nature of the Soul

1. Aharon Meir Altshuler, compiler, *Klalei Hatechalat haChokhmah*, chap. 4:1, no. 98, see the section beginning: "in the lower human being there are five aspects of light." See also Talmud, *Berakhot* 10a, section beginning: "What I meant to tell you is this: To whom did David refer in these five verses beginning with 'Bless the Lord, O my soul'?"
2. See Moses Maimonides, *The Guide for the Perplexed*, 2nd ed., trans. M. Friedlander (England: Hebrew Literature Society, 1904), part 1, chap. 41, where he identifies the *nefesh* with the intellect.
3. Shlomo of Radamsk, *Sefer haGilgulim*, part 2, chap. 2: "there is no death except for the *nefesh*."
4. Elijah ben Solomon (Vilna Gaon), in his commentary on *Sefer Yetzirah*, chap. 1:1, no. 3, writes that the main aspects of a human being are his *nefesh* and *ruach*, but mostly the *ruach*. And it is the *ruach* that receives reward and punishment. See Chayim of Volozhin, *Nefesh haChayim*, shaar 1:15, 17, and 18. (See Altshuler, *Klalei Hatechalat haChokhmah*, part 1, chap. 9:1, no. 208.)
5. *Zohar* 2, section titled *Sabah deMishpatim*, pp. 104b–105b, "the supernal tribes."
6. See Vital, *Shaar haGilgulim*, introduction 11; also Moses Cordovero, *Pardes Rimonim*, shaar 31, *Shaar haNeshama*; the *Zohar*, Torah portion *Acharei Mot*, and Chayim of Volozhin, *Nefesh haChayim*, shaar 1, chap. 17.

Chapter 4: Our Soul Family

1. Though Chayim Vital does not use the term "soul family" in *Shaar haGilgulim*, he speaks about the relationship between the different parts of the same *shoresh neshama* (soul root) in much the same fashion. See introductions 11, 12, 13, 30, and many other places in the text.
2. See Vital, *Etz haChayim, Hekhal 5, Hekhal Zeir Anpin*, shaar 14, shaar 20, *Shaar Partzufim*, drush 2. For a more detailed explanation of the Ari's teaching about this process, see chapter 15 of my book *Living the Life of Jewish Meditation*, "The Dynamics of Inner Experience."
3. Vital, *Shaar haGilgulim*, introduction 39. Section beginning: "know, without exception, each and every tzaddik has two souls, as is recalled in the *Zohar* in the beginning of the Torah portion of *Noach*." Vital describes how every tzaddik

has two souls: a *neshama penimit* (inner soul), which incarnates with him; and a *neshama makefet* (surrounding soul), which rests above him in the higher worlds and acts as a pathway by which he can connect with the higher worlds, receive emanations from them, and ascend unto them.

4. Shlomo of Radamsk, *Sefer haGilgulim*, part 2, chap. 1. According to Rebbe Shlomo, the Ari teaches that we all have two angels that accompany us on our left- and right-hand side and that we can ascend at night into the higher worlds with the help of these angels. Gikatilla, *Shaarei Orah*, shaar 3/4 (the name of *yachin*) mentions that in the *Hekhalot* section of the *Zohar* there are two supernal beings named after the two pillars of the Temple—*Yachin* and *Boaz*. The souls that enter the "higher temple" ascend up into the spiritual realms via the intermediary of these great beings.

5. Talmud, *Sotah* 36b. See also *Zohar* 1:192a, section beginning: "Joseph, in whatever he was doing."

6. Interestingly, there is an alternative reading in the *Yalkut Reuveni*, Torah portion *Vayeshev*, which states that it was the image of his mother, Rachel, that came to Joseph in his moment of temptation.

7. Gikatilla, *Shaarei Orah*, shaar 8; see the name of *Shekhinah ilah*, "Supernal Divine Presence."

8. Vital, *Shaar haGilgulim*, introductions 1, 2, 3, and 5 about how the *ruach* or *neshama* of a tzaddik can overshadow a person through the process of *ibbur* (intercalation). See also Nachman of Breslov, *Likutei Maharan* 21.

9. See Talmud, *Berakhot* 5a. Also see Talmud, *Shabbat* 29b, *Eruvin* 41b, *Pesachim* 111a, *Yoma* 83b, and *Sanhedrin* 75b. The Rabbis also refer to negative spirits as *mazikin*, or demons.

Chapter 5: The Garments of the Soul

1. The use of the terms "astral body" and "astral plane" has become common parlance in New Age circles and also in the Jewish Renewal movement, where the Kabbalistic world of *Yetzirah* (Formation) is linked to the realm of emotions (see the section "The Universe of *Tikun*" in chapter 9). The modern usage of these terms appears to go back to nineteenth-century French occultist Eliphas Levi. They were then taken up by Madame Blavatsky and the Theosophists. In Judaism, as we shall see later in this chapter, the Kabbalah speaks of the *chaluka derabanan* (robe of the sages), a spiritual garment that we wear in the higher worlds that is formed out of the mitzvot, commandments or positive spiritual acts that we do. It is clear from the book of the *Zohar* and writings of the Ari that the building of this spiritual garment is contingent on much more than the physical act of doing one of the traditional commandments. In *Shaar haGilgulim*, introduction 17, for example, Vital writes how the physical fulfillment of a commandment is

not enough to achieve a full *tikun* (repair) of the soul; each commandment must be fulfilled during our journey of incarnation on the level of thought, word, and deed. The *chaluka derabanan*, therefore, would appear to be formed from both our astral and our mental bodies, and perhaps even the body of *sefirot*, or centers. Hindu teaching speaks of the *linga sarira*, a subtle body that is composed of similar elements to those we have ascribed to the *chaluka derabanan*. Some schools of Hinduism divide the subtle body into several different bodies. In any case, there is clearly a teaching about a subtle body or bodies in many religions. The opinions concerning its makeup are diverse.

2. *Zohar* 3:214a.

3. *Zohar* 2:210a, section beginning *"trei ratikhin ilayen"*; Cordovero, *Pardes Rimonim*, shaar 31, *Shaar haNeshama*, chaps. 2, 5; Vital, *Shaarei Kedushah*, part 1, shaar 1; *Tana deBei Eliyahu*, hakdama derav Kashisha verav Yanikah.

4. Cordovero, *Pardes Rimonim*, shaar 31, *Shaar haNeshama*, chap. 11.

5. There is also an opinion that there are two *tzelems*: a *tzelem* and a *tzelem* for the *tzelem*. This opinion may be referring to the body of spiritual centers: everything else is cast in the form of the Tree of Life, so to speak. The body of *sefirot* is the basis for our linkage with the higher aspects of the soul. Regarding the *tzelem*, see *Zohar* 104b, Torah portion *Emor*, beginning: "The Book of King Solomon"; *Zohar* 1:217b, Torah portion *Vayechi*, beginning: "Rabbi Yossi said"; Cordovero, *Pardes Rimonim*, shaar 31, *Shaar haNeshama*, chap. 4.

Chapter 6: Incarnation and Evolution in the Human Kingdom

1. *Zohar* 2:99b–100b.

2. See, for example, Dov Baer of Mezeritch, *Lekutim Yekarim*, no. 112 (Jerusalem: Yeshivat Toldot Aharon, 1973); and also Dunner and Wodnik, *Baal Shem Tov al haTorah*, Torah portion *Mishpatim*, footnote 1, where it recounts a story about reincarnation involving the Baal Shem Tov and Rebbe Dov Baer.

3. *Idra Rabba*, *Zohar* 3:136b; see also *Shaarei Orah*, shaar 6, which speaks at length about the role of the *bet din shel malah* (celestial court) and *bet din shel mata* (earthly court) in overseeing karma (reward and punishment) and in organizing the life of the kingdoms and all of their creatures. The passage recounts how all the creatures and human beings come before the *bet din* (court) and acknowledge that they are happy with how they were created. This whole process is a good example of the workings of karma.

4. *Zohar* 2:144b–162b.

5. Cordovero, *Pardes Rimonim*, shaar 31, *Shaar haNeshama*, chap. 11.

6. See entry by David Godman on his blog *Arunachala and Sri Ramana Maharshi*, the interview with Annamalai Swami posted September 23, 2008—comments on the post for February, 1, 2009, http://sri-ramana-maharshi.blogspot.com/2008/09/

annamalai-swami-interview.html. See also Munagala S. Venkataramiah, *Talks with Sri Ramana Maharshi*, 8th ed. (Tiruvannamalai, India: Sri Ramanasramam, 1989), talk 155, where Sri Ramana compares different aspirants to gunpowder, charcoal, and coal.

7. "M," *The Gospel of Sri Ramakrishna*, trans. Nikhilananda, p. 831.

8. V. Ganesan, *Ramana Periya Puranam: Inner Journey of 75 Old Devotees* (Tiruvanammalai, India: Ganesan, 2013), available at www.aham.com/Ramana PeriyaPuranam/RamanaPeriyaPuranam.pdf, pp. 242–43.

9. For example, in the *Shaar haGilgulim*, introduction 38, Chayim Vital tells the story of an outing with the Ari to the location where the *Idra Rabba* was taught by Shimon bar Yochai. The Ari went to a spot where there was a large rock with two deep clefts in it. The Ari sat down in a cleft on the north side of the rock, where he says Rabbi Shimon sat, and he told Chayim to sit in the cleft on the south side, where Rabbi Abba, who wrote down the *Zohar*, sat. The Ari then proceeded to tell Chayim that Rabbi Abba was the *shoresh* (spiritual source) of Chayim's *nefesh*, or soul. Though the Ari does not expressly declare himself to be a spark of the soul of Rabbi Shimon, it is quite self-evident from his choice of place to sit.

10. Dunner and Wodnik, *Baal Shem al haTorah*, introduction—*Kuntris Meirat Einayim* 4.

11. The *Zohar* 1:76b, *Zohar* 2:96b, *Zohar* 3:43a, *Zohar Chadash*, *Shir haShirim* 84b and *Tikkunei Zohar*, *Tikkun* 70, 136b all talk about what happens before a soul incarnates, about the Torah it learns and the visions it is shown, as well as its dispute with God about not wanting to incarnate in this world. All of these passages are meant to teach us that the soul goes through a variety of preparations for each incarnation in conjunction with those who are looking after it in the higher worlds.

12. See chapter 5, "The Garments of the Soul," note 1. The original meaning of the word "astral" is "of the stars," an expression of this body's usage as the vehicle we use to ascend through the heavens or celestial realms.

13. *Zohar* 2:99a–100b, the section beginning: "because when a human being is in this world."

14. Kirpal Singh, *The Mystery of Death*, 2nd ed. (Blaine, WA: Ruhani Satsang, 2007), pp. 85–92.

Chapter 7: Key Factors in Spiritual Evolution

1. Ya'acov Yosef of Polonnoye, *Toldot Ya'acov Yosef*, Torah portion *Ki Tissa*, first teaching.

2. *Zohar* 1:77b, section beginning: "at the time they went, what is written, 'to go to the land of Canaan.'"

3. Yoel Glick, *Seeking the Divine Presence: The Three Pillars of a Jewish Spiritual Life* (Victoria, BC: Trafford Publishing, 2009), pp. 204–206.

4. Reb Yaibe, Torah portion *Terumah*.
5. *Midrash Mekhilta*, Torah portion *Yitro* 19:5.
6. Nachum of Chernobyl, *Meor Einayim*, Torah portion *Yitro*.
7. Yitzchak Yaakov Rabinowicz of Biala, *Divrei Binah*, Torah portions *Mishpatim* and *Beha'alotekha*.
8. Ya'acov Yosef of Polonnoye, *Hanhagot Yisharot*, p. 10a, quoted in Dunner and Wodnik, *Baal Shem Tov al haTorah*, Torah portion *Mikketz* 11.
9. Dov Baer of Mezeritch, *Or Torah*, *likutim*, quoted in Nachman of Tcherin, *Derekh Chasidim*, *Yirah veAvodat haShem* 105.

Chapter 8: Larger Group Souls / The Soul of Israel

1. Glick, *Living the Life of Jewish Meditation*, p. 106.
2. See, for example, the commentary *Or haChayim*, by Chayim ben Moshe ibn Attar, on Exodus 1:12, "But the more they afflicted them, the more they multiplied and grew."
3. Gikatilla, *Shaarei Orah*, *shaar* 5, where he describes the tribes of Israel as the *merkavah*, chariot of God, and the *chotamot*, seals of God, with twelve permutations of the name *Yud Heh Vav Heh* as the basis for this chariot. The tribes are divided into four camps and twelve flags—each camp is one letter of the Name, with three permutations of the Name as the three flags. Each of the permutations of the Name, camps, and flags is also linked to one of the twelve constellations.
4. Gikatilla, *Shaarei Orah*, *shaar* 1, the name *Knesset Yisrael*. Also see Chayim of Volozhin, *Nefesh Chayim*, *shaar* 1, chap. 17, the section beginning: "and the soul also connects and binds itself to the aspect of the root soul."
5. Abraham Isaac Kook, *Orot, Orot Yisrael*, 5th ed. (Jerusalem: Mossad Harav Kook, 1971), chap. 8:8, pp. 169–70.

Chapter 9: The Organization of the Heavens

1. Chayim Vital, *Etz haChayim*, *Hekhal* 1, *Hekhal Adam Kadmon*, *shaar* 1, *anaf* 2.
2. This idea is stressed repeatedly in the Kabbalistic literature. One well-known and often quoted example is the section called *Petach Eliyahu* in the second introduction to the *Tikunei Zohar*.
3. Rav Kook, *Orot haKodesh*, vol. 2, *Hitalut haOlam, Nishmat haKol haMitallah*, 3rd ed. (Jerusalem: Mossad Harav Kook, 1971), chap. 4, pp. 519–20 and 555.
4. Gikatilla, *Shaarei Orah*, *shaar* 1, the name of *Etz haDaat* (Tree of Knowledge), note 6 at the beginning of this name, and also in the introduction, section beginning: "Because God wanted to reveal the divine unity and attribute of goodness in the creation, the world below was created in the model of the world above."
5. *Zohar* 3, *Idra Rabba*, 128a–b.

6. *Zohar* 3, *Idra Rabba*, 127b–145a.

7. Though most people no longer consider Shimon bar Yochai to be the author of the *Zohar*, it would have been someone like him, who spent many years meditating in solitude, that had this extraordinary vision of the nature of divinity. It is interesting to compare the vision of God in the *Idras* with the vision that Arjuna sees in the Bhagavad Gita 11:9–30.

8. *Zohar* 2:178b, *Sefer Detzinutah*, chap. 5:2, section beginning: "in the beginning, is an utterance." For a description of the Higher and Lower Gardens of Eden and the interaction between them, see, for example, *Zohar* 2:209b–212a, *Zohar* 3, *Idra Rabba*, 129b. See also Chabadpedia: http://chabadpedia.co.il/index.php/גן_עדן.

9. *Zohar* 2, *Sefer Detzinutah*, chap. 4, 178; *Zohar* 3, *Idra Rabba*, 135.

10. For a look at the relationship between *Arich Anpin* and *Zeir Anpin*, see *Zohar* 3, *Idra Rabba*, 128b.

11. There is a component of the *daat* of *Arich* that belongs directly to *Zeir Anpin* and does not come from *Abba* and *Imma*. The Ari speaks of this energy as *Zeir Anpin's yerusha* (inheritance), so to speak, from *Arich Anpin*. Riki, *Mishnat Hasidim, Shaar Abba veImma*, chap. 1, *mishnah* 6, note 30, "*sugiyat ha'achsanatot.*"

12. *Zohar* 3:128b, section on the supernal dew.

13. Riki, *Mishnat Hasidim, Shaar Abba veImma*, chap. 1, *mishnah* 4, and *mishnah* 5, note 28. The "body" of *Abba* and *Imma* is said to extend from the throat down to the chest. This indicates the area of their influence. They "reside" in the throat (their *keter* is there) and emanate down to the chest—the heart—of *Zeir Anpin*. For a more elaborate explanation of the role of *Abba* and *Imma* in the "birth" of *Zeir Anpin*, as well as their role as transmitters of energy, see *Mishnat Hasidim, Masekhet Zivug Abba veImma*, chap. 3, *mishnaot* 1–4.

14. Riki, *Mishnat Hasidim, Shaar Abba veImma*, chap. 1, *mishnah* 4.

15. *Zohar* 3, *Idra Rabba*, 130b–134b.

16. *Zohar* 3, *Idra Rabba*, 132b and 139a. See also Vital, *Shaar haKavanot, Kavanah* for Hanukkah.

17. Vital, *Etz haChayim, Hekhal Ketarim, Shaar Arich Anpin, shaar* 13, chap. 9.

18. *Zohar* 3, *Idra Rabba*, 130b–134b. See also Riki, *Mishnat Hasidim, Shaar Arich*, chap. 7, *mishnah* 1, as well as notes 207 and 208.

19. Gikatilla, *Shaarei Orah, shaar* 7, the name *El*, on the interpretation of the thirteen attributes of compassion and the power of the tzaddik to call down God's compassion.

20. Godman, *The Power of the Presence*, in the glossary.

21. *Zohar, Idra Rabba*, 133b–134a (seventh *tikun*). See also Gikatilla, *Shaarei Orah, shaar* 10, on the prayer "*El Melekh hayoshev al kisay rachamim.*"

22. Riki, *Mishnat Hasidim, Shaar Arich*, chap. 7, *mishnah* 2 as well as note 216. See also Vital, *Etz haChayim, Hekhal Ketarim, Shaar Arich Anpin, shaar* 13, chap. 9.

23. See, for example, *Tikunei Zohar, tikun* 22, 64a, "There is a supernal Torah"; also *Zohar* 3:81a, section beginning: "The Torah dwells in and is sustained by the supernal wisdom, and all of Her [the Torah's] roots are planted there." For an example of this idea in Hasidism, see also Nachum of Chernobyl, *Meor Einayim*, Torah portion *Tetzavveh*, the first teaching.

24. See, for example, the *Zohar Chadash, Shir haShirim*, 74d, where it states that the 600,000 letters in a Torah scroll correspond to the 600,000 souls of the twelve tribes of Israel. Also see Nathan Nata Spira, *Megalei Amukot* 186, where he states that the soul of everyone in Israel comes from one of the 600,000 letters in the Torah, and Nachman of Breslov, *Likutei Maharan* 14:3, where he states that there are 600,000 letters in the Torah for the 600,000 souls of Israel, and that each soul has its source or root above in the "thoughts of God." See also Vital, *Shaar haGilgulim*, introduction 17. Here Vital discusses the subject of the link between each soul and a letter in the supernal Torah. He also states that each soul must reveal the truth of his letter on all four traditional levels of interpretation of the Torah: *peshat*, the literal meaning; *drash*, the homiletic meaning; *remez*, the psychological meaning; and *sod*, the mystical dimension. This presents us with quite a large scope for action.

25. Dov Baer of Mezeritch, *Likutei Amarim* 134, ed. Rivka Shas Oppenheimer (Jerusalem: Magnus Press, 1976).

26. Vital, *Etz haChayim, Hekhal 2, Hekhal Nekudim, shaar* 9: *Shaar Shevirat Hakalim*, and *shaar* 10: *Shaar haTikun*.

27. *Etz haChayim, Hekhal 2, Hekhal haNekudim, shaar 4, shaar 11, Shaar haMelakhim*, chap. 5. See also Yisrael Yitzchak Dancyger, *Yismach Yisrael*, on Lag B'Omer, the first teaching, where he quotes the Maggid of Mezeritch on this subject.

28. *Zohar 2, Sefer Detzinutah*, 176b.

29. Altshuler, *Klalei Hatechalat haChokhmah*, part 1, chap. 9. See also Gershon Scholem, *Major Trends in Jewish Mysticism*, 7th ed. (New York: Schocken Books, 1973), p. 272. See also Chayim Vital, *Etz haChayim, Hekhal 7: Hekhal Atzilut, Briah, Yetzirah*, and *Asiyah, shaar* 2, chap. 1.

Chapter 10: The Angelic Kingdom

1. The *Hekhalot* are described in *Zohar* 2, Torah portion *Pekudei*, 244b–262b, and in *Zohar* 1, Torah portion *Bereshit*, 40b to 45b.

2. Gikatilla, *Shaar haGilgulim*, introduction 25.

3. Lobsang P. Lhalungpa, trans., *The Life of Milarepa* (Boston: Shambhala, 1984), pp. 17–43. This version of the story is also told in my book *Living the Life of Jewish Meditation*, pp. 26–27.

Chapter 11: Incarnation and Evolution in the Divine Kingdom

1. For more on this concept, see Abraham Isaac Kook on two types of divine perfection: *Orot haKodesh*, vol. 2, chaps. 14–18, pp. 528–533.

2. A year of Brahma is 365 days and nights. In the Bhagavad Gita 8:17, it states that a day of Brahma is a thousand *yugas*. A cycle of *yugas* is 4,320,00 years. See Arvind Sharma, "Time: Our Hindu View," *Hinduism Today* (January–March 2013), www.hinduismtoday.com/modules/smartsection/item.php?itemid=5350.

3. Gikatilla, *Shaarei Orah, shaar* 8, talks about the *sefirah* of *binah* (understanding) and creation, and how it is hard to understand its role. See the corresponding note 3 in the commentary, which explains that there are two levels of creation: *Atzilut*—spiritual creation on the level of energies; and then *Briah*—the physical creation.

4. See, for example, the Baal Shem Tov, *Keter Shem Tov*, part 2, p. 2a–b, quoted in Dunner and Wodnik, *Baal Shem Tov al haTorah*, Torah portion *Bereshit* 82; and Yehudah Aryeh Leib Alter of Ger, *Sefat Emet*, Torah portion *Ki Tissa*, quoted in Dunner and Wodnik, *Baal Shem Tov al haTorah*, Torah portion *Ki Tissa* 7.

5. Riki, *Mishnat Hasidim, Masekhet Ibbur Zeir Anpin veNukva, Masekhet Yenikah, Masekhet haGadulat deZeir Anpin*. See also Scholem, *Kabbalah*, p. 141.

6. Vital, *Etz haChayim, Shaar haKlalim*, chap. 2, *Seder haTikun*. Here the different aspects of *Atik* are explained in brief. Also see *Etz haChayim, Hekhal 3, Hekhal haKetarim, shaar* 1, *Shaar Atik,* chap. 1, where these ideas are explained in detail. And *Etz haChayim, Hekhal 7, Hekhal Atzilut, Briah, Yetzirah,* and *Asiyah, shaar* 1, chaps. 1–3, for an overview of how the different aspects of the four worlds and five *partzufim* connect with the five levels of the soul.

7. Riki, *Mishnat Hasidim, Masekhet Atik*, chap. 1, *mishnah* 3. Vital, *Etz Hachayim, Hekhal 3, Hekhal haKetarim, shaar* 1, *shaar* 12, *Shaar Atik*, chaps. 1, 2, 3.

8. For example, see the hymn of the Ari for the meal of Shabbat day, where he refers directly to *Atika Kadisha* as the sun. It should be noted that the *ruach, nefesh,* and intellect of *Atik Yamin*, taken together, is sometimes also referred to as *Atika Kadisha* in the Kabbalah. This reference is not to be confused with the One who overshadows the solar system.

Chapter 12: Fundamental Forces at Work in Human and Divine Evolution

1. Dov Baer of Mezeritch, *Lekutim Yekarim*, quoted in Dunner and Wodnik, *Baal Shem Tov al haTorah*, Torah portion *Bereshit* 91.

2. R. Dov Baer of Mezeritch, *Maggid Devarav LeYa'acov* 152, *Likutei Amarim*, p. 36., quoted in Tcherin, *Derekh Chasidim, Yirah veAvodat haShem* 55.

3. Sivananda, "Pranayama," in *Bliss Divine*, 3rd ed. (Shivanandanagar, India: Divine Life Trust Society, 1974), pp. 430–31.

4. Dov Baer of Mezeritch, *Lekutim Yekarim*, quoted in Dunner and Wodnik, *Baal Shem Tov al haTorah*, Torah portion *Bereshit* 91.

5. See David Altshuler, *Mesudat David* and *Mesudat Tzion* commentaries on Malachi 3:2–3.

6. See Ezekiel 36:25–6.

7. Ya'acov Yosef of Polonnoye, *Ketonet Pasim*, Torah portion *Beha'alotekha*, quoted in Dunner and Wodnik, *Baal Shem Tov al haTorah*, Torah portion *Bechukotai* 5. See also Menachem Mendel of Vitebsk, *Peri ha'Aretz*, Torah portion *Ki Tissa*, where he speaks of how all the impurities must be purified from two pieces of silver in order to join them together.

8. Talmud, *Yoma* 85b, section in the Mishnah: "Happy are you, O Israel, before whom is it that you become purified?" See also Yisrael of Kosnitz, *Avodat Yisrael*, Torah portion *Parah* on the red heifer, section beginning: "In *Midrash Tanchuma*."

9. See Dunner and Wodnik, *Baal Shem Tov al haTorah*, introduction *Kuntris Meirat Einayim* 69.

Chapter 13: The *Shekhinah*—the Feminine Divine Presence

1. Riki, *Mishnat Chasidim*, *Hekhal* 1, *Masekhet Briat Adam Kadmon*, chap. 2, *mishnah* 1.

2. Sivananda, *Kundalini Yoga*, p. 20. See Avalon, *The Serpentine Power*, pp. 110 and 113. See also "M," *The Gospel of Sri Ramakrishna*, trans. Nikhilananda, p. 499.

3. In both Kabbalistic and Indian thought, the right-hand side is associated with God and the left-hand side is associated with the forces of evil. The left-hand or psychic powers, however, are not so much linked to evil, but rather are vulnerable to misuse for evil purposes unless there is the protective power of the divine attributes of the right-hand side. Psychic power is energy that is of a higher vibration than physical energies, yet it still has a form. The divine energies are formless or pure spirit.

4. Louis Ginzberg, *The Legends of the Jews*, 9th ed. (Philadelphia: Jewish Publication Society, 1982), vol. 1, p. 123.

5. Gikatilla, *Shaarei Orah*, *shaar* 1, names of *Eretz haChayim* (the Land of Life)—connected to force of life (even after death), and *Sefer haChayim* (the Book of Life).

6. See "M," *The Gospel of Sri Ramakrishna*, trans. Nikhilananda, pp. 499–500, and Sivananda, *Practical Lessons in Yoga*, pp. 85–87.

7. Gikatilla, *Shaarei Orah*, *shaar* 1, the name of *bracha* (blessing), regarding *malkhut* as the channel for all blessings and *shefa* (divine flow). See also the names of *koh* (thus) and *kol* (everything). Also see the section on the *Shekhinah* in Scholem, *Major Trends in Jewish Mysticism*, pp. 230–31.

8. Gikatilla, *Shaarei Orah*, *shaar* 1, on how the *Shekhinah* protected Abraham, and also how when the *Shekhinah* departed, the Temple was destroyed. The angelic

hosts of the *Shekhinah* are called *nesherei hamerkavah* (the eagles of the chariot), which guard and protect Israel under their wings.

9. Gikatilla, *Shaarei Orah, shaar* 1, the names of *tzedek* (justice) and *Elohim*, which discuss the *Shekhinah* as a destructive force. Also the sections on the names *be'er sheva* (seven wells) and *yovel* (jubilee), which discuss the *Shekhinah* as the destructive force of the plagues in Egypt, and on the name of *malkhut Beit David* (kingdom of the House of David), which explains that it was the *Shekhinah* that fought King David's wars for him.

10. *Zohar* 2:50b–51a.

11. Parts of this first section also appear in my book *Living the Life of Jewish Meditation*, p. 111.

12. One of the names in the Kabbalah for the *sefirah* of *malkhut*, the source of this energy, is *Beit haMikdash* (the Temple). See Gikatilla, *Shaarei Orah, shaar* 1, the name of *Beit haMikdash* and the name of *Shekhinah*.

13. Gikatilla, *Shaarei Orah, shaar* 1, the names of *koh* (thus) and *keter elyon* (supernal crown) on the priestly blessings.

14. Gikatilla, *Shaarei Orah, shaar* 1, the name of *Beit haMikdash* and the name of *Shekhinah*.

15. In fact, the wives of lamas are often referred to as their *khadro*—Tibetan for *dakini*. It is interesting to note in this regard that the Talmud tells us that the High Priests would marry the daughters of the tribe of Asher. One might speculate that this was because they were carriers of the *Shekhinah* energy. See the commentary of Rashi on Deuteronomy 33:24.

16. See, for example, Dunner and Wodnik, *Baal Shem Tov al haTorah*, Torah portion *Ekev* 32, and *Amud haTefilah* 128, 131, and 154.

17. See, for example, *Zohar* 3:209a–b, section beginning: "we have learned, when She is crowned from the side of the Mother," and *Zohar* 2:135a, section beginning: "the secret of the Shabbat." See also Gikatilla, *Shaarei Orah, shaar* 1, name of *kalah* (bride), and footnote 3 there.

18. See, for example, *Zohar* 3:150a, *Zohar* 3:296a–297a, and *Zohar* 1:151b–152a. Also see Gikatilla, *Shaarei Orah, shaar* 1, the names of *even sapir* (sapphire stone) and *be'er* (well).

19. Gikatilla, *Shaarei Orah, shaar* 1, explains that in this state the *Shekhinah* is called *yabashah* (the dry land), implying that there is nothing flowing through Her. When She is flowing, the *Shekhinah* is called *mikveh mayim* (the pool of flowing waters). See also the elaboration in *shaar* 2 on the name *makor mayim chayim* (the source of living waters). Also see in *shaar* 1 where the *Shekhinah* is called *nesher* (the eagle), soaring in the wind, carrying blessings on Her wings, when the energy has been raised and She is flowing; and *nashar* (fallen off), when She is in the lower state, like a tree whose fruit and leaves have all dropped off.

20. *Bereshit Rabbah* on Genesis 1:16.

Chapter 14: The Evolution of the Concept of the Temple

1. *Midrash Tanchuma,* Torah portion *Pekudei* on Numbers 38:21, and *Zohar* 2:240a.
2. Ya'acov Yosef of Polonnoye, *Ben Porat Yosef,* introduction pp. 8–9, quoted in Dunner and Wodnik, *Baal Shem Tov al haTorah,* Torah portion *Pekudei* 1.
3. Baal Shem Tov, *Keter Shem Tov,* part 2, p. 7a, quoted in Dunner and Wodnik, *Baal Shem Tov al haTorah,* Torah portion *Pekudei,* see footnote 3.
4. Johannes Jorgensen, *Saint Francis of Assisi,* trans. T. O'Conor Sloane (New York: Image Books, 1955), pp. 85–86.
5. Baal Shem Tov, *Keter Shem Tov,* part 2, p. 7a, quoted in Dunner and Wodnik, *Baal Shem Tov al haTorah,* Torah portion *Pekudei,* see footnote 3.
6. Shmuel Bornstein of Sochatchov, *Shem meShmuel,* Torah portion *Terumah,* teaching for the year 1911.

Chapter 15: The Manifestation of the Divine Thoughtform in the Four Worlds

1. Chayim Vital, *Etz haChayim, Hekhal* 7: *Hekhal Atzilut, Briah, Yetzirah,* and *Asiyah, shaar* 2, chap. 1, and *shaar* 3, introduction. See also Altshuler, *Klalei Hatechalat haChokhmah,* part 1, chap. 9. See also Gershon Scholem, *Major Trends in Jewish Mysticism,* p. 272.
2. Tzvi Elimelekh of Dinov, *Benei Yissaskhar, Chodesh Kislev, Ma'amar* 4:49, quoted in Dunner and Wodnik, *Baal Shem Tov al haTorah,* Torah portion *Beha'alotekha* 1; also see note 1.
3. See *Shir haShirim Rabbah* 7:5, "Your neck is as a tower of ivory." The Talmud, *Hagigah* 12b, states that *Yerushalayim shel malah* (heavenly Jerusalem) and the *Mikdash shel malah* (heavenly Temple) are focused on the fourth heaven, the plane of *tiferet* (beauty). From here divine livingness flows out to the whole body of *Atik Yamim.*
4. See Talmud, *Taanit* 5a.
5. *Midrash haNe'elam,* Torah portion *Noah* 20d–21a, section beginning: "Rabbi Judah said: 'The Holy One, blessed be He, made the heavenly Jerusalem.'"
6. See Talmud, *Hagigah* 12b.
7. For a look at how the Kabbalah connects the higher work of building the Temple with the three categories of *cohen, levi,* and *yisrael,* see Gikatilla, *Shaarei Orah, shaar* 1, names of *Adonai* and *bracha.*

Chapter 16: The Messianic Soul

1. Dharma Haven, www.dharma-haven.org.
2. Another source for this idea is Vital, *Shaar haGilgulim,* introduction 38, where the Ari states that the soul of Moses was divided into 600,000 sparks. See also

Zohar 3:216b, section beginning: "Come and see, the sun is revealed during the day." According to the tradition, Moses is part of the soul of the Messiah. The Ari regarded himself as a spark of the Messiah son of Joseph. The Gra, Vilna Gaon, also wrote that there are many souls over many generations that are part of the Messiah son of Joseph. He also saw himself as a spark of the soul of Messiah son of Joseph. The Baal Shem Tov went so far as to say that the soul of the Messiah is composed of the 600,000 soul sparks of all of Israel and that each person has a spark of the Messiah that he has to raise up and fulfill. See also Nachum of Chernobyl, *Meor Einayim*, Torah portion *Pinchas* on this subject in the name of the Baal Shem Tov. Also see Abraham Isaac Kook, *Orot, Orot Yisrael*, chap. 6:6, p. 160, on how the Messiah son of Joseph fulfills the national aspirations of the Jewish people and the Messiah son of David fulfills the universal aspirations. Therefore, the Messiah son of Joseph must die (as it states in the Midrash) before the Messiah son of David can come; that is, the narrow nationalistic perspective needs to fall away for the universal redemption to come.

3. See the letter from the Baal Shem Tov to his brother-in-law Gershon Kutover, the section beginning with "On Rosh Hashanah, the year 1746, I made an ascension of the soul," quoted in *Baal Shem Tov al haTorah, Amud haTefilah* 15, footnote 13. See also the story about Rebbe Elimelekh of Lizhensk and a man who saw the prophet Elijah, in Martin Buber, *Tales of the Hasidim*, trans. Olga Marx (New York: Schocken Books, 1991), vol. 1, pp. 257–58.

Suggested Resources

I t is extraordinary how many books have been written about the Kabbalah in the last few decades. There has been an explosion of creative work in the field as Jewish mysticism has been studied from almost every possible angle. In these recommended resources, I have tried to reflect this richness. The list includes both translations of primary sources as well as a variety of approaches to the wisdom of the Kabbalah. I have also suggested several texts from other traditions. Each book provides a different perspective on the nature of the inner life and the spiritual realm. Each offers a unique view of God and of the relationship between humanity and the Divine. Together they create a broad spectrum of ideas and paths to expand and deepen your understanding of this most lofty of subjects.

Avalon, Arthur [John Woodroffe]. *The Serpent Power: The Secrets of Tantric and Shaktic Yoga*. New York: Dover Publications, 1974.

Evans-Wentz, Walter, ed. *The Tibetan Book of the Dead*. 4th ed. By Karma-glin-pa. New York: Oxford University Press, 2000.

Fine, Lawrence, ed. *Essential Papers on Kabbalah*. New York: New York University Press, 1995.

Gikatilla, Joseph. *Gates of Light*. Translated by Avi Weinstein. Walnut Creek, CA: AltaMira Press, 1994.

Giller, Pinchas. *Reading the Zohar: The Sacred Text of the Kabbalah*. New York: Oxford University Press, 2001.

Green, Arthur. *Ehyeh: A Kabbalah for Tomorrow*. Woodstock, VT: Jewish Lights, 2003.
———. *Seek My Face: A Jewish Mystical Theology*. Woodstock VT: Jewish Lights, 2003.

Hellner-Eshed, Melila. *A River Flows from Eden: The Language of Mystical Experience in the Zohar*. Translated by Nathan Wolski. Stanford, CA: Stanford University Press, 2009.

Kaplan, Aryeh. *Innerspace: Introduction to Kabbalah, Meditation and Prophecy*. Edited by Avraham Sutton. Brooklyn, NY: Moznaim Publishing, 1990.

————. *Sefer Yetzirah, The Book of Creation: In Theory and Practice*. Rev. ed. York Beach, ME: Samuel Weiser, 1997.

Matt, Daniel C. *The Essential Kabbalah: The Heart of Jewish Mysticism*. San Francisco: HarperCollins, 1996.

Matt, Daniel C., trans. *The Zohar*. 9 vols. Pritzker ed. Stanford, CA: Stanford University Press, 2003–15.

Ponce, Charles. *Kabbalah: An Introduction and Illumination for the World Today*. Wheaton, IL: Theosophical Publishing House, 1973.

Scholem, Gershom. *On the Mystical Shape of the Godhead: Basic Concepts in the Kabbalah*. Translated by Joachim Neugroschel. New York: Schocken Books, 1991.

Singh, Kirpal. *The Mystery of Death*. 2nd ed. Blaine, WA: Ruhani Satsang, 2007.

————. *The Wheel of Life*. 2nd ed. Blaine, WA: Ruhani Satsang, 2007.

Vital, Chayim. *Gate of Reincarnations*. Translated by Peter Winston. Telstone, Israel: Thirtysix.org, 2014. Kindle edition.

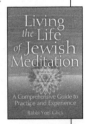
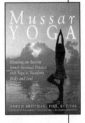

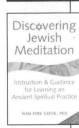

About Jewish Lights

People of all faiths and backgrounds yearn for books that attract, engage, educate, and spiritually inspire.

Our principal goal is to stimulate thought and help all people learn about who the Jewish People are, where they come from, and what the future can be made to hold. While people of our diverse Jewish heritage are the primary audience, our books speak to people in the Christian world as well and will broaden their understanding of Judaism and the roots of their own faith.

We bring to you authors who are at the forefront of spiritual thought and experience. While each has something different to say, they all say it in a voice that you can hear.

Our books are designed to welcome you and then to engage, stimulate, and inspire. We judge our success not only by whether or not our books are beautiful and commercially successful, but by whether or not they make a difference in your life.

For your information and convenience, at the back of this book we have provided a list of other Jewish Lights books you might find interesting and useful. They cover all the categories of your life:

Bar/Bat Mitzvah	Life Cycle
Bible Study / Midrash	Meditation
Children's Books	Men's Interest
Congregation Resources	Parenting
Current Events / History	Prayer / Ritual / Sacred Practice
Ecology / Environment	Social Justice
Fiction: Mystery, Science Fiction	Spirituality
Grief / Healing	Theology / Philosophy
Holidays / Holy Days	Travel
Inspiration	Twelve Steps
Kabbalah / Mysticism / Enneagram	Women's Interest

Stuart M. Matlins, Publisher